DESIGNING EARLY LITERACY PROGRAMS

Designing Early Literacy Programs

Strategies for At-Risk Preschool and Kindergarten Children

LEA M. MCGEE
DONALD J. RICHGELS

THE GUILFORD PRESS
New York   London

© 2003 The Guilford Press
A Division of Guilford Publications, Inc.
72 Spring Street, New York, NY 10012
www.guilford.com

Printed in the United States of America

This book is printed on acid-free paper.

Last digit is print number: 9 8 7 6 5 4 3 2

Library of Congress Cataloging-in-Publication Data

McGee, Lea M.
  Designing early literacy programs : strategies for at-risk preschool and kindergarten
  children / by Lea M. McGee & Donald J. Richgels.
     p.   cm.
  Includes bibliographical references (p.   ) and index.
  ISBN 1-57230-890-7
  1. Language arts (Preschool)—United States—Case studies.   2. Children with social
disabilities—Education (Preschool)—United States—Case studies.   3. Literacy programs—
United States—Case studies.   I. Richgels, Donald J., 1949–.   II. Title.
LB1140.5.L3M36 2003
372.6—dc21

                                                                    2003004009

About the Authors

Lea M. McGee, EdD, is Co-Director of the High/Scope Early Childhood Reading Institute and a Professor of Literacy Education at the University of Alabama. She teaches graduate and undergraduate courses in children's literature, beginning reading and language arts, and foundations of language and literacy development. She received her doctorate from Virginia Tech and has previously taught at Boston College and Louisiana State University. In addition to the current volume, she has coauthored another book with Donald J. Richgels, *Literacy's Beginnings: Supporting Young Readers and Writers* (4th ed.) and is the coauthor, with Gail Tompkins, of *Teaching Reading with Literature*. She has published numerous articles in a variety of journals, including *The Reading Teacher*, *Language Arts*, and *Reading Research Quarterly*. Her research interests include the role of fingerpoint reading in making the transition from emergent to conventional reading and young children's responses to literature. She frequently works with teachers in their classrooms and is currently President-Elect of the National Reading Conference.

Donald J. Richgels, PhD, is a Professor in the Department of Literacy Education at Northern Illinois University, where he teaches undergraduate and graduate courses in language arts, reading, and language development. He is the author of *Going to Kindergarten: A Year with an Outstanding Teacher* and is the coauthor, also with Lea M. McGee, of *Literacy's Beginnings: Supporting Young Readers and Writers* (4th ed.). His work has appeared in *Language and Speech*, *Reading Research Quarterly*, the *Journal of Reading Behavior*, *The Reading Teacher*, the *Journal of Educational Research*, and the *Early Childhood Research Quarterly*. His current research interests are preschool and kindergarten classroom practice and the relationship between spoken language acquisition and literacy development.

Preface

As we wrote this book, we were keenly aware of the unprecedented attention that is now being paid to the importance of early literacy instruction in preschool and kindergarten. Historically, beginning reading instruction, not early literacy instruction, was the major focus of concern. That is, the instruction provided to most 6- and 7-year-olds during first grade in the United States was considered to be the most critical period of literacy development. However, recent legislation (the Early Reading First section of the "No Child Left Behind Act" of 2002) has acknowledged that literacy experiences in the preschool and kindergarten years provide a foundation for later successful beginning reading and writing. This legislation draws heavily on the research reviewed and policies recommended by the National Research Council, published in *Preventing Reading Difficulties in Young Children* (Snow, Burns, & Griffin, 1998). Two conclusions are made clear in this report: Literacy development before and during kindergarten does matter, and some children are behind in literacy development even before they enter kindergarten.

Rather than being a frill, certain literacy knowledge acquired prior to the initiation of beginning reading instruction is necessary for early reading success. Unfortunately, children who are from low-income families and who are likely to attend schools with low reading performance are less likely to have acquired such knowledge. According to *Preventing Reading Difficulties in Young Children,* "reducing the number of children who enter school with inadequate literacy-related knowledge and skill is an important primary step toward preventing reading difficulties" (Snow et al., 1998, p. 5). The purpose of this book is to help educators and caregivers in kindergarten, preschools, nursery schools, and child-care centers reach the goal of providing every young child with the language and literacy foundation they need to become successful readers and writers.

We believe that the good news about the current attention to early literacy instruction is that more children—especially those children who most need early literacy experiences—may have access to high-quality early literacy programs. But we have grave concerns about the nature of literacy experiences and activities that will be the outcome of such unprecedented attention to literacy instruction in preschools and kindergarten. Like many others, we have long advocated for early literacy programs and instruction that balance child-initiated experiences with teacher-planned activities and instruction.

We have argued that the best early literacy programs are based on attention to children's literacy development and respect for children's intellectual capacity. We have written this book to provide the best possible advice for designing effective early literacy programs. To that end, we have carefully reviewed case studies of young children's literacy development and critically examined research on the effectiveness of early literacy intervention programs. We have drawn together insights from high-quality research and from our collective 50 years of experience working with young children and their teachers. We make recommendations about the nature of instruction best suited to help all young children have a strong and successful start in reading and writing. *Designing Early Literacy Programs* is intended to provide guidance for literacy supervisors, principals, teachers, and other early childhood caregivers as they implement early literacy programs for young children at risk for reading difficulties.

We would like to acknowledge several teachers and supervisors who have welcomed us into their classrooms and shared with us insights about their teaching craft. We would especially like to thank Mrs. Karla Poremba, kindergarten teacher extraordinaire, who has taught us how to listen better to children. We also wish to thank Dr. Judy Walis, language arts supervisor of the Alief, Texas, Public School systems, as well as the prekindergarten and kindergarten teachers in that system. We thank especially Ms. Michelle Bellamy and Ms. Suzanne Ballard of the Heflin Elementary Shool in Houston, Texas, for sharing samples of their children's writing. We also acknowledge Dr. Vicki Dick, Curriculum Coordinator of Talledaga Public Schools, and all the prekindergarten and kindergarten teachers in Illinois, Massachusetts, Texas, and Alabama who willingly opened their classroom doors to us.

Contents

CHAPTER 1

Who Is at Risk for Reading Difficulties?

Implications for Early Literacy Programs

Children's literacy experiences prior to first grade are critical for their success in learning to read and write. During these years they must acquire foundational understandings about the uses of reading and writing, strategies for understanding the meaning of various kinds of texts, and the rudiments of how our alphabetic writing system works in order to become successful early readers and writers. In this chapter we describe how researchers predict which young children are at risk for later reading failure. We discuss risk factors which are conditions that historically have predicted failure or success in reading, including factors that are related to the family, community, and the child. We use this information to make recommendations about selecting children for an early literacy program that primarily serves children at risk for reading failure. Then we consider issues related to the nature of such an early literacy program.

LITERACY FOR ALL: READING ON GRADE LEVEL BY THIRD GRADE

At no time in history has learning to read and write at high levels of proficiency and with great insight been both more valued and more hotly debated in our society. Many believe that our children's futures—and the economic future of our nation—in part depend on how well children learn to read and write, especially during the early primary grades. Educators are urged to prepare children for a future that will demand ever higher levels of literacy.

Literacy Matters, but Who Receives Instruction?

Whether or not we believe that high levels of literacy serve the economic good of society, statistics demonstrate that failure to achieve high levels of success in reading and writing is related to children's future, albeit indirectly.

- Poor skills in reading and writing are associated with poverty. While national adult illiteracy rates range from 11% in some states to as high as 30% in other states, 40% of the adults living in poverty are functioning at the lowest levels of literacy (Chandler, 2000).
- Poor skills in reading and writing are associated with unemployment. Unemployment rates are highest for high school dropouts (9.8%), compared to high school graduates (5.4%) or college graduates (2.6%) (U.S. Department of Labor, Office of Employment and Unemployment Statistics, quoted in National Center for Educational Statistics, 1995, p. 401).
- Poor reading and writing skills are related to dropping out of high school. At least one researcher predicted school graduation from third-grade reading achievement scores (Slavin, Karweit, Wasik, Madden, & Dolan, 1994).

For many children, especially children living in poverty, the future is bleak. In fact, living in poverty is one of the highest predictors of the probability of low reading and writing achievement. Despite our awareness of the high correlation between living in poverty and low reading achievement, few children receive educational services during their early childhood years that could ameliorate much of the impact of growing up in families of low socioeconomic status (SES). Statistics show that:

- Five and a half million children (23%) in the United States are living in poverty (National Center for Children in Poverty, 1998). The percentage for African American and Hispanic children is even higher.
- Only 40% of the eligible 3- and 4-year-olds are enrolled in Head Start programs.
- Five million children in the United States attend child-care centers daily but only one in seven child-care centers provides adequate language and learning experiences (Helburn, 1995).

Children's failure to receive high-quality early childhood services is related to poor achievement in elementary school. Recent data from the National Assessment of Educational Progress (NAEP) revealed that 40% of fourth graders failed to comprehend well because they did not make inferences or connections between the text and their experiences; the failure rate is even higher for children from low-income families (NAEP, 1996). However, research on early literacy intervention programs has demonstrated that higher percentages of children struggling to learn to read and write can make significant progress with the appropriate instructional support (Hiebert & Taylor, 2000).

Shifts in Beliefs: Ability versus Opportunity to Learn

Historically, the goal for all children was to read and write on grade level; however, in reality few educators believed this goal was possible (Allington, 1995). Even logical thinking suggests this goal is ludicrous. For example, it is statistically impossible for all children to score at the average level on any normed assessment of reading because the tests *are designed* so that scores range above and below the average. This artifact of normed standardized tests even affects children's grade-equivalent score. The grade-equivalent score, like the raw score, also ranges above and below grade level. However, if the term "on grade level" is interpreted not as an average on a norm-referenced test nor as a grade-equivalent score, but rather as children's ability to read with comprehension and fluency "texts generally considered appropriate for children's age or grade, . . . then the notion of *almost all children reading on grade level* may not be dismissed on purely logical grounds" (Klenk & Kibby, 2000, p. 684, emphasis in original).

There is a second reason that historically we have, at least intuitively, rejected the notion that all children would learn to read and write at the same time as their peers. Reading achievement was long believed to be related to ability. That is, we assumed that some children could read better than other children because they had better reading ability. Ability was conceived of as an inherent trait—one endowed at birth but certainly enhanced by particular experiences or made to atrophy by the lack of those experiences.

Ability was a critical determinant of reading instruction. The type of instruction and its pace were determined by the reading group in which children were placed. Reading groups were assigned by a teacher's determination of ability. Scoring well on a reading-readiness test in kindergarten was interpreted to mean that the child had high ability. Scoring low on the reading-readiness test was interpreted to mean that the child had low ability. Children in the "high"-ability group were provided reading instruction, and the pace of instruction was fast. Children in the "middle"-ability group were provided some reading-readiness activities before reading instruction was initiated (to catch up on the skills the readiness test indicated children had not acquired). Instruction then proceeded at a moderate pace. Children in the "low"-ability group received a great amount of reading-readiness training, and instruction in conventional reading was considerably delayed. Once it began it moved at a slow pace. It was not surprising that, over the elementary school years, children who started in the "low" group rarely left it and made significantly fewer gains in reading than children who started in the "middle" or "high" reading groups. In defense of this practice, it is true that many children did need additional opportunity to learn the foundational literacy skills critical for beginning conventional reading. Realization that it was *opportunity to learn* that many children in the "middle" and "low" groups were missing rather than ability only came slowly.

However, our thinking about reading ability has shifted drastically in the last decade. Instead of assessing children's reading abilities, we ask questions about their prior experiences or opportunities to learn in literacy events at home, in preschool, and in kindergarten. We know that most children, although not all, who have had intensive early experiences with reading and writing have higher reading and writing achievement scores on a variety of measures even at the time of school entry than children who have had relatively few literacy experiences. Instead of viewing these children's high achievement as being directly related to their high reading ability, we now recognize that these children have high achievement levels as a direct result of their extensive early literacy experiences—they have had many opportunities to learn. The advantage enjoyed by many middle-class children is often an advantage of experience and opportunity to learn rather than inherited ability. Middle-class children are more likely to have attended a high-quality preschool with frequent informal literacy experiences (Cochran-Smith, 1984; Rowe, 1998). They are also more likely to have parents who encouraged, supported, and provided direction for early writing experiences (Baghban, 1984; Bissex 1980; Schickedanz, 1998). However, the advantage of early and intensive experiences with literacy is not limited to middle-class children. Children from low-income families and from diverse cultural backgrounds who have had high levels of literacy support in the home or in preschool also display high levels of reading and writing knowledge at school entry (Barone, 1999; Taylor & Dorsey-Gaines, 1988).

Providing the Support Needed for Reading Success

Today most educators acknowledge that the goal of having nearly all children reading on "grade level" by the end of third grade is not the impossible ideal of a politician seeking votes. Rather, we believe that this goal is achievable. However, we recognize that "ensuring success in reading requires different levels of effort for different segments of the population" (Snow, Burns, & Griffin, 1998, p. 16). The Committee on the Prevention of Reading Difficulties in Young Children (Snow et al., 1998) differentiated among three levels of prevention and intervention needed to support the reading achievement of all children. Good classroom instruction is at the first level of support for literacy success. All children need coherent and effective reading and writing instruction delivered by a well-qualified, caring teacher. At the second level of support, children who are in groups that have been identified as having higher incidences of reading failure need prevention programs that deliver enriched and enhanced instruction that is focused and highly effective. Ideally, this instruction occurs prior to the onset of reading difficulties during preschool and kindergarten. Finally, children who are identified as already having reading difficulties need intensive, individualized instruction from highly trained reading specialists. Intervention instruction can begin as early as kindergarten and needs to extend through the primary years as long as the child requires this level of support.

The purpose of this book is to describe a prevention program designed for young children prior to receiving formal instruction in reading in the first grade. The Committee on the Prevention of Reading Difficulties in Young Children noted that preschool and kindergarten programs can be highly effective in preparing children for success in beginning reading. Many states are considering mandated preschool programs for 4-year-old children in an attempt to reduce the numbers of children who fail at reading and increase the percentages of upper-grade children who can read at high levels of proficiency. In the years to come, we anticipate that more efforts will be directed toward providing early education for preschool children and redesigning kindergarten curricula to better meet the needs of children who are at risk for reading difficulties.

Ironically, the Committee on the Prevention of Reading Difficulties in Young Children noted that we cannot predict with much accuracy which particular young children will have difficulty in learning to read prior to the onset of actual reading and writing instruction in first grade. Instead, they recommended that *prevention efforts be available for all young children.* Further, they cautioned that prevention efforts should "not, as a rule, require qualitatively different instruction from [that provided to] children who are 'getting it' " (Snow et al., 1998, p. 12). Therefore, the purpose of this book is to describe elements of effective early literacy programs for all 3-, 4-, and 5-year-olds, including those who are in groups that have been identified as having higher incidences of reading failure.

Ideally, early language and literacy experiences will be available to all children both in their homes and in high-quality preschool and kindergarten programs. School systems would provide quality preschool programs for all preschool children in the district and support high-quality parent-involvement programs. However, even when this is the case, we need to know which children are most at risk for reading failure, that is, which children will most likely need special consideration within early literacy prevention programs. We have some ideas about how to identify such children. But, unfortunately, our knowledge of risk factors is not complete.

RISK FACTORS: THE CHILD

The best use of limited educational funds would be to target particular children who are most in need of literacy prevention instruction. In other words, money would best be spent when we could predict with 100% accuracy that a particular child would struggle in learning to read without prevention or intervention. While we cannot predict with 100% accuracy reading success and failure, research has shown that certain conditions and characteristics are considered risk factors: these conditions and characteristics are highly related to whether a child later develops reading difficulties. For example, some physiological conditions are considered risk factors. Children who have severe cognitive deficits, extreme developmental delays, hearing impairments, or visual impairments are at greater risk for reading difficulties. Children with severe cognitive deficiencies and developmental delays usually attain only low levels of reading and writing abilities. Children with hearing impairments as a whole develop lower levels of reading achievement (Waters & Doehring, 1990). Similarly, children with visual impairments make slower progress in reading than sighted children (Tompkins & McGee, 1986). However, more promising conceptions of risk factors are related to levels of children's language development and literacy experiences. One way to identify children at risk for reading failure would be to assess their language development and the amount and quality of their early literacy experiences.

Language Development

During the preschool years the onset and pathway of language development allows for wide variation from child to child. Nonetheless, children are expected to achieve certain milestones of language development within that wide normal range. In particular, three language abilities are moderately correlated with reading achievement in the early grades: mean length of utterance (the average number of morphemes–that is, meaning units such as root words and prefixes and suffixes—in a speaking turn), syntactic complexity of utterance, and number of different vocabulary words (Scarborough, 1991; Walker, Greenwood, Hart, & Carta, 1994). Language ability at kindergarten entrance—including the abilities to repeat sentences or recall stories and to name objects in pictures (expressive vocabulary)—continues to be related to success in reading achievement during the early primary grades (Snow et al., 1998). Therefore, children with delayed spoken language development are far more likely to experience reading difficulties than children with well-developed spoken language abilities.

Another language factor—children's ability to produce extended *decontextualized* accounts, explanations, and narratives—is also related to later reading achievement (Dickinson & Smith, 1994). An example of decontextualized language is when children describe a past event (or an event only in the imagination) without the support provided by another speaker within a conversation. For example, with decontextualized language, children would describe how they helped their grandmother wash dishes over the weekend. They might talk about how they played with the soap bubbles, the stool they needed to stand on, and the dollar reward they received for their work. In contrast, most everyday conversations are about activities occurring in the here and now—about washing dishes as they actually do the task rather than a day or two later. Children who are able to produce decontextualized accounts of past events are more likely to succeed in reading than children who are not able to produce this kind of talk.

Phonological awareness is another language factor that has been shown to be highly related to reading success. Phonological awareness is necessary for reading development because of the alphabetic nature of our system of written language. The alphabet letters in written English words are related to *phonemes* (roughly, sounds) in spoken words. Readers, at least beginning readers, must grasp the notion that the letters they see in written words are related to the sounds they speak and hear in spoken words. They must be able to attend to these individual sounds or phonemes and use them during reading and spelling. While research has shown that phonemic awareness is related to later reading achievement, this does not necessarily mean that lack of phonemic awareness at kindergarten entrance dooms a child to reading failure (Adams, 1990; Snow et al., 1998). Children who have strong understandings about the phonemic structure of spoken language (that spoken words are comprised of phonemes that can be segmented) are very likely to become good readers. On the other hand, children who begin kindergarten with little phonological sensitivity can develop it in kindergarten and learn to read without difficulties.

Awareness of the Alphabetic Principle

Research has shown that children who acquire a strong knowledge of letter–sound relationships in kindergarten are more likely to become successful readers (National Reading Panel, 2000). Learning about letter–sound relationships is related to children's phonological awareness. Phonological awareness is part of what children need to know in order to grasp the *alphabetic principle*, the awareness that the letters in written words represent phonemes or sounds in spoken words. Children generally are introduced to the alphabetic principle by being taught *letter–sound relationships* in *phonics* instruction. Most children do not receive this kind of instruction until they enter kindergarten. However, many parents and some preschools provide an introduction to this activity. Again, strong knowledge of letter–sound relationships in kindergarten, particularly at the end of kindergarten, is related to reading success.

Early Literacy Experiences and Knowledge

Children who have many high-quality literacy experiences at home and in preschool are also more likely to become proficient readers and writers. Early literacy experiences include occasions when children observe family members reading and writing for purposes critical to their daily lives, when children interact with parents or others in activities that include emergent reading and writing, or when children engage in literacy activities on their own (Purcell-Gates, 1996). Clearly, such experiences provide children with many opportunities to learn. Children who have had these opportunities acquire stronger early literacy concepts and, therefore, learn to read and write more successfully than children who lack these opportunities (Purcell-Gates & Dahl, 1991). The effect of literacy experiences on children's literacy knowledge holds regardless of family SES level, ethnicity or race, culture, home language, and other physiological factors, such as exposure to crack or cocaine (Barone, 1999; Lesman & deJong, 1998; Purcell-Gates, 1996).

Thus, one way to identify children at risk for reading failure would be to measure the quantity and quality of children's early literacy experiences. However, researchers have found that collecting information about these experiences is problematic. For example, data from parents about their children's early literacy activities is fairly unreliable and has low predictive value (Senechal, Le Fevre, Thomas, & Daley, 1998). More importantly, reports from parents do not predict with accuracy children's actual knowledge of early literacy concepts.

A more effective approach to identifying children who are and are not at risk for reading failure is to assess their early literacy concepts. Research has helped to identify some concepts that are related to later reading achievement (Snow et al., 1998). These concepts include children's ability to identify and write their names (Bloodgood, 1999), identify and write some alphabet letters (Heibert, 1981), point out concepts about print (Clay, 1985; Yaden et al., 2000), demonstrate phonological awareness (Lonigan, Burgess, Anthony, & Baker, 1998), and retell stories with well-formed narrative structure (Morrow, 1989). Young children's knowledge of alphabet letters is one of the strongest predictors of reading, very closely followed by phonological awareness, concepts about print, memory for stories or sentences, and vocabulary. However, wide-scale assessment of young children is time-consuming and costly.

Learning to "Do" School

A risk factor that we are just beginning to understand relates to children's ability to move successfully from home to school. Schools are social settings with special rules, both stated and unstated, about how to enter and be accepted in the peer culture, how to interact with the teacher and with the content of instruction, and ultimately how to be seen as a capable learner. Children bring with them their characteristic ways of interacting with the world, including their dispositions toward certain kinds of children, activities, and interactions with adults.

Many children come to school with dispositions, behaviors, and ways of interacting with others that are congruent with most teachers' expectations. "Some children may appear 'ready' for school because they come with a selective repertoire of social and communicative practices upon which school literacy learning is contingent. In contrast, other children may appear 'unready' for school literacy learning because their participative repertoires are different from those required for literacy lessons" (Comber, 2000, p. 40). That is, some children, including some from middle-class backgrounds, have behaviors, dispositions, and ways of interacting with others different from those that are expected in school. Their difficulty in "fitting in" the classroom culture may actually impede learning. Even when they do possess moderate or even high levels of literacy knowledge at school entry, they are at risk for being identified as "immature," having "behavior problems," or "lacking literacy knowledge" (McMillon & Edwards, 2000). Children from diverse backgrounds are particularly at risk for being identified as having low levels of literacy knowledge because of their difficulties in "doing school" rather than because of actual low levels of knowledge.

RISK FACTORS: FAMILY AND COMMUNITY

Although we have described a number of risk factors that can be related to particular children, wholesale individual screening may not be practical or even highly effective when identifying preschool children for an early childhood literacy program. With the exception of obvious language delays (or specific language impairments), hearing impairment, or visual impairment, individual risk factors rarely emerge with high levels of predictability until children have already begun instruction in literacy. Therefore, the Committee on the Prevention of Reading Difficulties in Young Children suggests that early identification of young children might "proceed better by considering target groups rather than by assessing individuals" (Snow et al., 1998, p. 119). Group factors include minority status, SES, and limited English proficiency. These factors are usually overlapping and interactive.

Minority and Socioeconomic Status

In general, nonwhite children's reading achievement, despite gains in recent decades, continues to lag behind that of their white peers (NAEP, 1996). This factor is compounded by SES since significant numbers of minority children are also in low-SES families. SES is usually identified through level of household income and level of parents' education and occupation. The socioeconomic level of a school is usually estimated by the percentage of children who receive free or reduced lunch.

Regardless of how SES is determined, there are significant differences in reading achievement among children who vary by SES. Children from middle- and high-SES families enjoy greater reading and writing success than children from low-SES families even before entering school (Lonigan et al., 1998). However, the SES of the family and of the school interact. Regardless of the family's SES, children who attend school in affluent suburban neighborhoods score significantly above children who attend school in poor urban or rural schools. Therefore, family SES alone is not a strong risk predictor. That is, children who come from low-SES families but attend school with high percentages of middle- and high-SES children tend to have higher achievement scores than other low-SES children.

School SES data can predict children's reading and writing achievement. In general, children who live in poor neighborhoods attend school with other children living in poverty. These schools have chronically low achievement scores compared to schools where more children come from low-to middle-income families. Unfortunately, school systems may support the cycle of low achievement. In general, schools in poor neighbors have lower-quality libraries and fewer books in the classrooms (Duke, 2000). Children there have school experiences with literacy that involve less focus on extended texts (such as fewer discussions of the meanings of texts they read and hear read aloud) and more time completing worksheets. While these experiences certainly affect the literacy lives of children within the school, they can also have an impact on the literacy experiences offered to younger siblings. Older children bring home fewer books and may view literacy as copying or completing worksheets rather than thinking deeply about texts that are interesting. Thus, younger siblings of children attending schools in low-SES neighborhoods may be afforded even fewer and less powerful opportunities for early literacy development. Therefore, SES seems to have an accumulative effect. Children from low-SES families who attend schools with high percentages of low-SES children tend to have the lowest achievement scores. Children who live in low-SES families and attend low-SES schools are most at risk for reading difficulties.

SES is related to still another risk factor: the amount and quality of print materials found in the neighborhood environment and in public institutions such as libraries. Many low-SES parents have the same desire for their children's future academic success as middle- and high-SES families. However, limited literacy resources in low-SES extended neighborhoods and communities can shape the nature of literacy experiences that are afforded young children within that environment. In other words, we know that, in general, children in low-SES families have fewer book-reading experiences than children in middle-SES families, although there is a great variation in the frequency of literacy events in low-SES families, with some engaging frequently in literacy events and others rarely doing so (Purcell-Gates, 1996). Most explanations focus on the resources of the family as an explanation for low-SES children's fewer experiences with books. Yet research has shown inequity in

> the number of [literacy] resources, choice and quality of materials available, public spaces and places for reading, amount and quality of literacy materials in child-care center resources—even in the public institutions, the schools, and local public libraries in the com-

munity. Long before formal schooling begins, considerable variations in patterns of early literacy development are likely to be evident based on the ways in which print is organized in communities. (Neuman & Celano, 2001, p. 24)

Where families already have so few private resources to devote to literacy activities, low-SES neighborhoods compound the problem by providing relatively few public resources. Low-SES neighborhoods have few readable environmental print signs, few public spaces that encourage lingering over a good book, preschools with few and low-quality books, public elementary schools with limited libraries and few trained librarians, and public libraries with few books and short hours of operation (Neuman & Celano, 2001).

Limited Proficiency in English

Having limited proficiency in English is a strong risk factor. Despite recent gains in achievement, Hispanics, the largest group of English-language learners, score lower on reading achievement tests than whites (NAEP, 1996). This issue is of special concern in that approximately 8% of all kindergartners are English-language learners (August & Hakuta, 1997).

The difference in achievement between non-English-speaking and English speaking children is due to more than the simple difference in language of instruction and assessment. Even when Hispanic children are instructed and tested in Spanish, they exhibit low reading achievement (Goldenberg & Gallimore, 1991). It is also too simple to infer that children from non-English families have lower achievement because their parents have different beliefs about the importance of reading achievement and the role of parents in reading development or have low educational aspirations for their children. Some researchers have found high motivation for educational achievement in bilingual communities (Goldenberg & Gallimore, 1995) as well as parents who are willing and able to help their children improve reading abilities.

The cumulative effect of risk factors can be applied to minority status and speaking limited English as well as low SES. Higher percentages of children who are nonwhite and non-English speaking are living in poverty. These three factors, alone and in combination, are the best predictors of groups of children who will fail to learn to read and write well.

The Need to Look beyond Risk Factors

When school systems cannot provide prekindergarten programs for all 4-year-olds in the district, then the best and most efficient predictors we currently have for identifying target preschool children are that they (1) will attend a school with low achievement levels, (2) reside in a low-income family and neighborhood, and/or (3) have limited proficiency in spoken English (Snow et al., 1998). Unfortunately, these risk factors will eliminate many children who are middle-class and English-speaking but who will later develop difficulties in learning to read and write. At kindergarten entry, children can be screened for level of language and literacy knowledge, including letter naming, concepts about print, phonological awareness, story recall, vocabulary, and knowledge of letter–sound correspondences as additional indicators of risk factors.

Unfortunately, the way in which these risk factors are currently understood emphasizes the negative consequences of being poor and/or non-English-speaking rather than the positives associated with working with children from diverse backgrounds with rich cultural capital. Children who are poor and/or non-English-speaking are active learners as they engage in problem solving in their environment. They bring specialized funds of knowledge to early childhood settings (Neuman & Celano, 2001). However, current conceptions about early literacy clearly privilege certain kinds of decontextualized and school-like literacy behaviors and knowledge over the more contextualized and functional knowledge about literacy that all young children possess. Despite the often-heard refrain from teachers that "we meet all children where they are," actually capitalizing on all children's funds of knowledge can be a challenge. (See Ballenger, 1999, for a detailed description of a preschool teacher's thoughtful reflection on teaching bilingual children in a minority-neighborhood, inner-city preschool.)

Teaching other people's children, children who come from different cultural, socioeconomic, and racial backgrounds than most teachers, is perhaps the most critical element of the challenge of helping all children achieve high levels of success with reading and writing. Regardless of how children are selected for an early literacy program, it is critical that teachers resist seeing the children merely as "problem[s] to be solved and [their] literacy as an output to be measured" (Comber, 2000, p. 48). High-quality early literacy programs will be more than vehicles to get children "ready" to achieve high scores on later high-stakes tests of reading and writing. They will not focus narrowly on developing a few literacy skills that have been shown to be the best predictors of success. As we noted earlier in this chapter, early literacy programs designed to prevent reading difficulties are not qualitatively different from programs offered to children who are obviously well along on their road to reading and writing. Embedded in the early literacy programs that we describe in this book are rich experiences that address a broad array of a child's development needs. They comprise a wide range of literacy activities, while recognizing, valuing, and extending children's diverse home literacies.

IMPLICATIONS FOR EARLY LITERACY PROGRAMS

The purpose of this book is to help teachers, supervisors, principals, and others develop high-quality early literacy programs that primarily serve children at risk for reading failure. Much of what we describe in the book does not differ from the recommendations that we have made for the literacy development of all young children (McGee & Richgels, 2000). This is because high-quality instruction supports the learning of all children. However, when the program is designed specifically to meet the needs of children who are at risk, teachers need to keep in mind certain factors that may influence a variety of decisions about assessment, instruction, curriculum, and classroom environment.

One consideration is the nature of children to be served. The first step in planning an early literacy program for at-risk children is identifying children who will be included in the program. We have argued that most selections for preventative early literacy programs will be based on family income, home language, and minority status. An easy mistake is to overgeneralize that all these children have low levels of literacy knowledge when they enter the program and, therefore, require the same instruction. Some kindergarten teachers have operated in this manner for many years. Children are provided academic instruction only in whole groups, and all children receive the same instruction. Teachers might begin the year by studying one alphabet letter a week. All children learn the letter *a* regardless of whether they already know the letter, whether the letter is at all salient to them, or whether they have had previous experiences with alphabet books or writing. This is instruction that many call "one-size-fits-all."

In order to be effective in bridging the gap between what at-risk children know and what they need to know in order to be successful early readers, teachers cannot provide same-size-fits-all instruction. We know that at age 4 (Smith & Dixon, 1995) and even by age 3 (Lonigan et al., 1998), children from low-SES families know fewer literacy concepts and have fewer words in their vocabularies (Hart & Risely, 1995) than their middle-class peers. We also know that language and literacy knowledge usually remains stable from preschool to kindergarten and into first grade (Whitehurst & Lonigan, 2001). What this means is that many, although not all, children will enter early literacy programs already lagging behind their middle-class peers. Without instruction that *accelerates* their language and literacy learning, they will remain behind.

Accelerating learning is a difficult task and requires much energy, flexibility, and commitment on the teacher's part. In order to accelerate learning, teachers must take the time to consider a child's strengths, how that child seems to learn best, and how to arrange the classroom schedule to provide time to meet that child's individual needs–while also individualizing instruction for as many as 18 other children. Whole-group instruction must be supplemented with daily small-group instruction. Teachers will need to draw upon the resources of the community and parents in order to accomplish their task well. This may mean that teachers will need to develop new skills in order to work effectively with parents and other volunteers.

Language and cultural differences may provide another challenge for teachers. Many teachers, especially those in high-need, rural communities, find resources for English-language learners (ELL) to be unavailable. Other teachers, especially in large urban centers, can expect children to have a variety of home languages and represent several cultures. Reaching out to the community to provide information and guidance will be critical. One way teachers can extend their abilities to work well with diverse children and families is to read case studies of other teachers who have described how they faced these challenges (e.g., Ballenger, 1999; Meier, 2000). This book is designed to provide guidance to the teachers who willingly take on the many challenges of providing accelerated instruction for those children most in need of high-quality literacy experiences.

CHAPTER SUMMARY

We began this chapter by emphasizing the goal that all children could and ought to learn to read and write proficiently by the end of their primary-grade elementary school experiences. We argued that this goal was possible, but that children would need a variety of support systems in place in order to achieve it. The purpose of this book is to describe preschool and kindergarten programs that will provide all young children with the quantity and quality of experiences needed to support accelerated language and literacy growth. While the best approach is to provide all young children with extensive and high-quality early literacy experiences, including universal prekindergarten programs, most school systems will not find this approach practical. Therefore, school systems will need to employ screening procedures for identifying target groups of preschool and kindergarten children most in need of prevention programs. We noted that there are many factors related to how much support young children may need as they reach for the goal of full literacy. Individual children are more or less at risk for failing to achieve high levels of reading and writing proficiency based on physiological factors such as hearing or visual impairment, language development, and literacy experiences. However, group factors including low SES and limited proficiency in English are the most reliable predictors of future reading and writing difficulties for preschool children. These can be viewed as factors both for identifying children as at risk and for recognizing the rich potentials children from diverse backgrounds bring.

CHAPTER 2

Understanding
Literacy Development

In this chapter we describe some of the many literacy accomplishments that all young children, whether considered at risk or not, could be expected to achieve during the critical period of early literacy development. First we present an overview of a continuum of literacy development (adapted from the International Reading Association and National Association for the Education of Young Children, 1998). Then we use the continuum to describe some of the literacy accomplishments (called benchmarks) we would expect young 3-, 4-, and 5-year-olds to achieve and that seem to have the most direct relationship to later success in reading and writing. Many of these accomplishments are unconventional; nonetheless, we discuss their value in providing a foundation for children's later conventional reading and writing accomplishments. Children who truly are at risk for reading failure will need access to high-quality preschool and kindergarten literacy programs in order to achieve many of the benchmarks we describe in this chapter.

DEVELOPMENTAL CONTINUUM OF LITERACY ACQUISITION

Literacy development begins early in life, before children enter preschool and certainly before they can conventionally read or write. For example, young preschoolers who pretend to read favorite storybooks or use scribble writing to write a telephone message in their play are engaging in literate activities that are part of a continuum of literacy development. These emergent reading and writing activities are as valid as more conventional reading and writing abilities that also are a part of the literacy continuum.

In order for teachers to know where children fall on such a continuum and to appreciate what children can do on their own and what they can do with the right kinds of adult support, experts have described phases of typical literacy development. One such description is found in a joint position statement of the International Reading Association (IRA) and the National Association for the Education of Young

Children (NAEYC) titled *Learning to Read and Write: Developmentally Appropriate Practices for Young Children* (IRA/NAEYC, 1998). In this statement IRA and NAEYC describe five phases of literacy development. Children in preschool and kindergarten usually fall somewhere along the early part of this continuum—in the first phase, Awareness and Exploration, or the second phase, Experimenting Reading and Writing. We expect that some kindergartners might reach the third phase, Early Reading and Writing.

Although the IRA/NAEYC (1998) attach grade-level designators to each phase, they emphasize, "Children at any grade level will function at a variety of phases along the reading/writing continuum" (p. 200). Their use of the word *phases* rather than *stages* is consistent with an important caution about any such continuum: Children do not proceed along the continuum in a lock-step manner. The continuum is a guide; it gives teachers rough indicators of children's current notions about literacy and skills with reading and writing. It suggests potential next steps for children under appropriate supportive conditions, the sorts of conditions that this book will present.

AWARENESS AND EXPLORATION

With Awareness and Exploration, children take their first steps in literacy development. *Awareness* suggests a new kind of attention to the phenomena of written language to which children in most modern cultures are everywhere exposed. They become aware of print written on T-shirts and graffiti written on subway walls. They notice captions on television programs and print in children's books. *Awareness* implies a conscious knowing that print itself is a special category of marks different from other visual displays. From parents' reactions to print, children become aware that print carries a message, is related to certain activities, and serves specific purposes. For example, on a trip to K-Mart a parent might exclaim, "Look at that big *K*!" Children know that the "big K" is related to the activity of going to K-Mart, and that the printed *K* is related to the words *K-Mart*. Through these and other activities children become aware of print, that print *says* a message, and that the message print conveys is related to previous experiences.

Conscious Attention

The key to children's growing print awareness is consciousness. This consciousness about print is different from their everyday uses of language, which draw upon *unconscious* rather than conscious knowledge. For example, children unconsciously know how to participate in a conversation; they take turns and perhaps in their culture establish eye contact with their conversation partner. Similarly, they unconsciously use *phonemes* (basic sound units in spoken words) to produce and understand spoken words. Children clearly understand the message when someone says to them, "I have a candy bar, and I'll share half with you." They automatically, unconsciously, make use of the single difference between speech sounds in the words *have* and *half* . They are not conscious that the words *have* and *half* differ by only one phoneme: /v/ versus /f/. Nor do they need consciously to segment those words phoneme-by-phoneme (an ability that is usually called *phonemic awareness*). Without such conscious work with phonemes, they nonetheless are able to distinguish in the stream of sounds that is the whole sentence the different words *have* and *half* and use the meanings of those words in building an understanding of the message that someone is willing to share half a candy bar with them! Learning to read and write, however, frequently does require conscious work with phonemes and other attention to print and to language features. (Phonemic awareness is just one example of such conscious attention in reading and writing to something that is automatic and unconscious in spoken language.)

Children's conscious attention to print is a very significant development, one often obscured by the seemingly limited or primitive, certainly unconventional, products of their reading and writing. Figure 2.1 presents 3-year-old Marie's attempt at drawing a picture of herself and writing her name. Because the drawing and writing are so unconventional, at first glance we might assume that Marie knows very little beyond scribbling. Upon closer inspection we notice that she makes marks that are drawing and marks that are writing. Her signature has the feature of *linearity* (arrangement of marks in a line across the paper) and resembles cursive writing (often called *mock cursive*). As she was writing, her teacher noticed that Marie was familiar with *directionality*; that is, she wrote the mock cursive from left to right. After writing Marie announced to her teacher, "It says 'Marie.'" From this we know that Marie intended for her writing to be meaningful, was aware that her writing *says* "Marie."

Marie's example highlights another feature of the Awareness and Exploration

FIGURE 2.1. Marie's self-portrait and signature.

phase—*intentionality*. Marie intended to write, and she intended her writing to say something. Intentionality can be observed in many ways. A child, for example, who says, "Here's Skippy's coin" as she draws a circle is intending to convey meaning with her writing (McGee & Richgels, 2000, p. 195). That her writing is in the form of drawing is typical at this stage and should not obscure the significance of her intention to communicate. Writing by drawing is as important as the writing of a child who makes scribbles or mock cursive and announces that he is writing a letter to his grandmother. Similarly, children who tell a story about something found in a book's illustration are intentionally trying to connect print with meaning.

Concepts about Print

Being aware of print and exploring it through reading and writing allows children to construct *concepts about print*. These concepts are related to the visual characteristics, features, and properties of written language. Marie's discovery of print's linearity and left-to-right directionality is one example. Another of these concepts is that "print carries a message" (IRA/NAEYC, 1998, p. 200). Print, not illustrations, is what is read in a book.. Furthermore, children learn that these words are the same each time a book is read—print conveys not just any message, but a specific message. *Concept about words*—that print is composed of written words surrounded by spaces, and speech is composed of spoken words—is also a critical concept about print that children only begin to acquire during this phase of literacy development.

As children learn to write their names, they discover many concepts about print and alphabet letters. They become aware that words are composed of alphabet letters written left to right in a particular order. For example, Figure 2.2 presents 3-year-old Eric's signature. Most of the letter-like forms in his signature are not conventional,

FIGURE 2.2. Eric's signature.

although they have some features of conventional alphabet letters. These *mock letters* are found in many children's name-writing attempts. Eric's signature suggests he does not yet understand several concepts about print: that a signature should have linearity and that each letter should be written only once. Nonetheless, his name writing demonstrates a growing fine-motor control that has enabled him to produce recognizable letter features.

Children signal their growing awareness of print and written words and their role in reading and writing in ways other than through their signatures. Children frequently notice words in stories that begin with the first letter in their names. One preschooler insisted that Marcus had to read with him. When his teacher asked why, he explained, "There's all these words with *M* and Marcus has to be there for his words." Other children signal an understanding of concepts about print when they move their hands below a line of text as they retell a story. *Fingerpoint reading* (retelling a story from memory while pointing to the print) demonstrates children's awareness of the directionality of print—that it is read from left to right and top to bottom. At first, children's ability to track print is very global. They point at print and sweep across the lines of text without attempting to point to individual words.

Alphabet Recognition

Learning to recognize all the alphabet letters by name and to write them is an especially crucial concept about print that plays a major role in the Awareness and Exploration phase of literacy development. This accomplishment takes young children 1 or even 2 or more years to complete (Bloodgood, 1999). Many children begin this process as they learn to write their names. Although Eric's name writing (presented in Figure 2.2) includes many mock letters rather than conventional alphabet letters, it indicates that he is well on his way in alphabet learning. Writing mock letters shows that children are attending to features of letters—and it is the features of alphabet letters that distinguish one letter from another. For example, the only difference between an a and a d is the length of the vertical line. Therefore, to learn alphabet letters, associate a name with the letter, and discriminate between similar letters, children need to attend to letter features.

Alphabet letters are not learned in a particular sequence. The first letter of a child's name is often recognized early. However, letters in other family members' names or in the names of friends are also early-learned letters. Once children learn some letters, especially the letters in their names, they use these letters in their writing (e.g., see Jeremy's writing, presented in Figure 3.3). However, during Awareness and Exploration, children do not understand the role of alphabet letters as representing sounds in spoken words. Instead they hold many unconventional concepts about the relationship between alphabet letters and messages. For example, 3-year-old Santiago said about the letter *s* in his name, "That's Santiago's" (Ferreiro, 1986, p. 19). His concept about the letter *s* was that it belonged to him because it was in his signature. Tatie, another 3-year-old, hid all the plastic and magnetic letter *t*'s in her school cubby presumably because they were *her* letters (Ballenger, 1999).

Phonological Awareness

Another literacy construct developed during Awareness and Exploration is the beginnings of *phonological awareness*. Phonological awareness includes the ability to pay attention to the sound properties of spoken language apart from its meaning. This ability begins early for some children. Parents of toddlers sometimes comment how their children rock back and forth along with the beat produced by the accented syllables in favorite nursery rhymes. Children as young as 3 years old memorize parts of favorite nursery rhymes (Maclean, Bryant, & Bradley, 1987). However, enjoying and memorizing nursery rhymes may not reflect conscious awareness that words can be segmented into syllables or that words rhyme. On the other hand, children who can say a new rhyming word at the end of a rhyming poem are indicating their more conscious awareness of sound units in spoken language (IRA/NAEYC, 1998).

Awareness of *alliteration*, words that have the same *beginning phoneme*, is another phonological awareness that develops during Awareness and Exploration. One child, who has some awareness of alliteration, made up the following nonsense chant as she hopped on her neighborhood playground hopscotch grid: "Boogle, bumbum, boo—bee, boogle, bumbum, boo—bee." This child's relatively unconscious ability to make up nonsense words with the same beginning phoneme (in this case /b/) represents phonological awareness. But being able to match pictures of a *bat, balloon,* and *book* with a picture of a *ball* rather than with a picture of a *telephone* requires a more conscious awareness of beginning phonemes and may be more critical for children's later reading and writing achievement. So is the ability to identify, isolate, and pronounce the common phoneme /b/ in the beginning of the words *bat, balloon,* and *book*. Eventually children must learn to associate alphabet letters with phonemes. However, during the Awareness and Exploration phase of literacy development, children's attention is on the fun of making up interesting nonsense words, creating rhyming words, and playing games with alliteration rather than acquiring knowledge about letter–sound relationships.

Constructing Meaning: Engagement with Books and Other Printed Texts

During the Awareness and Exploration phase of literacy development, children learn how to respond to a variety of printed texts, from storybooks to grocery lists, from informational books to McDonald's signs. Most 3-year-olds cannot read a McDonald's sign, but they do construct an understanding of the big yellow arches in its sign. Similarly, many 4-year-old girls understand the meaning of the printed word *Barbie*. Children's awareness of the print in their environment and how it is used often is reflected in their dramatic play. Children pretend to read a telephone book and call a friend as part of their play in a Home Living center of a preschool. As preschoolers, they construct understandings of stories, poems, and nursery rhymes that are read aloud to them.

Because our culture organizes texts in particular ways, one way that preschoolers become better at understanding storybooks or informational books is by becoming aware of how these texts are organized. For example, children acquire a rudimentary awareness of the ways that stories are organized (Stein & Glenn, 1979). By listening to many stories, children's *concept about story* gradually includes the notion that stories have characters that are sustained throughout the story. Stories have actions or events that lead up to an ending. Later, children's concept about stories is refined to include an understanding that story characters have problems, that they attempt to solve their problems, and that settings can influence problems and their solutions. Table 2.1 presents a *story grammar*, a representation of a fully developed concept about story. Preschoolers and kindergartners are not likely to have acquired an understanding of all the knowledge specified in this story grammar. Stories they make up and tell to their teacher often lack problems and goal-directed actions. Nonetheless, all young children acquire some of the knowledge about stories that is presented in this story grammar. Their growing awareness of story grammar and ability to understand stories is demonstrated when they

TABLE 2.1. Story Grammar

All stories have

Characters
People, animals, or animate objects
Sustained throughout the story
At least one well-rounded character (with many traits)

Settings
Time, place, weather

Problems
Introduced in an initiating event
Cause one or more characters to set a goal (conflicting goals among characters
frequently occur)
Motivate the character to action

Goal of the main character
Is often implied rather than stated

Plot (sequence of events, tightly connected through cause-and-effect relationships)
Attempt
Action taken by main character
Aimed at achieving the goal and solving the problem
Obstacles/complications
Events that thwart the main character from obtaining the goal
Usually brought about by conflicting goals
Climax
Event just prior to resolution
Usually most suspenseful moment
Resolution
Event in which goal is reached and problem is solved
Suspense is resolved
Reaction
Character's feelings about ultimate resolution

Note. Adapted from Stein and Glenn (1979).

attempt to retell a favorite story. Gradually, children's retellings shift from merely including words or phrases to describing salient objects in pictures to using simple sentences to tell the sequence of actions in the story.

Children also develop concepts about informational books and how they are organized (Duke & Kays, 1998). For example, stories are about specific characters such as Tacky, a penguin in *Tacky in Trouble* (Lester, 1998). Informational books, on the other hand, are about generic rather than specific characters, such as "the penguins" in *The Penguin: A Funny Bird* (Fontanel, 1989). Stories are told in the past tense ("Tacky waddled ashore . . . "; Lester, 1998, unpaged); informational books are told in a timeless present tense ("The penguins leave the ocean . . . "; Fontanel, 1989, p. 6). In the Awareness and Exploration phase of literacy development children acquire only a few concepts about the organization and features of stories or informational texts, but these concepts provide a foundation for the later refinement and elaboration called upon in the early elementary grades.

Vocabulary Development

The preschool years are a time of vocabulary explosion; children acquire thousands of vocabulary words. The particular vocabulary children acquire is related to their language experiences at home and school (Dickinson & Tabors, 2001). Children whose parents and teachers share books frequently with them develop larger and more varied vocabulary than children who have little exposure to books (Wells, 1986). Books have more unique words, words that appear infrequently in everyday spoken language. Therefore, books allow children to develop understandings about words they do not hear while listening to television or engaging in everyday conversations. Perhaps because of differences in frequency of book experiences, as early as 3 years of age, children from low-income families have smaller vocabularies than children growing up in middle-class families (Hart & Risley, 1995). Clearly, one of the important tasks of all phases of literacy development is expanding vocabulary—learning new meanings for known words and acquiring new words.

EXPERIMENTING READING AND WRITING

With supportive home and classroom activities, children gradually begin to operate with print in more sophisticated ways that suggest a new level of conceptual understanding about written language. Teachers will notice that children show increased involvement in literacy activities by frequently pretending to read and write during play, participating more readily and more frequently during book read-alouds, and attempting to fingerpoint-read familiar texts.

The Experimenting Reading and Writing phase of literacy development is similar to what we have described elsewhere, also using the word *experiment* (McGee & Richgels, 2000). We have argued that the key to experimenting is an even keener awareness than in the previous phase. Now young readers and writers are not only aware of literacy around them, but know more about the processes of reading and writing. However, they also know that they do not know everything that readers and writers need to know. The Experimenting Reader and Writer approaches reading and writing more tentatively, more thoughtfully, in a more testing way than before. In particular, during Experimenting Reading and Writing two new concepts emerge—*concept of written words* and the *alphabetic principle*.

Concept of Written Words

As Experimenting Readers fingerpoint-read, they deliberately and carefully attempt to point to one written word for each spoken word. Unlike children in the Awareness and Exploration phase of literacy development, who make broad sweeps across the text with their hands, children with emerging concepts about written words realize that spoken words need to match up with the printed text in a systematic way. As children deliberately point to each word in a printed text, they demonstrate an awareness of how words are marked—through spaces. Early on children miscalculate how to point when spoken words have more than one syllable and may use the ends of text lines to self-correct. This self-correcting is an early form of monitoring that will come into play more critically as children begin to read conventionally.

In order to reach this level of understanding about print, children must memorize small bits of text—and most children easily memorize bits of favorite songs, poems, and books during the Awareness and Exploration phase of literacy development. This is a simple task for children who have had numerous experiences with pattern books that have repeated words and phrases. In *Silly Sally* (Wood, 1999), for example, the words "dancing backwards, upside down" are repeated many times. However, Experimenting Readers' new awareness of the match between printed text and spoken words allows them to go beyond pretend reading. As they reread memorized parts of text, match spoken words with written words in fingerpoint reading, and even apply knowledge of letter–sound relationships, they gradually acquire a few *sight words*. Sight words are words that children recognize without using memory of the entire text. Taken out of familiar context, children still recognize sight words. Although Experimenting Readers and Writers do not acquire many sight words (perhaps up to 25–30), their ability to read some words in a conventional manner indicates their growing sophistication with written language.

Alphabetic Principle

Children in the Experimenting Reading and Writing phase gradually acquire the alphabetic principle. It first appears when they can manipulate small sound units in spoken words to blend them together to pronounce a word. For example, in guessing games children can blend the spoken segment /b/ pronounced separately from the spoken segment /eat/ to form the word *beat*. The ability to blend an *onset* (the spoken segment of a word that occurs before the vowel) with a *rime* (the spoken segment of a word that includes the vowel and all the phonemes following it) indicates a rudimentary level of *phonemic awareness*. Successful blending of spoken onsets and rimes requires children consciously to hold smaller-than-a-word sound units (including single phonemes) in memory, blend them together, and retrieve from memory a meaningful word matching the blended product.

However, phonemic awareness is not all that is required for children to discover the *alphabetic principle*. They also must recognize the role that alphabet letters play. They must realize that alphabet letters in written words match up to the phonemes that are heard in spoken words. Learning such letter–sound relationships comes easily once children know at least some alphabet letters and can recognize words with the same beginning phoneme (alliteration). Children who have many opportunities to see their teacher or parents write the words *boy, baby,* and *birthday* eventually realize that the letter *b* that appears at the beginning of those written words is related to the /b/ phoneme that they hear at the beginning of the spoken words. They are poised to discover the letter–sound relationship between the letter *b* and its sound (the phoneme /b/). In fact, some children discover letter–sound relationships on their own because most letter names include the phoneme associated with that letter (i.e., the letter name *d* is comprised of two phonemes, /d/ and long *e*). Other children need teachers who will point out these relationships during shared writing (see Chapter 7) and during small group instruction focusing on this skill. The ability to use knowledge about letters and sounds to spell is a process called *invented spelling*. When children invent spellings they listen carefully to a word, segment some of its phonemes, and associate letters with those phonemes. At the beginning of invented spelling, children may only hear one phoneme for a word and spell it with a single letter.

How Experimenters Spell

Calling it "experimenting" is especially apt as we examine how these children spell. In the Awareness and Exploration phase, young writers compose messages without an understanding of the alphabetic principle. Instead, their compositions are constructed from writing the few letters they know, especially letters in their names, or mock letters (see Figure 3.3 in Chapter 3). In contrast, Experimenting Writers use their increasing knowledge of letter–sound matches (matches taught during instruction and matches children discover for themselves) to invent spellings. For example, Kyung wrote, "My favorite ride is the roller coaster" (presented in Figure 2.3). His writing does include many sound–letter matches (*m* for *my*, *f* for *favorite*, *z* for *is*, and *r* for *roller coaster*). In this composition Kyung ignores word spaces, only spells one or two of the most salient phonemes for each word, and includes many letters that are merely *place holders* (they do not have any letter–sound relationships with words they are intended to represent).

Spelling only a few sounds, running words together, and using place holders are characteristics of early invented spellings, sometimes called *late emergent spellings* (Bear et al, 2000). As children gain more experience trying to hear phonemes within words and acquire more information about conventional sound–letter correspondences, their invented spellings mature. They begin to hear both the beginning and ending phonemes in words (called *boundary phonemes*). They use consonants and vowels (but only to rep-

FIGURE 2.3. "My favorite ride is the roller coaster." M (my) fREtf (favorite) RT (ride) Z (is) RDEf (the) RKHCDR (rollercoaster).

resent long vowel sounds). For example, a child may make a birthday card for her father with a picture of a birthday cake and write the message, *HPEBRFDA DE* ("Happy Birthday, Daddy"). Experimenting Readers and Writers are likely to ask their teachers, "Will Daddy be able to read this?" Even when they have worked hard to match letters with sounds in the words they want to write, Experimenting writers may not be able to read their own writing and may remain unconvinced that what they have done is considered real writing.

Inventive spellers often realize that they do not know how to spell like grown-ups do. Sometimes they will ask how to spell words, but, especially with encouragement and example, they will begin to experiment with what they do know to produce spellings. An Experimenting Writer, for example, who wants to write the word *poison* may realize that she does not know how to spell that word. She may ask, and a grown-up or older child may be willing to tell her. (The following is a nonverbatim reconstruction of the conversation based on later notes made by the child's father.)

CARRIE: [who has drawn a skull and crossbones] How do you spell *poison*?

FATHER: I think you can figure that out. What do you hear in *poison*? Start to say *poison*.

CARRIE: Puh, puh.

FATHER: Yeah! What letter has that sound?

CARRIE: (*Recites the ABC's until she arrives at the letter P.*)

FATHER: That's right! Can you write a *P*?

CARRIE: (*Writes P.*)

FATHER: What other sounds do you hear in *poison*?

CARRIE: Poisonnn. Nnn. I hear nnn.

FATHER: Yes. Can you think of a letter that has nnn?

CARRIE: (*Discovers that the name of the letter N has the sound she is trying to spell, and now her spelling is PN.*) Is that *poison*?

FATHER: Well, I can tell that that's what you wrote. (*Points to Carrie's word and reads*) "Poison."

CARRIE: But *is* that how you spell it?

FATHER: Well, you could listen for more sounds. Do you hear anything in the middle of *poison*? Poizzz-un. Poizzz-un.

CARRIE: Zzzzz.

FATHER: Yes! What letter do you need for zzzz?

CARRIE: (*Arrives at the letter Z and inserts it between her P and N, so that her final invented spelling is PZN.*)

In this writing event, Carrie displayed several characteristics of an Experimenting Writer. She can name letters of the alphabet; she knows the alphabet well enough to discover when a letter's name contains a phoneme that she is attempting to spell. Her increasing phonemic awareness allows her to concentrate on one sound at a time in the word *poison* and one sound in the names for the letters as she searches for a letter–sound match. She is aware that she does not know how to spell *poison*, but she is willing to experiment with what she does know. Even when she has a good invented spelling, *PN*, she is aware that it may not be a conventional spelling ("But *is* that how you spell it?"). She is willing to do more with adult assistance, attempting a spelling for a middle sound in *poison*. Her father was willing to help her with this last task, but was also willing for Carrie to choose not to spell that sound. He knows that at this phase of literacy development, a spelling with a beginning and ending is fairly sophisticated.

Carrie's spelling of *poison* suggests that teachers must know some linguistics. For example, they must know that the letter *s* often spells the unvoiced phoneme /s/ (as in *sat*), but it can also be used to spell the voiced /z/ phoneme in the middle of the word *poison*. However, the letter *z* also spells that voiced phoneme, as in the word *puzzle*. When an inventive speller spells the voiced /z/ sound with a *z*, as Carrie did in *PZN*, she is attending to features of phonemes and making important discoveries about the nature of spelling, such as that letters are not used haphazardly, but in a systematic way that has to do with matching letters and sounds. A teacher who knows these things about the sound structure of English—and again, it should be emphasized, this is more than the teacher would go into with children—will not be concerned that Carrie did not spell the middle consonant in *poison* the same way that adults do. Carrie chose one of the two ways available in conventional English spelling for representing the voiced /z/ phoneme; her spelling should not be corrected. In fact, her spelling reflects a more regular letter–sound association than is used in the conventional spelling of the word *poison*.

Constructing Meaning: Engagement with Books

Experimenting Readers and Writers, because of their experiences with constructing meaning of books during Awareness and Exploration, can construct more complex understandings of stories and informational books. They begin to employ a wider range of strategies for understanding what is read aloud to them, including asking questions, making inferences, recalling details, predicting, and connecting book information with their lives or with other books. The emergence of these strategies is due in part to children's maturing cognitive abilities, prior experiences with books, and teachers' modeling (in Chapter 6 we discuss how teachers can model sophisticated strategies for understanding stories and informational books).

Just as experimenters are more conscious of the patterns found in words, they are also more conscious about the patterns found in stories, informational books, and poems. Being conscious about patterns in words allows experimenters to discover letter–sound relationships. Being conscious about patterns in stories, informational books, and poems allows experimenters to discover and use their repetitive patterns to construct their own compositions. A kindergartner used the pattern found in *Brown Bear, Brown Bear, What Do You See?* (Martin, 1967) to compose a *pattern innovation* (a composition using the pattern found in literature but substituting new content). Michael located and copied words he can read, invented spellings, and used some known conventional spellings to construct his composition:

| E A rth | E Arth | *Earth* | *Earth* |
| Wtdoyou | cic Mars | *What do you* | *see? I see Mars* |

EARLY READING AND WRITING

We do not expect all, or even many, children to reach the phase of Early Reading and Writing before they enter first grade. Nonetheless, we do discuss some of what children will do as they enter this phase in literacy development because effective teachers always prepare instruction that nudges children toward the next step. We use the term *Early Readers* in this section of the chapter to describe what young readers are capable of doing during this phase of reading because *Early Reading* is in the name for this phase in the IRA/NAEYC (1998) continuum. However, we preface the usage of the word *Early* with this warning: *Early Reader* may be a problematic label for children whose performance falls mainly in this phase. *Early* is often interpreted to mean *earlier than usual* or *precocious*, when all it means here is a phase that looks more like conventional reading than in the Awareness and Exploration or Experimenting Reading and Writing phases. Some 7-year-olds may be characterized as Early Readers, just as some 5-year-olds may be; all that matters is that their abilities and performances be mostly consistent with benchmark abilities characteristic of this phase.

Text Reading by Early Readers

Early Readers are more prolific and fluent than are Experimenting Readers. The Early Reader, for example, acquires a sufficient number of *sight words* (words read automatically, on sight, without sounding out or otherwise deliberately analyzing) so that many easy-reading texts are readable. Most of such sight words are *high-frequency words*— words such as *the, was, are,* and *can* that appear frequently in all texts. Texts for early reading instruction have many high frequency words, words that are repeated, and words that children are capable of decoding. *Decodable words* use expected relationships between letters and sounds (see Appendix A for A Primer on Phonics for Teachers). As children read and reread these texts with the support of their teacher, they acquire several hundred sight words and become more fluent in decoding words and using comprehension strategies such as predicting, asking questions, and rereading.

For example, consider the easy text *Danny and the Dinosaur* (Hoff, 1958), which has long been a favorite of many Early Readers. Page 18 of this book presents an illustration of Danny riding on the neck of his friend, a dinosaur. The text is

"Bow wow!" said a dog,

running after them.

"He thinks you are a car,"

said Danny. "Go away, dog.

We are not a car."

Experimenting Readers may be able to remember many of the words of the story during a fingerpoint reading, especially if they have heard it read many times. In contrast, Early Readers will attempt to read the entire book even if it is not familiar. In order to be successful in reading this text, children must know many of the words in the text by sight, including the words *Said, a, after, them, He, you, go, we,* and *No. Bow wow* may be decodable if children know the sight word *how,* use what they know about this word, and apply sound–letter correspondences to decode the new words *Bow* and *wow.* Context will help with the words *dog* and *car;* most readers know that what says "bow wow" is a dog, and many readers know that what dogs sometimes bark at is cars. Knowledge of word structure may help with decoding the word *running;* readers may notice the word part *run,* recognize it as a sight word, and also recognize *-ing* as a common, readable word ending.

Spelling by Early Writers

Early writers are beyond merely using letter–sound correspondences of the consonant letters (usually taught during the Experimenting phase of Reading and Writing). They learn to decode and spell short vowels, especially in frequently occurring word families (i.e., the short *a* in the *ad, an,* and *at* families). Their spellings reflect an awareness that every word includes a vowel, although the vowel they use in spelling may be unconventional. As shown in Figure 2.4, Ryan wrote, "Jim gave the giant a wig" in response to *Jim and the Beanstalk* (Briggs, 1970); he spelled the word *wig* as *weg.* Notice that Ryan has control over word spaces, and in addition to inventing spellings, he uses conventional spellings for high-frequency words. Spelling at this level is called *alphabetic spelling* (Bear, Invernizzi, Templeton, & Johnston, 2000). Children who spell alphabetically include a letter for nearly every phoneme in a word, as Ryan did. Such spellings are called *fully phonemic* because the complete phonemic structure of the word is represented. Children who can construct fully phonemic spellings are also likely to use *fully phonemic decoding* when reading; they decode a written word by producing a phoneme

FIGURE 2.4. "Jim gave the giant a wig."

for each letter or letter combination. However, fully phonemic decoding requires that children have learned long vowel and other vowel spellings as well as consonant digraphs and blends (see Appendix A for more information about these elements of phonics).

THE LITERACY CONTINUUM REVISITED

Children acquire dozens of benchmark concepts as they move through the phases of Awareness and Exploration, Experimenting Reading and Writing, and Early Reading and Writing. We know that later concepts arise from earlier concepts, but not all children acquire all the benchmark concepts we have described. Instead, *a grasp of many of the concepts within a phase seems to allow children to move toward the next phase.*

Literacy Benchmarks

The benchmarks within each phase of literacy development can be grouped broadly into three major categories. The first category we call the print category; it includes concepts about print and alphabet letter knowledge. This category represents everything children come to know about the visual properties and characteristics of written language, including sight words and conventions of writing such as capitalization and punctuation. The second category we call the alphabetic principle category. It includes everything children need to know to employ alphabetic principle knowledge. This category includes children's strategic use of early phonological awareness concepts and knowledge of letter–sound correspondences to spell and decode. Together these two categories of knowledge eventually allow children to read and write printed words. The last category includes children's concepts about language and meaning. This category includes strategies for understanding the meanings of texts, vocabulary knowledge (words children understand and can use in speech rather than read by sight), and understanding of the different ways reading and writing are used. This category allows children to bring meaning to connected texts they read. All three categories of literacy knowledge (language and meaning, print, and alphabetic principle) are necessary in order to learn to read and write successfully. Table 2.2 presents an overview of the three categories of literacy knowledge acquired during the first three phases of literacy development.

Overlap from One Phase to Another

We hope that our descriptions of the early phases of literacy development show that no one phase is discrete from the others; there is some overlap from one phase to the next. In both the Awareness and Exploration and the Experimenting Reading and Writing phases, for example, children are expected to develop some rudimentary forms of phonemic awareness. Likewise, in both the Experimenting and Early Reading and Writing phases, children are expected to acquire knowledge of letter–sound correspondences and some sight words. Development of letter–sound correspondences and fluency in word reading from the earlier to the later phase is a matter of degree. Similarly, some children may display in a rudimentary way one literacy ability that is found on the continuum way beyond the phase that characterizes most or all of their other literacy activities.

It is important to remember, too, that development is elastic; children will move back and forth between neighboring phases, often in response to the amount of support they receive in a reading or writing event, and depending on other task features such as their purposes for reading and writing. What matters to a teacher is an appreciation of a child's general place on the continuum of development and his or her progress over long periods of time, measured in months or even years.

CHAPTER SUMMARY

In this chapter, we have given an overview of literacy development using the first three phases of the IRA/NAEYC's (1998) continuum: Awareness and Exploration, Experimenting Reading and Writing, and Early Reading and Writing. In the phase of Awareness and Exploration children turn conscious attention to print. They acquire concepts about print such as linearity and directionality. They learn to write their names and recognize and write alphabet letters. They develop early phonological awareness through playing games with rhyming words and alliteration. They learn to listen to and talk about books that are read aloud to them. They construct understandings about a variety of kinds of books and print in the environment and begin developing a concept about story. Their vocabulary grows as they acquire understandings of new words through their experiences, including experiences with books. As Experimenting Readers and Writers, chil-

TABLE 2.2. An Overview of the Literacy Continuum

Awareness and Exploration	Experimenting Reading and Writing	Early Reading and Writing
Meaning/Language		
Construct meaning of print found in environment.	Participate in read-alouds by recalling, asking questions, predicting, inferring, connecting.	Use strategies during reading, including predicting, inferring, drawing conclusions, recalling, connecting.
Construct meaning from read-alouds of stories, informational text, and poems.	Fingerpoint-read using memory and tracking.	Read with use of sight words, letter–sound decoding, and monitoring meaning.
Acquire vocabulary from read-alouds.	Retell familiar text with some technical and literate vocabulary (informational books may include some timeless present verbs; stories may include events with cause–effect relationships).	Retell text with some complex syntax, more literary and technical vocabulary (informational books will include some timeless present verbs; stories will include problems and events with cause–effect relationships).
Retell and pretend to read informational books, stories, and poems (from words and phrases to simple sentences to complex sentences; from unconnected random ideas to sequence of ideas).	Use copying, gathering known spellings, and invented spellings to write messages.	
Use print functionally in play.	Notice and use repetition of events and words to compose pattern innovations.	Read easy texts with increasing level of difficulty.
Pretend to read and write in play.		Reproduce, analyze, and use literary patterns to write pattern innovations.
		Use known spellings and invented spellings to write messages.
Print		
Notice print versus pictures.	Recognize alphabet letters fluently.	Acquire 200–300 sight words.
Recognize that print carries the message.	Attend to print for reading and writing (ask for spellings, copy text, locate known words).	Spell by analogy (use patterns from short and long word families to spell unknown words).
Notice features of alphabet letters, words, and texts (mock letters, mock cursive, mock texts).	Track print from right to left (no match to nearly one-on-one match).	Spell and decode word endings such as *ing, ed*, and *s/es*.
Recognize and write alphabet letters.	Use tracking to identify words.	Use some conventional punctuation and capitalization.

Awareness and Exploration	Experimenting Reading and Writing	Early Reading and Writing
Write first name.	Acquire 25–30 sight words.	
Acquire concepts about print (book orientation, some directionality).	May ignore word spaces in writing.	Stable use of word spaces (concept of word matures).
Begin to track print with broad sweep.	Extend concepts about print (directionality, some letter and word concepts).	
	Alphabetic principle	
Acquire phonological awareness (tap out syllables, identify/produce rhyming words, identify/isolate beginning phoneme—alliteration).	Acquire phonemic awareness (segment/blend onset and rime, identify/isolate ending phoneme).	Use fully phonemic decoding and spelling strategies (segment/blend two- and three-phoneme words).
	Acquire consonant letter–sound correspondences.	Acquire letter–sound correspondences for consonants, short vowels, consonant digraphs and blends, and long vowels.
	Invent spellings with boundary phonemes (may include use of place of articulation and place holders).	Invent spellings in which short- and long-vowel spelling patterns may appear unconventionally.
	Use letter–sound correspondences to monitor tracking in fingerpoint reading.	

dren develop a concept about written words and acquire the alphabetic principle. They discover and learn letter–sound correspondences and use them to invent spellings. They use fingerpoint reading to acquire a few sight words. Early Readers and Writers use sight words to read easy text conventionally, and they use knowledge of more sophisticated letter–sound relations to decode unknown words. They write using conventional spellings of some words, and show understandings about vowels and awareness of the complete phonemic structure of words. As these phases of literacy development suggest, learning to read and write is a gradual process requiring the orchestration of many foundational concepts.

CHAPTER 3

Using Assessment to Make Instructional Decisions

In this chapter we discuss methods of assessing young children's literacy development that are particularly appropriate for 3-, 4-, and 5-year-olds. We recommend assessment tasks that are designed to measure children's literacy learning in six critical areas of early literacy development. However, we also recommend that teachers systematically and frequently observe children as they interact in centers and during instruction.

EFFECTIVE AND APPROPRIATE EARLY LITERACY ASSESSMENT

Experiences provided every day in preschool and kindergarten have enormous potential to support language and literacy development. However, in order for this to happen, teachers need to know each child's level of development and how to provide instruction that will nudge that child forward toward conventional reading and writing. Having a precise understanding of children's current language and literacy development is especially critical for at-risk children in order provide the personalized instruction that will accelerate their learning and development.

The Importance of Assessment for Accelerating Learning

Assessment is especially important in making instructional decisions for children from diverse backgrounds. Such children are likely to come to preschool or kindergarten with different understandings about the nature of print and its use depending on their family and cultural experiences. These concepts, like the concepts of all young children, are not likely to be conventional. For example, one preschool teacher observed that Tatie, a bilingual Haitian child who was not yet 3 years old, was walking around the classroom making the shape of the letter *T* with two fingers. When the teacher asked her what she was doing, she replied, "That's me." (Ballenger, 1999, p. 45). While Tatie did not seem to know the name of the alphabet letter *T*, she did demonstrate an awareness that letters are symbols representing meaning. Unconventional concepts such as Tatie's are important starting points for classroom experiences that will make sense to particular children.

Issues of Appropriateness, Reliability, and Validity

Despite the importance of assessment for making instructional decisions for young children, assessing young children is tricky. Three-, 4-, and 5-year-olds are still at early stages of language development and may have difficulty using language to express what they know. They may have difficulty understanding directions,which are also communicated through language. Thus, assessments of young children may not be highly reliable; the results may not reflect what the children actually know.

Consider assessing what a 3-year-old like Tatie understands about alphabet letters. Imagine Tatie, the young Haitian child symbolizing herself with two fingers in the shape of the letter *T*, being given a sheet of paper with all the alphabet letters printed in random order and being asked to name the letters. This alphabet letter identification task has been used frequently with young children and is considered a valid assessment of early literacy. In fact, children's knowledge of alphabet letters before entering school is related to their reading comprehension at the end of second grade (Catts, Fey, Zhang, & Tomblin, 2001). What might Tatie do when presented with this assessment task? Suppose she merely shrugged her shoulders. Does this mean that she does not have a concept of alphabet letters or that she does not understand the task? We already have seen that Tatie does have some concept of alphabet letters, so using the alphabet letter identification task alone, although valid, would not be a very reliable assessment of Tatie's early literacy concepts.

We could argue that using an alphabet identification task with a 3-year-old is never appropriate. We could claim that 3-year-olds could not be expected to know the names of alphabet letters. Instead, we might argue that 3-year-olds should only be assessed by being observed as they interact with their peers, teachers, and classroom materials. In fact, all of the preceding claims are true. Many 3-year-olds do not know any alphabet letters, but some do. Alphabet tasks have been used with 3-year olds (Bloodgood, 1999; Chaney, 1992); however, alphabet tasks do not tap all or even the most important conceptual knowledge that children must acquire about alphabet letters (Bloodgood, 1999; McGee & Richgels, 1989). Still, knowing whether children are acquiring the names of alphabet letters is important for preschool and kindergarten teachers.

Therefore, effective and appropriate literacy assessment needs to be carefully planned, keeping in mind the purposes for assessment as well as the possible misinterpretations that might arise because of issues of appropriateness, validity, and reliability. As teachers assess individual children, the best practice is to form tentative conclusions about that child's literacy awareness that need to be refined through multiple assessments. Teachers will use a combination of assessments, including observations of naturally occurring classroom events along with specially devised assessment tasks.

EFFECTIVE ASSESSMENT PRACTICES

Teachers are continually observing the relationship between the nature of classroom events and children's responses during those events in order to adjust their minute-by-minute interactions with particular children. However, in order to be most powerful, assessment should be more systematic than the informal observations teachers normally make as they interact with children. Assessment is more effective in helping teachers make instructional decisions when it is systematic, is guided by knowledge of a broad overview of literacy development, provides insights into children's underlying cognitive concepts and strategies, and is used to make plans for future instruction and classroom adaptations.

Developing an Assessment Plan

Systematic assessments are planned to meet specific objectives; teachers will have in mind particular literacy concepts that must be assessed (such as the benchmark concepts described in Chapter 2). Once they decide which concepts to assess, teachers select a valid and reliable method of assessment that provides the best information about children's development of those concepts. Finally, teachers schedule assessments to make sure information is gathered in a timely manner.

Teachers might want to schedule particular assessments early in the year, again at midpoint, and then toward the end of the year. For example, using a name assessment (Villaume & Wilson, 1989) at the beginning of a preschool class would provide information about several literacy concepts that could be used to plan more responsive instruction and classroom activities for 3- and 4-year-olds. In addition, teachers might want to plan observations of naturally occurring classroom events once a month for each child. Perhaps these observations would be taken on Tuesday. The first week of the month the teacher would designate three or four children for observation. During center time, the teacher could observe each child for approximately 10–15 minutes. During the second, third, and fourth Tuesdays of the month, other children would be designated for observation. So by the end of the month, all the children would have been observed and the cycle could resume again.

Keeping Records

Teachers will need a method of keeping track of the assessment data that they collect on each child and a plan for writing reflections. They may use a notebook with divider tabs for each child. As more information is collected, additional pages can be added to the notebook. Alternatively, teachers could use a folder for each child. Information can be added to the assessment notebook or file immediately after it is collected to reduce the opportunity for misplacing important information. One preschool teacher uses Tuesday afternoons to keep her assessment notebook up to date. She dates and makes copies of notes that she wrote during her observation of each child and puts them in her assessment notebook. She takes a few minutes to reflect on her observations by quickly reading through the previous month's observations and jotting down a few insights about the significance of what she observed (we discuss how to reflect on observations and write insights later in this chapter).

Refining Observational Skills

Observing young children is the most useful of all assessment strategies that teachers can use. However, in order for observation both to guide instructional decisions and to reflect children's growth over time, anecdotal records that teachers write about children's behavior and language must have sufficient detail, accuracy, and objectivity (Rhodes & Nathenson-Mejia, 1992). Anecdotal records are written accounts of what children do and say free from any inference about what children might be thinking and from any evaluation about what the behaviors might mean. They allow teachers, parents, or others who read the records even months later to picture in their minds what children were doing and saying. Anecdotal records use the fewest possible words to describe the classroom setting of an event and the children's critical actions; they use as many of the children's words as possible.

Using a Broad Overview of Literacy Development to Guide Assessment and Reflection

Knowing what to look for is one of the most critical components of effective assessment (Clay, 1998). Teachers who have deep understanding of the broad range of literacy concepts that children develop during the early childhood years are at an enormous advantage in knowing what to look for as they observe children. Many descriptions of young children's literacy development that provide information about a variety of literacy concepts are available, including the one presented in Table 2.2 in Chapter 2. However, it is important to keep in mind that individual children do not seem to go through predescribed sequences of concept acquisition (Clay, 1998). Instead, each child's journey through the wide and varied landscape of literacy development seems to be unique. Teachers can be guided by their awareness of possible emergent concepts that children might acquire as suggested by developmental sequences, but they should be cognizant that these developmental sequences provide only a rough guide to any one child's journey.

Despite the fact that no two children seem to follow the same path through developmental milestones, certain areas of literacy development seem to be more directly related to later literacy achievement than others. Researchers have found that before entering kindergarten, a child's level of language and expressive vocabulary development, ability to recall a story, concepts about print, knowledge of alphabet letters, and phonemic awareness can predict with some confidence that child's success or failure in learning to read at the end of first grade. By the end of kindergarten, children's knowledge of letter–sound relationships is another early literacy concept with a direct relationship to success in beginning reading (Snow et al., 1998). We recommend that teachers in preschool and kindergarten use a set of tasks to monitor these critical literacy constructs. However, we also recommend that teachers use other assessments, including observation of children as they engage in a variety of classroom activities, to supplement and expand these assessments. Furthermore, teachers should be aware of the complex nature of these six literacy constructs and the kinds of activities that will support children's growing knowledge of them.

Language, story understanding and recall, concepts about print, alphabet letter knowledge, phonemic awareness, and knowledge of letter–sound relationships are not straightforward concepts. Instead they are comprised of many underlying concepts (McGee & Richgels, 2000). For example, being able to learn alphabet letter names means that children must become aware of alphabet letters as a separate set of printed signs and that the printed signs consist of repeated forms with particular features. When children do not perform well on an alphabet recognition task, teachers may want to seek further information about the children's underlying concepts. Such concepts may be revealed best through observation.

Because the six key early literacy concepts are complicated constructs depending upon multiple underlying concepts, there is not a straightforward relationship between these constructs and instruction. That is, young children are likely to acquire the more complex constructs as a result of engaging in broader activities that allow children to develop a range of concepts. For example, many young children become aware of alphabet letters as they learn to recognize and write their names (Bloodgood, 1999). In addition to alphabet letters, name writing draws attention to directionality and linearity, concept of word, and the relationship between spoken and written words. Therefore, if a young child is not making progress in alphabet letter learning, having the child engage in an activity that provides opportunities to learn only a narrow range of concepts, such as practice matching or naming letters as they are presented in isolation on alphabet letter cards, may not be the most efficient way of helping the child develop the complex construct associated with alphabet letter recognition.

Using Reflection to Draw Insights from Assessment

Teachers can only observe behaviors and the language that children use as they complete a task or participate in a literacy event. Determining the significance of these behaviors and language means that teachers must make inferences about the underlying cognitive strategies and understandings that are reflected in the child's language and behavior (Clay, 1998). Figure 3.1 presents one teacher's anecdotal records about a play event that occurred in the Home Living center as three children pretended to go grocery shopping in the nearby Grocery Store dramatic play center. The anecdotal records describe the setting and the three children's behavior and language as teacher observed them play. Later, the teacher gathered up the three children's writing samples and placed a copy of her anecdotal records in each of the three children's assessment file along with their writing samples (also shown in Figure 3.1)

Then the teacher reflected on the significance of each of the children's writing, language, and behaviors. She drew upon her awareness of the broad array of literacy concepts that children develop in order to write tentative hypotheses about their underlying literacy concepts and strategies. Then she placed her written reflection for each child in the assessment notebook (as shown in Figure 3.1).

Jamie, Mary, and Tomika are playing in the Home Living center. Jamie says, "I need some milk and eggs and bread and cookies." He gathers packages of food from the Home Living center and writes a list. Mary says she's going shopping, too. She writes a list and says, "I'll buy candy." She gets a cart and goes to the Grocery Store center. Tomika writes a list. She takes her list and gets a cart.

Jamie's grocery list and the teacher's reflection.

Mary's grocery list and the teacher's reflection.

Jamie recognizes that print communicates specific messages related to the activity. He uses a strategy of thinking about what could be bought at a grocery store to plan what he intends to write. His strategy for writing is to select printed words from familiar food items to copy onto the list. However, he does not match the words that he says he will write with the words he does write. His writing demonstrates awareness of directionality and linearity, list format, words as composed of groups of letters, and recognizable (although not perfect) upper-case alphabet letter formats.

Mary recognizes that print communicates messages and uses her knowledge of food items in a grocery store to assign meaning to her writing after she has written. Her writing demonstrates awareness that writing consists of discrete symbols. No conventional letter formats are discernable although the number 5 is included.

Tomika's grocery list and the teacher's reflection.

Tomika is willing to join in the activity of writing with other children. She knows that writing carries a message, but does not use her knowledge of grocery items to assign a specific message to her writing. Her writing consists one line of linear mock cursive.

FIGURE 3.1. Anecdotal records of observation at the Home Living and Grocery centers.

Using Insights to Plan Responsive Instruction

Once teachers have written tentative hypotheses about their students' literacy concepts, they make decisions about instructional activities that will provide children with opportunities to push forward. Teachers consider how to use what children already know to provide bridges for the development of more complex concepts. They consider adjustments in current instructional activities, changes in materials and activities for particular centers, or alterations in classroom routines. They may decide to prepare particular instructional activities for some children or to spend a few minutes each day with one or two children in a particular center. For example, after observing Jamie, Mary, and Tomika play in the Grocery Store center, their teacher decided that Jamie and a few other children would benefit from fingerpoint reading to expand awareness of written word and strengthen understanding of the relationship between spoken and written words. She decided to spend time with Mary and Tomika as they wrote their names for morning sign-in to support their attention to linearity and conventional letter features and formations.

USING ASSESSMENT TASKS

Several assessment tasks can be used to evaluate children's emerging understandings of foundational literacy concepts. The most effective assessment tasks will be informal—using materials developed by teachers and similar to those used in instruction and center activities. They can be used for assessing children individually or in small groups.

Assessing Children's Constructs about Meaning

Being able to construct a thorough understanding of a storybooks or informational book is based on a variety of abilities, including oral language development, size of vocabulary, awareness of the basic structure of stories (concept of story) or informational books, and experience talking about and recalling information from books. Each of these components has a strong relationship to comprehension.

Assessing Language and Vocabulary Growth

Speech and language pathologists may be available to screen children for language development and identify children with language delays. These specialists are likely to use standardized language tests such as the *Peabody Picture Vocabulary Test—Revised* (Dunn & Dunn, 1981), *Test of Language Development: Primary* (TOLD; Newcomer & Hammill, 1988), or *Expressive One-Word Picture Vocabulary Text—Revised* (Gardner, 1990). These tests provide information about articulation difficulties, use of complex sentence structure, and level of vocabulary development.

When these services are not available, teachers can use children's *mean length of utterance* (MLU) as they engage in a variety of oral language tasks as one way to assess language development. MLU is the average number of morphemes that children use in a thought unit. A morpheme is a unit of meaning; a word is often one morpheme, such as *happy* or *walk*; but a word can be more than one morpheme when it has meaningful additions, such as *unhappily* (3 morphemes) or *walked* (2 morphemes). A *thought unit* (T unit) is similar to a sentence; it includes an independent clause and any dependent clauses connected to it (Hunt, 1965). Dependent clauses are indicated by use of connectives such as *then, because,* and *if.*

A child's MLU can be measured by tape recording a sample of the child's language during play in a center, while composing a story at the writing center, or when retelling a favorite informational book. Generally, a small unit of time is selected for this analysis—up to at most 5–10 minutes. Using the tape-recorded conversation, teachers count the total number of morphemes spoken by a particular child, count the number of T units, and divide the total number of morphemes by the number of T units to calculate MLU. With practice teachers will not need to tape record or even write a child's words; rather, they can count the number of morphemes spoken in several T units and find the average.

A conversation between Leslie, Delores, and Daryl as they played in their preschool Office center illustrates how to determine MLU. Daryl is stamping papers while Delores is pretending to write. Leslie picks up the phone and says (Neuman & Roskos, 1993, p. 111):

LESLIE: Cops? Come and get Daryl and Delores . . . Bye (Looks at others) Cops comin' to get you and Delores.

DARYL: Uh-uh

LESLIE: Is

DARYL: Uh-uh

LESLIE: Yes. Yes they IS! (Picks up telephone receiver).

DELORES: They gonna come get me? They gonna come get you 'cuz youse bein' BAD!

LESLIE: I'm calling the cops on you again.

DARYL: No you aint!

LESLIE: Yes I is. 1.2.3.4.5.5.6.6.9.9 (Dials some numbers)

In this short conversation Leslie says a total of 30 words (not counting the numbers) in 9 T units. Three of the words (*comin', I'm,* and *calling*) have two morphemes each, making the total number of morphemes 33. The MLU is 3.67 (33 ÷ 9). Delores says fewer words (14) than Leslie; four of them (*gonna, gonna, youse,* and *bein'*) have two morphemes each, for a total of 18 morphemes. She says 2 T units, and so her MLU is 9.0 (18 ÷ 2). Delores's MLU is much longer than Leslie's, reflecting the more complex sentence structure she uses. Of course, more language samples are need for both Leslie and Delores in order to gain an accurate estimation of their language complexity. Different tasks and settings often result in different measures of language sophistication. For example, having children compose stories or retell favorite storybooks or familiar informational books may allow them to demonstrate more sophisticated language use.

Vocabulary growth is another aspect of language development that early childhood teachers may want to assess. Certain literary, theme-specific, or technical words are essential components of theme activities or books read aloud to children (Duke & Kays, 1998; Levy, Wolfgang, & Koorland, 1992; Senechal, 1997). Teachers expect that children will learn these new words—both be able to understand their meaning and use them in their conversation during storybook read-alouds or theme activities. Vocabulary assessments indicate whether children are acquiring an understanding about specific words and are able to use them in their spoken vocabularies.

Teachers can prepare vocabulary assessments by selecting a set of target vocabulary words that are particularly relevant to a theme, unit, or book and to which children will be exposed on multiple occasions during the theme or book interactions. To assess children's vocabulary acquisition, teachers select several book illustrations that provide opportunities for children to use the target vocabulary. Teachers ask children to tell what is happening in the illustrations, noting whether children use any target vocabulary (Senechal, 1997), or they can have children retell informational or storybooks and then count the number of target vocabulary words children use in their retellings (Leung, 1992). One preschool teacher read *Rosie's Walk* (Hutchins, 1968) as part of a farm theme with her group of 3- and 4-year-olds. She used the illustrations in this book to determine whether her children were acquiring words she had talked about during several read-alouds, including the words *chicken coup, hen, beehives, haystack, goat, rake, tines,* and *tractor.*

Assessing Story and Informational Book Retellings

One way to assess children's understanding or comprehension of books is to have them retell stories or informational books that they have heard read aloud. Retelling checklists are effective assessment tools to gauge the amount and accuracy of children's recall. Teachers compose checklists by writing the major events in the story or informational book in a list format. Figure 3.2 presents a retelling checklist developed for the book *Owl Moon* (Yolen, 1987). As shown in this checklist, the main ideas and important details are divided into short phrases, leaving out most descriptive phrases. As children retell a text, teachers match the gist of the children's recounting with the events and information on the checklist. In order to keep track of the order of children's recall, teachers can use a numbering system on the checklist. Teachers can make note of when children make insightful inferences not included in the checklist or when they include literary language such as similes or metaphors. This indicates an abstract level of comprehension not usually measured in a retelling checklist. Over time, children recall more information from both informational books and storybooks (Pelligrini & Galda, 1982), and their retellings follow the order of events and use the language features as they are presented in the book (Duke & Kays, 1998; Newkirk, 1989; Purcell-Gates, McIntyre, & Freppon, 1995). Children's retellings shift from remembering just a few ideas in random order to recalling many ideas in a well-connected sequence.

Assessing Children's Constructs about Print

Concepts about print, knowledge of alphabet letter names, and concept of word are three critical components of children's print constructs. Concepts about print include

_____ Pa and I went owling

_____ Pa did not call out

_____ you have to be quiet if you go owling

_____ Pa stopped at the pine trees

_____ he called who-who-whoooo

_____ the sound of a great horned owl

_____ he was silent and we listened

_____ there was no answer

_____ we walked on and I felt cold

_____ you have to make your own heat if you go owling

_____ we went into the woods

_____ the woods were dark, black

_____ you have to be brave if you go owling

_____ we came to a clearing

_____ Pa called who-who-whooo

_____ an echo came through the trees who-who-whoooo

_____ Pa called back who-who-whooo

_____ the owls' shadow flew over us

_____ Pa turned on his flashlight

_____ we stared at one another

_____ then the owl flew back into the forest

_____ Pa and I walked back

FIGURE 3.2. Retelling checklist for _Owl Moon_ (Yolen, 1987).

book orientation concepts (how to hold the book right side up and turn the pages from front to back), directionality concepts (that print is read rather than pictures, that print is read from left to right), and letter and word concepts (that print includes such things as _letters_ and _words_) (Clay, 1993). Clay's concept about print assessment has been used with children as young as 3 years old. Many teachers make their own versions of the assessment using a familiar picture book.

Alphabet Knowledge

Alphabet knowledge is usually assessed by presenting children with the upper-case and then the lower-case letters typed in random order on a card (Appendix B presents administration and scoring sheets that can be used for assessing alphabet letter recognition). Children point to each letter on the assessment and identify its name. Teachers keep track of which letters children recognize on a scoring sheet. Clay (1993) presents norms for this assessment for children 5 years old and older. In general, children are expected to learn the names of some upper- and lower-case alphabet letters in preschool, especially the letters in their names. Children who begin kindergarten knowing many, if not most of the alphabet letters are at an advantage (Snow et al., 1998). At the end of kindergarten children should not only know all the upper- and lower-case alphabet letters, but also know them so well that they can identify letters fluently (Adams, 1990).

Another alphabet assessment is to determine how well children can write letters. Teachers name a letter (see Appendix B for an administration sheet for this task), and children write the letter. Teachers judge whether the letter is similar in form to the expected shape (although some orientation problems are acceptable). Using the assessment in Appendix B, teachers can observe whether children are able to write the letters quickly and accurately or whether they confuse letters and have some orientation problems. Children can write letters in either upper- or lower-case.

Younger children's concepts about alphabet letters can be assessed using a name writing task. Children are invited to write their names, and their attempts are scored according to a 7-point scale (adapted from Bloodgood, 1999, and Hildreth, 1936): (0) no response, (1) scribble, (2) linear scribble, (3) separate units (but no letters formed), (4) mock letters (letters shapes that are not conventional but share some features with actual letters) or mixture of mock letters and a few conventional letters, (5) first name generally correct (although all letter formations may not be well-formed or have correct orientation), (6) consistently well-formed name (smaller-sized letters with good legibility).

Concept about Word

Concept about word includes children's recognition that words are units of written language and that spoken words can match up with written words. This concept is assessed by having children attempt to fingerpoint-read a familiar text that can be memorized with moderate amounts of practice. The text of a familiar nursery rhyme can be used for this assessment by printing it in a small booklet. Each page of the booklet should include two or three lines of the nursery rhyme typed in a large font and with larger-than-normal word spaces. For example, the first page of a concept-about-word assessment book might include an appropriate illustration (perhaps using clip art) and the text:

Jack   and   Jill

went   up   the   hill

After children become familiar with the oral version of the rhyme, teachers can introduce the specially prepared concept-about-word nursery rhyme book that will be used with fingerpoint reading. Teachers demonstrate the fingerpoint-reading procedure by reciting the poem and pointing to each word. During the second reading, the child and teacher point together, with the teacher modeling and providing feedback on the child's pointing attempts. On the third attempt the teacher observes while the child attempts to read and point at the words. Children who have a concept of word will point to each written word one at a time (or self-correct when pointing gets off) as they say the corresponding spoken word. Children with a developing concept of word can be expected to exhibit the following behaviors, ordered here from more sophisticated to less sophisticated concept of word: matching correctly one-syllable written words with spoken words but not matching correctly two- or more syllable words, matching spoken syllables to written words, or stressing spoken words and attempting to point at units without correctly matching words. Children without a clear concept of word may point at the first letter and then glide across the line without attempting to point to separate written units, or they may quickly point across lines of text without a clear linear movement (adapted from Bloodgood, 1999).

Assessing Children's Constructs about the Alphabetic Principle

Concepts related to the alphabetic principle include children's awareness of rhyming words, alliteration (words with the same beginning phoneme), onset and rime, and letter–sound relationships. We recommend that teachers use puppets to engage children in assessment activities, making them more like games than tests.

Assessing Phonological and Phonemic Awareness

Assessment of children's phonological sensitivity to rhyme and alliteration can be accomplished in a variety of ways. Teachers can present children with a set of three pictures (*cat, fan,* and *hat*) and have children select the two pictures that rhyme (Lonigan et al., 1998), or children can pick the picture of the word that does not rhyme (called an *oddity task*; Maclean et al., 1987). Another way to assess rhyme is to give children a word such as *cat* and ask them to produce as many rhyming words as they can. Appendix B provides an example of a rhyme assessment sheet. First, teachers describe rhyming words and demonstrate pointing to rhyming pictures. Next teachers have children practice pointing to two rhyming word pictures. The children point to the two pictures that rhyme on the ten assessment tasks. Appendix B presents rhyming pictures that can be used in this assessment.

Alliteration (the ability to determine whether words begin with the same initial sound) can be assessed in the same manner as for rhyme: by selecting which two pictures begin alike, by selecting which picture does not begin like the others, or by producing additional words that begin with the same sound as a target word. Sensitivity to alliteration can also be assessed by giving children a word such as *Sam* and asking them to say just the little bit they hear at the beginning of the word (/s/). This task assesses whether children can identify and say the phoneme in isolation. Appendix B presents an example of an alliteration assessment sheet. The teacher copies the assessment sheet. First the teacher demonstrates by explaining beginning phonemes. The child practices selecting two pictures that begin with the same sound from three pictures. In the next ten tasks, the children point to the two pictures that have the same beginning sounds. Appendix B presents this assessment.

Ten sets of pictures are sufficient to determine whether a child has acquired a concept of rhyme or alliteration. Correctly matching seven out of ten pairs indicates concept acquisition, whereas matching fewer than three pairs indicates that children do not yet understand the concept.

Sensitivity to onset and rime requires a slightly higher level of phonological awareness. Teachers can assess children's ability to blend onsets and rimes by presenting words segmented into onsets and rimes. First teachers say the onset, wait 5 seconds, and then say the rime (Stahl & Murray, 1994). Children say the word blended together. For example, the teacher says /s/, pauses, then says /am/, and the child replies with the word *Sam*. Before presenting this assessment, teachers use a puppet to demonstrate the task several times. Appendix B presents a blending onset and rime assessment sheet. The teacher demonstrates with three words, saying the onset, pausing, then saying the rime. Then the teacher demonstrates saying the word blended together. The teacher then presents only the onset, pauses, and rime. The child must blend the word together.

Children's ability to segment onsets and rimes can be assessed in a similar fashion. In this case teachers would demonstrate saying a word and then segmenting it into its onset and rime, pausing between them. The teacher says a word such as *Sam*, and the child is asked to say it in little bits: /s/, pause, /am/. Appendix B provides an administration sheet with the words to be used in this assessment and a picture page for children. The teacher demonstrates with three words. Then the child is shown each picture and told its word; the child then must segment the word into two parts at the onset and rime. Again, using 10 words is sufficient to determine whether children can blend or segment onsets and rimes.

The ability to segment and blend all the phonemes in a word is the most difficult phonemic awareness task (Yopp, 1988). Most preschoolers and many kindergartners have difficulty with this task even after instruction. If children can segment words into onsets and rimes, teachers may want to assess if they can do the more difficult task of segmenting the word into all its phonemes. Appendix B presents a list of 4 practice and 10 target words that can be used to assess phoneme segmentation. The list includes words with two and three phonemes. Teachers demonstrate the task by saying the entire word, then saying the word a little bit at a time using a puppet, as they push up a penny or other object into boxes found on the assessment sheet. Then children practice saying the demonstration word segmented into phonemes and pushing up a coin as they say each phoneme. The teacher provides corrective feedback, demonstrating the word again correctly if the child does not perform the task. Then the child segments the 10 assessment words without teacher support. If the child does not segment the word entirely, then the teacher can observe which portions of the word he or she is able to segment. Pictures to use in this assessment are presented in Appendix B.

Assessing Letter–Sound Relationships

Children's knowledge of the relationship between letters and phonemes can be assessed in a variety of ways. Children can be shown a picture and asked to name the letter that is associated with the beginning sound of the word in the picture, or they can be shown a picture and asked to select one letter from a set of three that has the beginning sound associated with the word represented by the picture. Pictures and letters presented in Appendix B can be used to assess children's knowledge of letter–sound relationships. Teachers pronounce the name of the picture and have the child point to the letter that spells the beginning sound.

Children's use of letter–sound relationships can also be assessed by having children attempt to spell words (Bear et al., 2000; Johnston, Invernizzi, & Juel, 1998). Children can be encouraged to spell by keeping the activity game-like and assuring children that correct spelling is not the purpose—rather, the purpose is to see how many letters they can use in trying to spell the word. The spelling assessment is used to analyze components of words that children attempt to spell (including initial consonant, final consonant, vowels, blends and digraphs, and long-vowel markers). To assess children's awareness of these phonic elements, we suggest using words such as *bug, fan, sun, lip, vote, flag, skip, shape, cheat,* and *drive* for this assessment. Children may spell these words with random letters, indicating they are aware that words have letters but not which letters match with sounds in words. Alternatively, children might spell a word with some consonant letters in initial or final position, indicating a beginning ability to hear sounds in words and use letter–sound knowledge to spell some parts of the word. Sometimes children produce spellings using the expected, *conventional* letters (spelling the word *fan* with an *f*). However, with early invented spellings many children spell words with letters that have reasonable but unconventional relationships to phonemes (such as spelling the word *fan* with a *v*). When spellings have reasonable, but unconventional, letter matches, teachers can score these spellings as *unconventional.*

Children may demonstrate more sophisticated letter–sound knowledge if they spell both initial and final consonants and vowels. Even when vowel sounds are spelled unconventionally, the inclusion of vowels in spellings indicates a sophisticated understanding of the structure of words, the ability to segment medial sounds in words, and letter–sound knowledge beyond the consonant level. Even more sophisticated is when children attempt to spell consonant digraphs and mark long vowels using more than one letter (see Bear et al., 2000, and Johnston et al., 1998, for more information about how to analyze children's invented spellings).

Assessing Children's Reading Level

For children who have begun to read, teachers may want to document their level of reading and use of reading strategies. Teachers can assess children's ability to read easy text at the pre-primer, primer, or first-grade level. An informal reading inventory (a commercially published assessment that can be used to determine reading levels from pre-primer through middle or high school) can be used for this purpose. Teachers may have access to benchmark books such as those used by Reading Recovery teachers. Another commercially published assessment that is especially geared toward early readers is the *Developmental Reading Assessment* (Beaver, 1997). This assessment provides benchmark books for kindergarten through third-grade levels.

When using an informal reading inventory or benchmark books, teachers ask children to read the text aloud as they take a *running record.* A running record is a recording of the miscues that children make as they read. The easiest way to take a running record is to write notations of miscues on a copy of the text that the child reads. Teachers write words that children substitute (reading *yard* for *garden*), omit, or mispronounce (attempting to read *garden* by sounding out /j/). Notation is made when children self-correct their miscues, and self-corrected words are not counted as miscues. After reading, teachers ask children questions in order to assess comprehension. Then, teachers calculate the *accuracy rate*: the percentage of words read correctly (determined by subtracting the number of miscues from the total number of words in the passage and dividing this number by the total number of words). Finally, teachers determine level of comprehension by calculating the percentage of questions answered correctly. When books are at the independent level, children can read the words with 98% or better accuracy and answer 90% or more of the comprehension questions. At the instructional level, children read words with 90–95% accuracy and answer 70–90% of the questions. Texts read with less than 90% accuracy and 70% comprehension are considered at the frustration level.

OBSERVING CHILDREN'S USE OF LITERACY IN CLASSROOM ACTIVITIES

The most effective assessment plan combines literacy assessment tasks with observations of children as they engage in literacy activities during naturally occurring classroom events. Classrooms in which literacy materials and tools are readily available provide many opportunities for teachers to observe children engaging in literacy activities. Teachers may observe children as they select books and pretend to read in the Library center. Or, they may observe children as they play in special dramatic play centers such as a classroom hospital. Teachers can note vocabulary children use and the ways in which they pretend to use writing and reading materials. Children can be observed as they use retelling props to retell a familiar story or use the props to construct a new story. Teachers can observe children as they arrange rhyming word pictures in a pocket chart or as they play with alphabet letters in a Letter and Word center.

Through classroom observations teachers can note how children's unconventional concepts about reading and writing are moving toward more conventional ones (Whitehurst & Lonigan, 2001). In order to uncover children's emerging literacy concepts, teachers need to observe children as they attend to print, attempt to read and write, and talk about their literacy activities. In addition to observing children and writing anecdotal records, teachers can use photographs, tape recordings, and samples of children's writing as further assessment evidence.

Photographs and Tape Recordings

Photographs provide children, parents, and teachers with accurate accounts of classroom events that can be used to foster insights about development. Photographs are used when information cannot be captured using other assessment-gathering tools—when several children work on a paper that is too large to store easily or when they engage in activities not yielding samples, such as when they write street signs for a city constructed out of blocks. As with all assessments, photographs should be used to capture an event that documents a significant step in literacy development (Shores & Grace, 1998). For example, a child's first time pretending to read a magazine to a doll in the Home Living center by making up a version of a favorite story might warrant a photograph.

To make photographs more systematic, teachers can keep a notebook in the same bag as the camera. Immediately after taking a picture, teachers should record in the notebook the number of the picture on the roll of film, the day and time of the photograph, and a short description of any activity or words that will extend the information captured on film. We recommend that teachers use a 35mm camera with a modest telephoto lens (Shores & Grace, 1998). Grants or teacher gifts can be used to purchase the camera and film and for developing the pictures. Once photographs are developed, teachers can write reflections on adhesive notes and attach them to the backs of the prints.

We recommend that, over time, teachers make a 90-minute audiotape for each child in the classroom. Children can be tape recorded as they play in a Home center, recite a favorite nursery rhyme, or retell an informational book. As children are recorded, teachers note the date and activity on the label for each audiotape. Teachers can later calculate MLU and write reflections about children's literacy development.

Samples of Drawing and Writing

Collecting samples of children's attempts to draw and write provides a window into their emerging concepts about print, their understandings about alphabet letters and the alphabetic principle, and their control over the language of story and informational books. Children's first drawings are usually back-and-forth scribbles. Eventually they acquire the motor schemes necessary to produce lines, dots, and circles. As children learn to control their scribbles and as they gain awareness of symbolic representations, they draw people. These early representational drawings of people are quite primitive, with large circular heads sprouting lines for arms and legs.

Children continue to expand their repertoire of motor schemes as they experiment with writing alphabet letters and drawing other objects. Children's early attempts at writing their names resemble mock cursive writing or random written marks. Gradually children's writing includes the feature of linearity—when the letters or letter-like marks are written in a line across the page. Mock letters (unconventional letters with many of the features of alphabet letters) appear, along with nearly conventional letter formations. Children do not notice word spaces or use them in early writing. As children discover the relationships between alphabet letters and sounds in spoken words, they invent spellings.

In high-quality preschools and kindergartens, children have frequent opportunities to write a variety of genres. They may write menus in the Writing center and telephone messages in the Home Living center. They may write a label for a picture in the Art center or record an observation in the Science center. Each of these samples may be collected when the writing indicates children have made a new discovery or have moved to a higher level of writing development. After teachers collect writing samples, they can write a caption that describes the literacy concepts reflected in the sample (Feldgus & Cardonick, 1999). For example, Figure 3.3 presents a story written by John, a kindergartner. His teacher asked him to read his story, and John replied, "I like you to visit me.

You are nice." John's teacher jotted down some notes about his reading, collected a copy of his writing, and later wrote a caption for John's writing (see Figure 3.3).

CHAPTER SUMMARY

Assessing young children's concepts about literacy is a critical component of early childhood programs. The best assessments are systematic; they are planned to meet specific goals and purposes and draw upon close and careful observation of children. Taken systematically, anecdotal notes provide teachers with accurate records of the changes in children's engagement with literacy activities over time. Teachers reflect on the information in anecdotal records to make hypotheses about children's underlying understandings about reading and writing. Teachers also use assessment tasks to pay careful attention to children's development of six foundational literacy concepts: language and vocabulary development, understanding and recall of stories and informational books, concepts about print, alphabet letter knowledge, phonemic awareness, and knowledge of letter–sound relationships. Teachers supplement assessment tasks by frequently observing children and collecting photographs, tape recordings, and samples of children's drawing and writing. Assessments, when systematic and well planned, provide teachers with valuable information about adjusting classroom instruction and document each child's literacy development over time.

John demonstrates understanding of linearity and directionality. He uses mock letters formed from several of the letters in his name, especially the letters. He also writes some letters conventionally (letters D, W, and T). He repeats the few letters he can write in order to write long messages. When invited to read his message, he constructed two connected sentences but did not use past tense verbs as are expected in story texts.

FIGURE 3.3. John's writing sample and his teacher's caption.

CHAPTER 4

Language- and Literacy-Rich Classrooms

In this chapter we describe how to design classrooms that are rich in language and literacy learning opportunities. We describe six principles of literacy learning that guide decisions teachers make as they design classroom environments. Then we discuss the physical arrangements of center-based early childhood classrooms and explain how to expand language and literacy activities in every center. We describe dramatic play centers that are especially effective in encouraging children's pretend reading and writing, literacy-focused centers, and literature-based centers. Finally, we discuss the teacher's role in center activities and describe how teachers can interact with children within the context of language- and literacy-rich environments.

HOW CHILDREN LEARN ABOUT LITERACY

We know that young children learn a great deal during the first few years of their lives. Much of this learning occurs in the informal interactions between a parent and child as a natural part of living. This learning takes place during authentic activities—activities that occur during the ordinary routines of life (Neuman & Roskos, 1997). Authentic activities include going to lunch at a fast-food restaurant, stopping at the post office to buy stamps, and calling friends on the telephone to arrange for a ride. As a part of such meaningful activities, children acquire concepts about the nature and purposes of language and literacy practices as they are embedded in everyday life. Such knowledge-in-practice is powerful in socializing young children toward the particular literacy practices of their communities (Collins, Brown, & Newman, 1989).

Zone of Proximal Development

The term *zone of proximal development* is used to describe the interactions between parents and children as children learn about their family's literacy practices (Vygotsky, 1978). In the zone of proximal development the child cannot perform a process or task alone but can do so with the support of the other person. This explains how children learn in school as well as at home. In the zone of proximal development, teachers provide cues for where children should look, describe how actions are to be performed during the task, and monitor the success of children. As children internalize the teacher's language and behaviors and use these to control their own language and behaviors, they leave the zone of proximal development. Now children have learned to do the process independently. However, more learning occurs as children practice the learned process. Through practice they acquire the ability to accomplish the process or task automatically and fluently without conscious thought.

One example of learning in the zone of proximal development is described in the following interaction between a 3-year-old and her mother. This interaction began when Kristen decided she wanted to learn how to write the letter *K* herself. She had not previously written this alphabet letter, but had asked her mother to write it for her on numerous occasions.

Kristen Learns to Write *K*

Kristen's mother was writing at her desk, and Kristen was sitting on the floor drawing and writing with her markers. Kristen stood up and demanded that her mother show her how write the letter *K*: "I [with great emphasis] write *K*."

Her mother replied, "You write *K*? You want to write a *K*?" Kristen's mother picked up her pen and said as she wrote on a sheet of paper, "Line down [as she wrote a vertical line], now line in [as she wrote the diagonal line downward to meet the center point on the vertical line] and line out [as she wrote another diagonal line out and downward from the center point to complete the letter *K*]. Now you write it."

As Kristen wrote, her mother said, "OK, line down, then line in and line out." (Kristen's attempt at writing *K* is presented in Figure 4.1a.)

Kristen looked at the letter she had written and said, "No, no."

Her mother said, "Good job. I see a line down [she pointed at a line Kristen had written]. We need a line in and a line out [she said with emphasis as she pointed outward from the vertical line]." (Notice that Kristen's attempt has a vertical line and a diagonal line; however, the diagonal line goes beyond the vertical line to make the letter look more like the letter *X* than the letter *K*.). "Try again."

As Kristen wrote another letter her mother repeated, "Line down, line in, line out." (Kristen's second attempt at writing *K* is presented in Figure 4.1b.)

Kristen said in frustration, "No, that's an *H*!" (Notice that Kristen's attempt has two vertical lines that are prominent letter features of the letter *H*.)

Kristen's mother said, "Yes, it does look like an *H*. Try again with line in and out [with emphasis]."

Kristen attempted to write the letter *K* two more times (as shown in Figures 4.1c

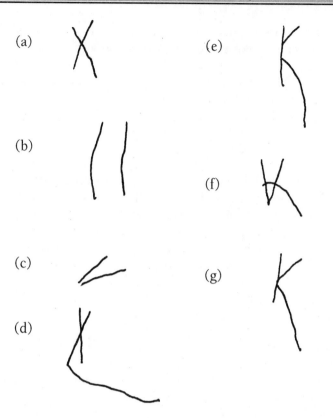

FIGURE 4.1. Kristen attempts to write the letter *K*.

and 4.1d), each time with her mother repeating, "Line down, line in, line out." Finally Kristen wrote the letter in Figure 4.1e and said, "Hey, I wrote *K*. Look, look, I wrote *K* [with great excitement]!"

Her mother replied with the same excitement, "A *K*! A *K*! You did it. Can you do it again?"

Kristen immediately wrote the letters that appear in Figure 4.1f and 4.1g. She said, "*K*" in a very satisfied tone. Her mother replied, "Yes, *K*," in the same satisfied tone.

Principles of Literacy Learning

This example illustrates the first principle of literacy learning: *Learning emerges from social interaction during joint participation in an authentic task.* Kristen needed her mother's help to learn to do a task she wanted to do but could not do on her own—write the letter *K*. However, this example illustrates two additional principles of literacy learning: *Learning is accelerated when instruction is responsive to the needs of the individual learner,* and *learning is refined through feedback.* Kristen's mother adjusted her directions and support to Kristen's attempts. She was responsive to what Kristen was doing and not doing. She realized that Kristen's problem seemed to be figuring out how to stop the first diagonal line at the center point on the vertical line and then changing directions to make the second diagonal line outward and downward from that center point. Kristen's mother provided feedback about what Kristen could do, "Yes, it does look like an *H* [in response to the two vertical lines Kristen had written]," and feedback on what needed to be adjusted, "Try again with line in and out [with emphasis]."

Over the next year Kristen demonstrated another principle of literacy learning: *Learning is extended through independent practice.* For several months Kristen experimented with writing many other alphabet letters. It took her over a year to learn to write nearly all the upper-case alphabet letters (and her mother continued to help her learn on infrequent occasions). It was not until the end of kindergarten that Kristen had independent control over writing both upper- and lower-case letters.

As a result of Kristen's independent and self-initiated writing of alphabet letters on hundreds of occasions during her preschool years, she learned more than merely how to write individual alphabet letters. She learned to write them quickly and fluently, without conscious attention to the direction or length of the lines she needed to write. Figure 4.2 presents some writing that Kristen produced when she was 4 years and 1 month old. When her mother found the paper on the floor of her bedroom, she asked Kristen about the writing. Kristen replied, "Well, that's my writing you know. I did it last night. But I think it might be something more like maybe a message. Can you can read it?" As shown in Figure 4.2, Kristen has written the letter *K* along with many other alphabet letters. However, what Kristen seemed to be focusing on during this writing was not forming letters, but actually writing, and perhaps writing a message. Because Kristen no longer needed to focus her attention on how to write alphabet letters, she could now attend to how writing functions to communicate with others.

Motivation to Learn

There are at least two additional principles of literacy learning that are illustrated in the example of Kristen's learning to write and use alphabet letters. One principle is that *learning is more likely to occur when materials are at hand at the time the learner is motivated to engage in reading and writing tasks.* Having paper, pens, and pencils conveniently on hand probably prompted both Kristen to want to write and her mother to spend 5 minutes on this task. Writing and reading materials could be found in most rooms of

FIGURE 4.2. Kristen's message writing.

Kristen's home, and each location suggested different purposes for reading and writing. Kristen copied menus in the kitchen and drew television guides in the family room. She pretended to read and browsed through books in her bedroom, and she enlisted her father's help in writing letters to friends on the computer in the home office.

The final principle of literacy learning illustrated by Kristen's case is that *learning emerges from tasks that are meaningful and motivating to learners.* A corollary to this principle is that *learners become motivated to do authentic tasks.* Kristen found the task of writing on her own very motivating and clearly knew how to participate in writing activities. But it is important to keep in mind that Kristen was not born motivated to engage in literacy activities such as learning to write alphabet letters. Instead, her motivation arose from the way Kristen's mother and father used literacy to entertain her.

One way that her parents entertained Kristen on long car trips or during waits at a doctor's or dentist's office was to engage her in writing games. Long before Kristen could write, her mother would take a pencil and paper and say, "Look, I'll write *Kristen*. Do you want *Kristen* to be big [in an exaggerated deep tone] or little [in a squeaky high tone]?" In this playful way her mother elicited Kristen's interest in the activity, then entertained her with writing using her voice, gestures, eye contact, gentle hugs, and much praise for attention to the task. Kristen could not escape print, watching her mother or father write, or paying attention during writing interactions. Because the interactions were playful and engaged Kristen's attention and participation, Kristen *became* motivated to write.

Conventional and Unconventional Learning

It is important for teachers to realize that the outcome of interactions within a child's zone of proximal development is not necessarily learning a conventional concept or skill. It just so happened that Kristen was prepared to learn how to write the letter *K* conventionally. She already knew what the letter *K* looked like because she knew when her attempts did not look like that letter. She had already developed many motor schemes for writing letter features because she had some control over the length and placement of horizontal, vertical, and diagonal lines. She merely needed to learn to put all these skills together to write a conventional letter *K*.

Chapter 2 presents another example of a parent and child interacting in the zone of proximal development in which the outcome was not conventional learning. Carrie's father helped her spell *poison* as *PZN* (see pp. 24–25). At first Carrie wanted her father to spell the word for her. However, with his guidance she was willing to attempt spelling it herself, and, further, to expand her spelling beyond her initial attempt that comprised only the beginning and ending phonemes to include a medial phoneme as well. Although *PZN* is not a conventional spelling, it does represent learning on Carrie's part.

These six principles of literacy learning (summarized in Table 4.1) can guide teachers in preparing the classroom environment and planning instructional activities. Teachers do not wait for children to be motivated to engage in reading and writing; they prepare authentic language and literacy activities that will be engaging and capture children's natural curiosity. They make sure that materials are accessible to children in a

TABLE 4.1. Six Principles of Literacy Learning

Literacy learning:

- Emerges from social interaction during joint participation in a task
- Is accelerated when instruction is responsive to the needs of the individual learner.
- Is refined through feedback.
- Is extended through independent practice.
- Is more likely when materials are at hand at the time the learner is motivated to engage in literacy tasks.
- Emerges when learners become motivated to do literacy tasks

variety of locations in the classrooms, and they suggest many different authentic purposes for reading and writing in those particular locations.

SPACE, MATERIALS, AND CLASSROOM ARRANGEMENT

Teachers are thoughtful about the arrangement of space and materials in the classroom because they influence how children behave (Christie, 1991). Children are more likely to engage in inappropriate running or rough-and-tumble play in large open spaces. They are likely to wander in and out of small spaces without sustaining activities when the materials and their arrangement are undefined (Isbell & Exelby, 2001). Children are more likely to engage in higher levels of social play and more dramatic play in small spaces with materials that suggest a specific theme. Therefore, careful arrangement of the classroom space, thoughtful selection of materials and their storage, and attention to simple routines for using classroom spaces and materials provide the foundation for effective learning.

Arranging the Classroom Space

Most early childhood classrooms include at least one well-defined large space for whole-group activities such as listening to the teacher read books aloud. This space is typically carpeted, includes a comfortable chair for the teacher, a pocket chart, and an easel for reading big books (enlarged copies of children's books) or displaying chart paper for writing. Many classrooms include small tables where children eat snacks or work on projects. These tables can serve multiple purposes by being part of an Art or Writing center. All classrooms include accessible storage areas for children's belongings and for classroom materials.

Using rugs, plants, pillows, and lamps softens classrooms that are in institutional settings, provides visual appeal, and can reflect the particular culture of local communities (Isbell & Exelby, 2001). Bringing in unusual and natural materials from the local community and beyond arouses children's curiosity and invites their active exploration of the classroom environment. Displays of photographs of children as they engage in classroom activities also allow children to make personal connections to the classroom.

Children notice when classrooms are appealing and include meaningful activities. Branscombe (1991) described one young African American boy's reaction to a summer lab classroom where he had many successful experiences reading and writing—unlike his earlier experiences in kindergarten, where he was considered a behavior problem: "It be play. See, you go and read and do stuff in de large group. Den you go to de choice board and choose your work. Den you do your art. Art . . . dat be my work. Then you do your journal and have snack. Play . . . you know. It be play. It be fun! You be learnin . . . " (pp. 111–112). This classroom was appealing because it included actual butterflies and turtles and colorful nonfiction books about butterflies and turtles that the teacher read aloud and then placed for children's independent exploration in the Safari center. It provided opportunities for choosing from various activities, including creating a 10-foot construction-paper tree—all on the first day of class.

Centers

Early childhood classrooms that support language and literacy learning include *centers*, small spaces sectioned off from other classroom space that are equipped with materials to encourage children's active involvement. Centers are designed for groups of three or four children to work and play independently or cooperatively. They allow for child-directed play, considered a critical part of early childhood classrooms. Effective centers are designed to provide connections between the children's world and the wider environment they will encounter in their later lives. In the safe environment of play within centers, children can try out new roles and rearrange events to fit their level of understanding. In this environment, they build confidence as capable learners (Isbell, 1995).

The Role of Centers in Children's Development

Centers are a critical component of early childhood classrooms for a number of reasons. At this stage of development children learn best when they are actively involved in constructing, playing, talking, and observing. The amount of time that children can sit still and listen is limited, although teachers continue to help children extend this time. Therefore, learning *can* occur in whole-group sessions (Dickinson & Sprague, 2001). However, learning is more likely to occur as children are actively engaged in completing a task—using materials, talking about the task at hand, and negotiating with peers and their teacher as they complete the task.

Young children—especially at-risk children—bring very different experiences to school, including their language use. When all children are expected to complete the same task in a prescribed way, with a correct answer, at the same time, the opportunities for failure multiply. On the other hand, centers that offer children choices, *open-ended activities* (activities without any one correct outcome) and activities on different levels of difficulty ensure everyone's success. Children who feel successful are more likely to try new things, sustain their interest and activity, and develop self-confidence and self-regulation. Helping children make choices and develop self-discipline is an important part of early childhood programs.

Centers encourage a great deal of play. Through play children develop problem-solving skills by trying out different solutions when conflicts arise. They develop social skills as they negotiate with the peers over differences of opinion and language skills as they talk with and listen to other children. Children learn to plan, carry out their plans, and persist in completing a task. Their attention spans are expanded as they sustain their play around common topics. The level of their play deepens as they move from manipulating props to using props in symbolic play to using imaginary props to extend play in new directions.

Centers can provide opportunities for teachers to accelerate individual children's learning. Using centers allows teachers to work and talk intensively with just a few children. As children play in centers, teachers can join in the activities for a portion of the time children spend in the center. At other times teachers need to conduct directed lessons with small groups of children selected for particular purposes. Well-designed center activities allow young children with various levels of experience to work independently so that teachers are free to work with small groups of children on these teacher-directed instructional activities.

Typical Early Childhood Centers

Centers are designed to engage children in particular activities, such as pretending to visit a veterinarian's office in a Drama center or retelling stories and browsing through books in a Book or Library center. Most classrooms include five to eight centers, depending on space and the number of children served. Common early childhood centers are the Home Living, Blocks, Art, Sand and Water, Nature and Science, and the Math center (the Math or Counting center may often consist of small manipulatives like beads).

Teachers select the centers that they will place in their classrooms based on the backgrounds of the children. Most classrooms will have children with a variety of different developmental levels and background experiences. Meeting children's needs, therefore, will require a range of typical early childhood centers along with some specially designed dramatic play centers and a few unique centers that will evolve from the curriculum. Each center will include materials and activities that appropriately challenge children with different levels of knowledge. Materials will be labeled and stored where they are accessible to children. Teachers will consider the size of the space and the nature of activities in order to establish rules about the number of children allowed in the center and acceptable behavior and material use. Activities in centers will change on a regular basis to maintain children's interest.

Library Center

One of the most important centers for children's language and literacy development is the *Book* or *Library center*. Figure 4.3 presents a Library center suitable for preschoolers and kindergartners. The components of a high-quality Library center (Fractor, Woodruff, Martinez, & Teale, 1993) include

- space large enough for three or four children;
- a display of objects and books arranged with their covers visible;

FIGURE 4.3. Preschool/kindergarten Library center.

- accessible storage for 100 or more books (The minimum number of books included in a classroom should be 10 times the number of children. However, not all books should be stored in the Library center; some will be located in other centers.);
- some books grouped into categories (e.g., books about animals, bugs, and favorite characters);
- equipment for at least two children to listen to recorded books, with storage for 10 or more books and tape bags;
- attractive wall displays, including photographs of children retelling stories and charts asking children to indicate their favorite animal and storybook characters;
- soft, comfortable seating; and
- a special display place for books recently read aloud by the teacher.

This center offers children several choices for activities, including looking through books, listening to books on tape, browsing through books on topics of recent study that their teacher has read aloud (animals and bugs), or writing on survey charts to indicate their favorite character (see Chapter 6). While the activities in the Library center may remain the same, the materials in the center are changed every 2 or 3 weeks. New books on tape are exchanged for old books, new objects and book displays are arranged, and tubs of books on more recent topics of study replace those on previous topics.

Enhancing Language and Literacy Activities in All Centers

With simple adjustments in materials, teachers can expand the opportunities for children's authentic use of language and literacy during their play in all typical early childhood centers. Recall that children's earliest experiences with literacy are embedded in their everyday life experiences. Familiar settings with authentic objects prompt children to step into dramatic play in which they use reading and writing as they have observed parents and others do in their communities. Children are likely to pretend to read and write during dramatic play at a Home Living center when the teacher carefully selects authentic literacy props that could be expected to be found in the children's homes. These might include telephone books, food coupons, play money, note pads and pencils, play checkbooks, calendars, cookbooks, recipe cards, pizza delivery menus, envelopes, stationery, and note cards. Teachers can also help children construct their own props for centers. For example, children enjoy making baby albums to place in the Home Living Center by bringing in their own baby pictures and dictating captions. Teachers may help children construct personal telephone books listing the names and imaginary or real (with parent permission) telephone numbers of all the children.

With careful consideration, teachers can add materials and activities that increase the opportunities for language and literacy activities in every center. Teachers can add schematic drawings and blueprints of buildings, large blank sheets for children's schematic drawings and blueprints, clipboards with pretend lumber order forms, and homemade books with captioned photographs of children and their block constructions in the Block center. Even outdoor play can be altered to include literacy opportunities when teachers provide appropriate materials. Children can become truckers, police officers, and race car drivers as they ride bikes, read maps, and write speeding tickets. They can open a drive-through window for a fast-food restaurant with paper bags, plastic food, credit cards, play money, and a menu. They can set up a car wash with buckets and soap, signs for the cost of a wash, tickets, and play checkbooks.

In addition to enhancing centers with authentic reading and writing materials related to the theme of the center, teachers can also read aloud story and informational books that will extend children's awareness of how to play in the centers. For example, *Building a House* (Byron, 1990) provides an illustration of a blueprint and describes how to construct a house, starting with digging the foundation. This book provides children with new vocabulary and an extended understanding of construction activities that can extend their play in a Block center.

Dramatic Play Centers

While all early childhood centers can be enhanced with literacy materials, centers that encourage dramatic play are particularly fruitful for stimulating preschool and kindergarten children's language and literacy experiences (Snow et al., 1998). *Dramatic play centers* encourage children to take on many different roles in an authentic activity. They are most effective when the theme is clearly defined and when a wide variety of literacy materials related to the theme is available. Play themes that elicit high levels of pretend reading and writing include an office, library, veterinarian's or doctor's office, post office, and restaurant (Morrow & Rand, 1991; Neuman & Roskos, 1997). Table 4.2 presents a description of props that encourage pretend reading and writing which can be included in dramatic play centers. Other possibilities include a Camping center, Mall, Gas Station, Construction Site, or Beach center (Isbell, 1995).

Teachers select themes for dramatic play centers based on the experiences of their children. Children need some familiarity with the theme in order for it to be effective, but teachers can extend children's ability to play in more complex ways by introducing children to the props included in the center and explaining their possible uses. They can read related books and mention connections between events in the book and possible play activities in the center. The most effective way to extend children's play in dramatic play centers is to take children to actual sites—a local fast-food restaurant or grocery store. When field trips are not possible, teachers can take children on pretend field trips. They can demonstrate and guide children in dramatic enactments of activities as if they were on a field trip.

Literacy-Focus Centers

Much of young children's literacy learning will occur in three classroom contexts: participating in center activities including dramatic play centers, exploring literacy concepts in specially prepared *literacy-focus centers*, and during large- and small-group teacher-directed lessons. So far in this chapter we have discussed children's learning in self-selected and self-directed activities in centers. Later in the book we will discuss teacher-

TABLE 4.2. Dramatic Play Centers That Encourage Pretend Reading and Writing

Theme	Dramatic props	Literacy props
Veterinarians'/ Doctors' office	Chairs and table Telephone White lab coats Masks Plastic gloves Cotton swabs Play stethoscope Bathroom scale Dolls and stuffed animals X-rays	Magazines Books/pamphlets on pet care Signs Payment forms on clipboard Appointment cards Telephone book Play checkbooks Pencils, pens, markers Patient forms Various pads of paper
Office	Chairs and table Telephones Racks for file folders Box for index cards Typewriter Calculator Computer keyboard In/out trays Clipboards Paper clips, rubber bands, scissors	Calendar and appointment books Message pads and various pens/pencils File folders and various types of paper Index cards and business cards Signs Date stamp Assorted business forms Post-it notes Ledger sheets
Post office	Tote bag for mail Mail carrier hats Shoe boxes (to sort mail) Mail boxes Telephones Paper clips, rubber bands, scissors Scale	Pencils, pens, markers Various envelopes Stickers and various gummed Shapes Calendar Telephone book Various forms from the post office Assorted stationery and postcards Catalogs
Library	Table and chairs Box for index cards Telephone Typewriter Computer keyboard Various pads of paper	Books and book cards Date stamp and stamp pad Magazines Blank library cards Markers, pencils, pens Post-it notes
Bank	Table and chairs Telephones Play money Calculator Box for index cards	Deposit and withdrawal slips Play checkbooks Loan and credit card application forms Pamphlets and brochures Index cards and various papers Pens, pencils, markers

Note. Adapted from Morrow and Rand (1991) and Neuman and Roskos (1997).

directed lessons that are designed to accelerate language and literacy learning. The most effective classrooms for diverse learners are those that strike a balance between teacher-directed instruction and child-initiated learning. Literacy-focus centers are one way teachers can maintain that balance.

Literacy-focus centers are designed to allow children to explore independently materials and concepts introduced in teacher-directed lessons. These centers put learning materials "in children's hands." Independent exploration of materials without teacher direction allows children to connect what they currently understand about literacy concepts with the new strategies and skills introduced by the teacher. Teachers will expect that children's explorations of materials in literacy-focus centers will not necessarily look conventional—and the purpose of literacy-focus centers is not to make sure all children reach the same level of conventional understanding about literacy concepts that have been introduced in lessons. Teachers keep in mind that preschool and kindergarten children expand their concepts about literacy by playing with literacy materials in unusual and highly creative ways (Ballenger, 1999; Meier, 2000). Literacy-focus centers will be used more frequently with kindergarten and older preschool children and less frequently with younger children.

Table 4.3 provides a list of possible literacy-focus centers, including Computer, Writing, Letter-and-Word, Sound, and Overhead-Projector centers. This list provides suggestions for materials and activities that might be found in these centers. Only a few of these centers will be available at any one time during the school year, although some centers may be in use most of the year (such as the Writing center). Activities in these centers will both remain stable and change to reflect the objectives and materials used in current literacy instruction. For example, children may have access to stationery, a variety of writing implements, small blank books, blank postcards, and alphabet stamps in the Writing center. However, as a result of an instructional activity, children may be also encouraged to use clipboards to write a list of names of children in the classroom or to cut words from coupons to use in composing an ABC book of foods.

Managing Centers

Teachers have many decisions to make related to managing centers and children's choices. Some teachers may allow children free choice about the selection of centers. They may allow children to sign their names on a sign-in sheet that indicates the number of children who may play. In other classrooms, children may select colored beaded necklaces, with the colors indicating the centers and the number of necklaces of a color indicating the number of children allowed to play at a center. Alternatively, teachers may prepare *planning* or *choice boards* to assign children to centers.

Regardless of whether centers are self-selected or assigned, teachers need to prepare children to play in centers. Teachers may prepare the children to use a choice board by demonstrating how to use the board to determine which center to play in. Teachers then set guidelines for how children are expected to interact with each other and use materials in each center. For example, teachers may expect children to select at least one activ-

TABLE 4.3. Literacy-Focused Centers

Center focus	Materials
Computer	Text and graphic programs such as Kidpix, KidWords 2, Kidwriter Golden Edition; learning programs such as A to Zapp, Kid Phonics, Wiggleworks, Letter Sounds; books on CD-Rom such as *Biley's Book House, Chica Chica Boom Boom, Curious George Learns the Alphabet, Living Books, Mixed Up Mother Goose, Tales from Long Ago and Far Away, Storybook Theater*; books and stuffed characters or animals to accompany CD-Rom books
Writing	Writing tools such as pencils, pens (with variety of shapes and toppers), markers (of different sizes, scented, and mixable), alphabet (stamps, tiles, cookie cutters, sponges, plastic, felt); crayons, chalk; writing surfaces such as clipboards, wipe-off boards, chalkboards, paper (lined, unlined, cut in shapes, various colors and textures), pads (Post-it notes; pads with printed notes; spiral-bound pads); reference materials (such as photo book with children's pictures and names, words related to themes, visual dictionaries, pictionaries, alphabet chart, copies of menus from local restaurants); environmental print (bags from grocery stores or fast-food restaurants, newspapers, coupons, catalogs)
Letter and word	Various upper- and lower-case alphabet letters (magnetic, plastic, tiles, cards in different fonts and sizes), ABC charts, clothespins and clothesline, pocket chart, shoe pocket organizers, wikki sticks, alphabet puzzles, words (children's names or theme-related), paper, crayons, markers, bingo or Concentration alphabet cards, large boxes (for sorting), word books, alphabet books, environmental print (e.g., bags from groceries or fast-food restaurants, boxes of food)
Sound	Laminated pictures (words that rhyme, words with the same initial consonants, words with the same final consonants), magazines, scissors, paper, glue, tape recorder and headsets, audiotapes of books with language play (many rhyming words or alliteration; sound games made by the teacher or parents), rhyming books, books with alliteration, pocket chart, boxes for sorting
Overhead-Projector	Transparent alphabet letters and words with pattern and word cards, transparent characters and objects for retelling stories, transparent nursery rhymes (with transparent words and alphabet letters to match), blank transparencies and pens, transparent alphabet chart and alphabet letters, small objects and plastic letters (to sort by rhyme or alliteration), transparent children's names and plastic letters

ity at each center and to complete that activity before moving to the next center. Many teachers have children complete a daily or weekly center checklist to indicate the centers they have visited and the activities they have completed each day.

Because center activities are such a critical part of early childhood programs, it is important for teachers to keep track of how children play and interact with others in centers and which centers children select. Having children participate in record keeping extends their ability to plan and review their activities. For example, teachers can prepare a *center record* by writing the list of centers across the top of a large chart and the list of children's names down the side. At the end of center time, teachers ask each child to briefly report which centers he or she visited that day. Teachers place a check by those centers. This quickly allows teachers to see if children are selecting a variety of centers or whether they are spending the majority of their time in only one or two centers.

Teachers also need to plan to observe each child in center activities on a regular basis. Observing each child closely for about 10 minutes at least once a month provides teachers with valuable information about the children's engagement in learning activities and their learning growth (see Chapter 3 for more information on taking anecdotal records and writing reflections about children's learning).

Materials

Along with arranging the classroom space, teachers carefully consider the kinds of materials to include in centers. We have already provided information about a variety of language and literacy materials that are appropriate for use in early childhood centers, dramatic play centers, and literacy-focused centers. An often overlooked, but crucial classroom material for children from diverse backgrounds is environmental print.

Environmental Print

Some of the most effective language and literacy materials are free—they are the print found in the wider environment of the world beyond the classroom. One of the reasons that *environmental print* is so effective is that it brings the everyday world of the children into the classroom. This is especially so for children whose home language is not English. Environmental print allows all children to share together the print in their homes and communities. Teachers can collect and ask children to bring from home environmental print items, including empty cereal boxes; toothpaste boxes; other product boxes; Sunday newspaper supplements with coupons and colorful advertisements, many featuring distinctive product logos; junk mail; old telephone books, especially yellow pages; maps; shopping bags with store names; photographs of street signs and store signs (one roll of film and a short drive around town can yield many usable images). These materials can be used in many ways: as props in play centers, as reading materials in the Reading center (e.g., a scrapbook of distinctive writing and logos from environmental print items), as writing models in the Writing center (children enjoy copying from an identical scrapbook), and as games.

Teachers can construct several types of *environmental print matching* and *sorting* games (Christie & Enz, 2002). An example of a matching game is a bag filled with pairs of laminated cards bearing logos cut from environmental print items and pasted on the cards (e.g., the fronts of two small Cheerio cereal boxes or sides of two boxes of toothpaste). Children dump out all the cards and find the matching pairs, again, identifying letters and words as they do so. The same cards can be used to play a memory game; the players' job with all the cards mixed up and face down is to take turns peaking at the faces of two cards at a turn, picking them up only if a match is found.

A variation on any matching game is to have one card bear the environmental print word in the form it is found on the item—usually in a logo-like, colorful, distinctive print—and have the other card bear the just the word in black-and-white (produced by making a photocopy of the original) without its distinctive logo. Alternatively, the match can be the word printed with marker in ordinary manuscript handwriting. Teachers demonstrate how to use the puzzles and games, especially reading the words (running their fingers under the words from left to right) and perhaps identifying some letters on the puzzle and game pieces. They do this both when they introduce the game into a center and when they join with a group of children to play the game during center time when the center is still new.

An example of another sorting activity is to have a boxful of environmental print word cards and several alphabet cards. Children make stacks of environmental print words that begin with the same letters that are on the alphabet cards. This requires having the word cards right side up, focusing on the first letter in the word, and matching that letter with the alphabet card letter even when the font and color probably are not identical. Teachers can also make *I can read bulletin boards* with environmental print items that they know many students can read. Students enjoy stopping by the bulletin board (especially if its items are changed regularly) and demonstrating their competence in naming all the print items.

Classroom Print

Another important kind of literacy material is the print found on the classroom walls, on bulletin boards, and on posted directions. The most effective *classroom print* is that which is dictated or written either by the teacher or children. Commercial displays usually have little appeal for children, whereas children highly value class-made pictures, charts, surveys, and lists.

Children's awareness of print is heightened when classroom objects bear printed labels, when bulletin boards and teacher-made posters include print as well as pictures, and when centers include print items, whether magazines in the waiting area of a Doctor's Office play center, or *Color, Cut,* and *Glue* directions in an Art activity center (Richgels, 2003). However, the power of classroom print does not reside in its merely being displayed or made available. Simply labeling the refrigerator, stove, and table in the Home Living center does not allow teachers to demonstrate how print functions. Instead, teachers need to place useful print in the classroom and demonstrate that usefulness frequently.

For example, before choice time, teachers can point to the *Color, Cut,* and *Glue* directions posted in the Art center and say, "Remember, if you choose to work at the Art center to make your own foods poster, it will work best if you work in this order. First color the foods on this sheet. See the word *color* here next to the picture of a crayon? Then cut out your food picture. See the word *cut* here next to the picture of a pair of scissors? And then last you do the gluing. See the word *glue* here next to a picture of a glue bottle? That way works best, and these words can help you to remember to color (pointing to the word again), cut (pointing to that word again), and last of all paste (pointing to that word again)." Through deliberate demonstration and explanation, teachers can promote both functional and meaningful use of classroom print.

The Teacher's Role
in the Language- and Literacy-Rich Classroom

One component of creating a language- and literacy-rich classroom is having the room arranged properly with the right materials. However, just putting appropriate materials in the classroom is not enough. Teachers must provide frequent and deliberate demonstrations of how to use the materials and make explicit why they are important for readers and writers. We have described a teacher who purposely prepared a *Color, Cut,* and *Glue* directions poster, demonstrated how to read it, and made explicit its purpose. Teachers can provide demonstrations in many different ways. They may join in children's play, for example, to make a telephone call and write a note, demonstrating these activities and simultaneously increasing the sophistication of the children's literacy interactions. Similarly, teachers can occasionally enter dramatic play centers and take on a role in children's ongoing play. During role play, teachers can name literacy materials, explain how or introduce new ways to use literacy tools, extend children's themes by suggesting new episodes, and contribute more sophisticated vocabulary related to the play themes (Neuman & Roskos, 1993).

However, teachers' contributions to children's literacy learning will not stop at merely demonstrating how and why to use literacy or joining in with children's play. Teachers will deliberately seek out children for conversation during center time. Rich conversation emerges naturally as a teacher and a child or small group of children talk together about their activities. Of course, such one-on-one conversations must not become an invasion of children's play. Instead, effective teachers drop in on children's center activities so that they can join in conversation that is already ongoing. This means that teachers will frequently talk with small groups of children about topics of interest to them.

Teacher–child conversations such as the ones that arise during center activities are critical to children's language development (see Chapter 5). However, good teachers are careful not to take over or correct children's language or products. Rather, they sit in on, collaborate with, and respond to children's ongoing conversation and activities. For example, a teacher visiting the Writing center may say, "I'm writing about Joey's mom's visit. What are you writing about?" Teachers also keep track of whom they have spoken with and how the conversation has gone so that no child is neglected and so that the teacher can keep track of children's spoken language development.

Another important role that teachers play when they interact with children in center activities is to judge whether a child's activities provide a *teachable moment*. A teachable moment is when a teacher realizes that with just a suggestion, an offer to help, or a demonstration, the child will use a new strategy. For example, when playing a matching game with environmental print cards, the teacher may notice that one child has matched two cards that include pictures as well as print and placed them side by side with the print conventionally oriented; however, the child does not seem to realize that the print on the cards is the same. A teacher might notice this, comment on what the child has done, and offer a new strategy: "I see you have the cards right side up so that it is easy to see if these words are the same [running her finger under the words—tracking words from left to right]. Let's check the first letter [pointing to the first letter of each word]. Yes, I see that they both have the letter [pausing for the child to name the letter]." Later, this child may be able to use this strategy independently to match environmental print words.

CHAPTER SUMMARY

This chapter introduced six principles of literacy learning. Literacy learning emerges from social interaction during joint participation in an authentic task, is accelerated when instruction is responsive to the needs of the individual learner, is refined through feedback, is extended through independent practice, is more likely when materials are at hand at the time the learner is motivated to engage in literacy tasks, and emerges when learners become motivated to do literacy tasks. These principles guide the space, materials, and arrangements of classrooms. Literacy-rich classrooms are center-based. They are well stocked with literacy materials and tools. Conversations among children as well as between the teacher and children are considered an integral part of the classroom environment. Teachers provide frequent demonstrations of how and why to use literacy during the ongoing activities in the classroom. They engage children in conversation during center activities and are attuned to the possibilities of the teachable moments when children are poised to learn a new concept or strategy. Within such classrooms, at-risk children from diverse backgrounds acquire the language competencies and literacy skills they need in order to become highly successful readers and writers.

Language Development
Gateway to Literacy

Chapter 5 extends our discussion of the classroom environment. In this chapter we demonstrate that effective literacy teaching is embedded in a classroom environment that arises from thoughtful, responsive dialogue between children and their teacher. We describe how to improve the quantity and quality of language interactions that occur during whole group activities and in more informal one-on-one conversations during center activities and other classroom events. We discuss issues that teachers need to consider when talking with children who come from diverse backgrounds—children whose home language is not English, children who speak a dialect of English different from the dominant dialect of their community, and children whose families represent a variety of cultures. At the end of the chapter we describe how children use their spoken-language competencies in their first encounters with written language, such as when parents or teachers read books aloud to them. We also discuss new language strategies that children need to acquire in order to become competent users of written language.

ESTABLISHING A HIGH-QUALITY LANGUAGE ENVIRONMENT

Classroom environments consist of more than just an arrangement of space and its materials. Instead, it is the interaction among people (children, teacher, aide, volunteers, parents) and the materials in the classroom that create environments (Roskos & Neuman, 2001). Some environments provide all children access to activities and resources that allow them to acquire new vocabulary, new strategies for using language to meet social and academic goals, and a new sense of competence (McGill-Franzen & Lanford, 1994). Other environments provide opportunities for some children to learn, but not all. One of the most constraining factors in an environment is whether children have access to a teacher who provides high-quality literacy activities and talks with them frequently. That is, a critical component of classroom environment is the quality of its language interactions. Through high-quality classroom conversations, children acquire new concepts at the same time as they become more competent language users.

Although preschoolers and kindergartners have already acquired much competence with their native spoken language, their language development is, nonetheless, not complete. They have still to learn many new words and many new meanings of old words. They have still to acquire greater ability with word parts and sentence structures, or *syntax*. High-quality preschool and kindergarten classrooms help children acquire better spoken language as well as learn the foundations for literacy development. Spoken language is one of the critical underlying conditions that support children's later reading and writing achievement.

Language Development and Dialect

At 3, 4, and 5 years of age, young children are acquiring the ability to communicate their meanings in ways accepted as more conventional in their language environments. Many at-risk children about whom this book is written are dialect speakers. They speak a form of language different from the mainstream language spoken by highly educated members of their communities. While dialects differ in form from language that is considered standard, dialect speakers are just as capable of communicating complex, abstract messages as are speakers of language considered standard.

The purpose of the language activities that we describe in this book is not to require children to speak in standard language. Rather, it is to expand their ability to use language to express meanings. Children will acquire ways of speaking more like the dominant ways in their community by being included in conversations in which teachers use such language and through listening to books as they are read aloud. The focus of conversations in preschool and kindergarten should always be on the meaning being conveyed rather than on the form in which meaning is conveyed. Teachers can use many of the strategies we describe later in this chapter to extend and elaborate on children's responses in ways that will demonstrate a more complex form of their communicated message.

Second-Language Development

Just like English-speaking children, non-English-speaking children have acquired competence as language users by being included in conversations with parents or other caregivers, siblings, and peers. They have been socialized into their family's, community's, and culture's ways of using language to accomplish everyday routines. As a result, children, including English-speaking children, bring to preschool and kindergarten an understanding of how to use language that is appropriate in their family, community, and culture. Teachers can expect that for children from diverse language and cultural backgrounds there will be differences between their understandings of language use and appropriateness and mainstream expectations (Delgado-Gaitan & Trueba, 1991). Teachers will need to be sensitive to possible miscommunications due to differences in expectations and understandings (see more about this later in the chapter).

Some children will be lucky enough to enter a preschool or kindergarten in which their home language is the primary language of instruction. For other children, they will begin school with the additional task of also acquiring competence in English. As English-language learners (ELL), they will need to acquire a new vocabulary, a new awareness of how to enter and interact within a conversation, and new ways of seeking and obtaining help. They must also learn how to behave appropriately in this new setting so that they can be viewed as competent learners.

Learning English is accomplished in the same context as learning a first language—through conversations. Learning English is dependent upon many factors, but key is children's willingness to attempt to communicate through English. Language is learned through conversations in which an ELL child attempts to communicate a meaning and a teacher uses gesture, pointing, dramatizations, and repetition to confirm and extend the child's meaning. A teacher's attempt to understand and communicate through simplified language is called *comprehensible input* (Krashen, 1982). Teachers need to focus on making themselves understood and making sure they understand children's attempts. Just as with dialect differences, the concern cannot be on the correctness or conventions of language. Rather, the focus must be on the message. Communicating a message successfully and frequently naturally extends children's ability to use more complex sentences that gradually become more conventional.

Many ELL children seem to move through several stages as they acquire English (Tabors & Snow, 1994). During one of the earliest stages, children memorize phrases that allow them to seek help from the teacher or peers or to enter into ongoing play. The number of these formulas that children can use increases as ELL children attempt to gain more information and more interaction with others. Children frequently repeat words and phrases they have heard and pay close attention to words and actions to connect meanings with words.

There are many concerns related to using English as the language of instruction in preschool and kindergarten, to second language acquisition, and to language development, in general. What is important here is for teachers to understand that all children are still developing language competence during their early childhood years. Regardless of whether children speak English or another language, they still need frequent opportunities to engage in conversations with others in order to continue to expand their native language competence. The best opportunities for this occur when teachers are bilingual and are able to talk with children in their home language. In some preschools and kindergartens, aides are carefully selected to provide language resources for the children in the classroom. For example, one preschool classroom of 19 children included five children who were native Spanish speakers and four who were Khmer (language of Cambodia) speakers. This classroom was fortunate to have two classroom assistants—one was bilingual in Spanish and the other in Khmer (Brewer, 1998). However, even when teachers and aides speak only English, all children need language experiences in their home language.

The commonsense expectation is that, for ELL children, native language development can occur in the home; however, it often does not. Unfortunately, research (Fillmore, 1991) has shown that regardless of whether children enter a bilingual or an English-only preschool, ELL children are particularly at risk for language loss. They tend to rely more and more on English for communication, even in their homes. Therefore, even when teachers cannot help children further develop their home language, they need to find others who can. They must actively seek ways to bring speakers of other languages into the preschool or kindergarten setting. Parents and community resource persons can help teachers identify people in the community who would be willing to come to school as "conversation partners." Parents and other volunteers can tell stories, help children retell stories in their home language, and talk with children as they play in an Art center or Drama center. Teachers will also need to find children's books published in the children's home languages for volunteers to read aloud. When these are not available, teachers can draw upon the community resources to construct their own books.

CLASSROOM CONVERSATIONS

Rich experience with spoken language means conversation, that is, really talking with children. So among the most important things a teacher can do for preschoolers and kindergartners is to make time to converse with them, to engage them in real talk about their lives, their activities, and their interests. This may seem difficult because of the number of children in a classroom, and because often other matters, especially matters of classroom management, seem more pressing. Having real conversation with all children in a classroom is not easy, but it is necessary. Therefore, teachers must plan for it; they must make time and occasions for it.

Improving Whole-Group Conversations

Good-quality conversations are essential whether they occur one on one or in whole-group situations. Teachers can improve the quality of whole-group conversations by keeping track of the two biggest determinants of any conversation, turn taking (Who gets to talk and for how long?) and topic selection and maintenance (Whose topic gets discussed?) Teachers can consider the following questions: Who is dominating the talk? Who talks most frequently? In most classrooms, the answer is *the teacher*. Some teachers control conversations by asking questions whose answers are a single, short, right answer (often a *yes* or a *no*). Other teachers invite more open conversations, perhaps by suggesting a topic and then inviting responses. Some teachers really pause to listen to children. For example, teachers might say, "I noticed on the way to school today that some of the trees had little green dots on the branches. Those dots are called buds," or "I thought we might talk about something that worries me. There is a lot of trash blowing around on the playground lately." These are conversation openers that signal to children that they must really think and respond conversationally rather than participate in question–answer dialogues.

Teachers need ways of signaling to children when it is acceptable for several children to speak at once and when children need to listen to just one of their classmates at a time. Teachers need to be explicit about these things in order to monitor themselves (being sure that they are really doing these things) and in order to make their expectations clear to children. But teachers quickly must let the children know that it is their contributions that matter, that the teachers really want to know what the children have to say, that the teachers will listen, and that the children's ideas are important. Teachers might say, "I wonder what you know about those little green buds? I wonder what's going to happen to them?" or "I'd like to know what you think about that trash? Is there something we could do about that?"

Once children begin talking, teachers' responses are important. They may need to repeat, clarify, or expand a child's response, but they should be careful not to fall into the role of sole judge and manager of responses. It is not always their role to say whether or not every child's contribution is right or wrong and who gets to talk next. If teachers always convey this expectation, then true whole-class conversation will never occur.

Two things happen when children know that the teacher will not pass judgment on every response. First, they look to one another to continue the conversation; second, they know that contributions can be part of the mix without always being accurate, that one purpose conversation can serve is to entertain multiple ideas and eventually sort them out. That sorting out may mean determining together whether certain offered ideas are right or wrong. It may mean recognizing that in a particular conversation, with a particular topic, right and wrong do not matter. Or it might mean realizing that more work is needed, that they need to go to another activity or other sources to determine what is right. To do this, teachers can say about children's contributions, "That's important" or "That's interesting" or "I see" or just nod their heads and then say "Anybody else?" or look to another person for a contribution.

Sometimes teachers can loosen the reins of the conversation by saying "I can see you all have a lot to say about this. Let's take some time for you to talk to the person next to you about trash." Teachers have routines for reconvening the whole group. One teacher we know says, "One, two, three, kindergarten check time," and all the kindergartners know to return their attention to her. Teachers and classrooms will have their own conversational styles. It is important for teachers to learn what works best for them. Tape recording whole-class conversations and listening to them later can help teachers to see how they can accomplish these goals within the ranges of their own styles.

Improving the Quantity and Quality of Teacher–Child Conversations

As critical as the quality of whole- and small-group conversation is to children's language development, opportunities for one-on-one conversations are even more crucial. However, research has shown that many preschool children have little opportunity to talk with adult caregivers or teachers in child care or preschool settings (Snow et al., 1998). Where children did have opportunities to talk with adults, the quality of conversation was found to be low. We describe how teachers can increase the number of conversations they have with each child and how to improve the quality of those conversations.

Increasing the Number and Quality of Conversations

With responsibility for large numbers of children, preschool and kindergarten teachers are often hard-pressed to find time to talk with individual children. While teachers feel as if they do nothing but talk all day long, most of this talk is directed to groups of children and its purpose is to manage behavior or provide information for the whole group. Teachers can increase their opportunities to talk with individual children in two ways: set goals for having at least one or two conversations with each child each day, and make teaching in small groups more like conversations (Clay, 1998). Teachers need to be particularly concerned to have conversations with children who are least likely to initiate them: children whose home language is not English or children with poorly developed language who struggle to put thoughts into words. Clay advised teachers to "talk to the ones who are least able to talk. . . . Talk when the going is hard. Listen when the child wants to talk. . . . Reply, and extend the conversation" (1998, p. 11).

The best way teachers can expand the number and quality of conversations they have with individual children is to sit and stay with children and talk with them about their activities. *Sit and stay* means that teachers will spend lots of time during center activities in just a few locations rather than cruising around the room making sure children have materials they need and are engaged in worthwhile activities. *Sit and stay* to talk with children can occur during snack and other mealtimes, when children and teachers are most likely to have high-quality conversations (Dickinson & Tabors, 2001).

High-quality conversations are those in which the participants solve a problem, complete a task, learn something new, or share information. In a conversation, all speakers are sensitive to the other speakers' understandings. They seek to clarify and confirm one another's understandings in order to reach joint understanding. In such conversations, the focus is always on the meaning being communicated. This is especially true for younger children, children who speak a dialect different from the community's dominant dialect, and children for whom English is not their first language.

However, conversations can sometimes provide teachers with opportunities to expand children's language by modeling the use of more complex syntax and demonstrating ways of speaking that are considered more standard. In the context of conversation, teachers can sometimes use strategies that expand upon children's responses (Manning-Kratcoski & Bobkoff-Katz, 1998). One of the easiest strategies that teachers can use to expand children's language is to *recast* their responses. If a child says, "doggy bark" the teacher recasts the child's words into their expanded and more conventional syntactic form, "Yes, the dog is barking." Another strategy is to use *repetition*, in which teachers repeat their recasted response, "The dog is barking. The dog is barking loud!" When used carefully, *questioning* is another strategy that can extend children's responses. After giving a response, teachers ask a question calling for the child to provide the same information in a longer and more complex sentence. For example, the child comments, "Doggy bark," and the teacher asks, "Why is that dog barking?" The child may respond with the extended sentence, "Doggy bark at squirrel." *Elaboration* is another language-extending strategy. It also involves using some of the child's own words, but embedding those words in slightly more complex sentence structures and adding a bit more related information. For example, a child asked, "When Daddy comes home?" and his mother elaborated, "Daddy will come home soon when it gets dark" (Clay, 1998, p. 8).

Another way of enhancing the quality of conversations is to ask for further clarification—invite the child to tell more. The more children talk, the more likely teachers are to understand what they are trying to communicate. The more children talk, the more opportunities they have to practice language use. Simply replying with "Mmm" suggests that teachers are listening and ready to hear more. Conversations can be enhanced by letting children have more time to reply. After asking questions, the teacher can wait several seconds to provide children with opportunities to frame a response. One of the best indicators of the quality of a conversation is its length; good conversations involve many give-and-take interactions between two or more speakers.

Talking with children about past events provides particularly rich opportunities to engage them in high-quality conversations that are critical for literacy development. When children are asked to describe a past event in which they participated—such as a birthday celebration or a trip to the mall, they must talk about objects, people, and events that are not visible to the speaker or listener. In order to talk about the past, speakers must use decontextualized language because the words used will not refer to the objects or events in the immediate context of the speaker and listener. Language interactions in which children are coached as they try to retell past events are particularly helpful in preparing children for later reading and writing (Dickinson & Smith, 1994; Purcell-Gates, 1988). These conversations are even more powerful when teachers contribute by modeling their own retellings of past events. As teachers model recalling what happened, for example, on their trip to the mall, they can use relatively rare and unique words as a part of their conversation. When discussing a trip to the mall with children, teachers can use words such as *pedestrian walkway, vendors,* and *saunter.*

Using Conversation to Teach

Conversation is a model for teaching as well as for learning. Conversation requires that both participants (teachers and children) attempt to reach joint understanding. Children come to understand more of what the teacher means, and teachers come to understand what children know. Once teachers understand what children know and do not know, they can shape the conversation to further children's thinking and expand their concepts. In the following conversation, Mrs. Poremba asked two kindergartners to read plans they had written for building an incubator. Before writing the plans, the boys had carefully examined a photograph of an incubator found in *The Little Duck* (Dunn, 1976). Jason and Freddy used invented spelling to write a list of materials they would need in order to build their own incubator. Their writing appears in Figure 5.1.

As Mrs. Poremba prepared to read *The Little Duck* to the class, Freddy asked her if she would read the plan they had written for constructing an incubator. Instead, Mrs. Poremba invited Freddy to read it himself (from Richgels, 2002, p. 593).

> "Could *you* read it for us, Freddy?" she countered.
> "I don't think I can remember."

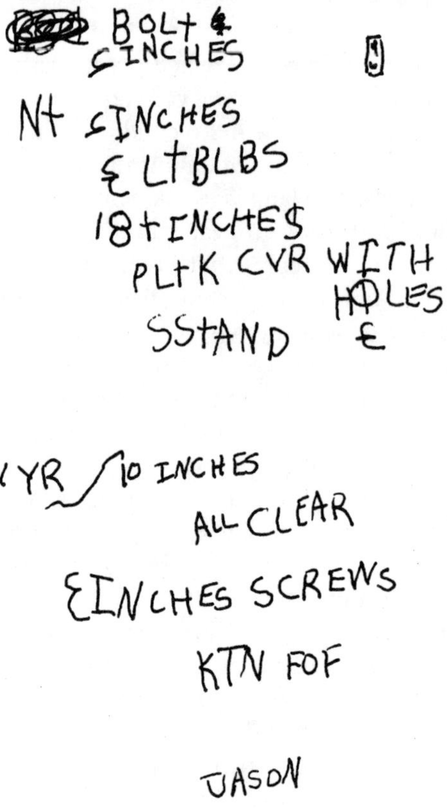

BOLt &
CINCHES

Nt CINCHES
& LtBLBS
18 tINCHES
PLtK CVR WITH
HOLES
SStAND   &

WYR / 10 INCHES
AllCLEAR
& INCHES SCREWS
KTN FOF

JASON

FIGURE 5.1. Jason's and Freddy's plans for making an incubator (Richgels, 2002, p. 592).

"Mmm hmm" said Mrs. Poremba.
"I can't remember either," said Jason.

Neither boy, despite both boys' sophisticated level of invented spelling, was willing to read his writing to the class. Mrs. Poremba, however, suspected that with help both boys could read their plan. She pointedly looked at the composition and thought aloud.

"Mmm, that's a good idea. Oh, I see. Okay. Okay. I remember they were talking about bolts."
"Two inches bolts," said Jason.

At this point Jason was also looking at the plan, including the text that Mrs. Poremba was reading. Mrs. Poremba continued to invite conversation while she looked at and sometimes read the plan.

"Two inch bolts, okay," said Mrs. Poremba. "And, [reading now] 'Two inches nuts.' [Conversing again now] Two inch nuts. And how many light bulbs did you need?"

"Two," answered Jason.

"Two, okay. And here you wrote an *18*, [reading again] 'inches—' " Mrs. Poremba paused in her reading.

" 'Plastic cover,' " read Jason.

" 'Plastic cover with—' " read Mrs. Poremba.

" 'Holes,' " read Jason.

" '—holes!' " continued Mrs. Poremba. [Back to conversation now] "Holes in the plastic cover. Okay."

They read in a similar manner about the stand and the wire.

Then Mrs. Poremba asked, [Reading] " 'All clear?' [Now conversing] What's that?"

"We wanted every single piece to be clear," Jason explained.

"Okay."

"So we could see all the things inside," explained Freddy.

By reading from the plan, Mrs. Poremba made explicit that the print was guiding her conversation. Next she pointed to the words KTN FOF on the plan but did not read. She paused and Freddy commented about the words.

"That's to put the egg on," Freddy hinted. "If you drop it."

" 'Cotton—' " read Mrs. Poremba.

" 'Fluff!' " read Jason.

[Continuing to read] " 'Fluff,' [Now conversing again] okay," said Mrs. Poremba. "What a good idea!"

In this conversation, Mrs. Poremba provided instruction as well as support for Freddy and Jason to read. Mrs. Poremba demonstrated several strategies that the boys could use later in rereading their own writing. She demonstrated thinking about and remembering what they had discussed while they wrote ("I remember they were talking about bolts"). She looked carefully at the printed text for words and numbers she could read ("and here you wrote an *18*, 'inches—' ") and paused to invite help from others in figuring out the part she could not read (Jason supplied "plastic cover"). As she demonstrated these strategies, Jason and Freddy looked at the text, recalled what they had discussed, and read their words.

Because she listened closely to the children's responses during the conversation, Mrs. Poremba was aware of Jason's and Freddy's level of literacy knowledge and sensitive to their thinking. This allowed her to draw their attention to things they overlooked when asked to read, to point out new strategies for reading, and to acknowledge the worthiness of their writing. While Mrs. Poremba clearly wanted Freddy and Jason to engage in reading, she was willing instead to engage with them in a conversation. Jointly negotiated, the conversation came to include reading as well as talking.

The conversation among Freddy, Jason, and Mrs. Poremba illustrates responsive instruction in which teachers personalize conversation so they are responsive to the specific needs of individual learners. Responsive instruction occurs when teachers know something about children's backgrounds and interests.

Using Conversation to Accommodate Cultural Backgrounds of Children

Conversation and instruction that specifically takes into account children's culture is called *culturally sensitive* (Diamond & Moore, 1995) or *culturally responsive* (Ladson-Billings, 1994). Culturally responsive teachers have high expectations for all children's learning but are aware that children from different cultural backgrounds may approach learning in different ways. They continually seek knowledge about the cultural backgrounds of their children and enlist the assistance of community members and parents as regular volunteers in the classroom or for special classroom projects.

Seeking Cultural Information from Parents and Community Experts

Learning about children's worlds outside of school allows teachers to adjust the classroom environment and instruction to be more congruent with children's worldviews. The place to begin understanding children's worldviews is with their parents. Parents transmit and interpret culture for their children. "Children learn the habits, traditions, and ways of life of their families" (Gibson, 1999, p. 19). Teachers who show respect for the worldviews of parents are more likely to garner their help in supporting their child's learning and in discovering critical information about family and community cultures. Respect is obvious when teachers acknowledge parents' high expectations for their children's academic success and their families' sacrifices for the good of the children's educations (Edwards & Danridge, 2001). Teachers also show respect for parents when they "avoid making sweeping generalizations [about children's home or culture] based on skin color or surnames" (Strickland, 1994). Wise teachers are aware that there is a great deal of diversity within every cultural group and among children in a single family.

Making home visits early in the year is an extremely valuable way to establish a respectful and supportive relationship with parents. Teachers who commit to visiting with the parents of every child in their classrooms have found that some parents prefer to meet at a neutral location such as a neighborhood fast-food restaurant, and most parents appreciate very short visits of 15–20 minutes (Edwards & Danridge, 2001). Parents give very insightful information when they are asked to a few open-ended questions such as

- Who are the important people in your child's life?
- What are the most important things I should know about your child?
- What is one of your family traditions (e.g., when someone has a birthday)?
- What is something important that you have taught your child to do? How did you teach that?
- What is most important that you want your child to learn this year? (adapted from Edwards & Danridge, 2001, p. 206)

Information from parents helps teachers understand the children's best way of learning, the nature of past and expected relationships with adults (including ways of "disciplining" children), and unexpected pools of knowledge that teachers may acknowledge and use in classroom activities (Ballenger, 1999). From conversations with parents, many teachers find that they must challenge their current beliefs about children from diverse backgrounds. More than one teacher has discovered, for example, that, contrary to his or her initial beliefs, children who live in urban poor neighborhoods are surrounded by loving, caring adults who provide rich language models (Edwards & Danridge, 2001).

Another avenue for discovering more about children's cultural backgrounds and family lives is enlisting the help of community experts. All communities have members who are able to negotiate their community for others who may not be familiar with it—for example, graduate students at a university who live in a Korean neighborhood, ministers in African American churches, bilingual parent–community liaisons in elementary schools, or local business owners. Seeking information from community experts may provide teachers with better strategies for contacting and communicating with parents and with insights into the cultural practices of communities (Edwards & Danridge, 2001).

Community experts are especially useful when the teacher does not speak the primary language used in the community or family. Parent involvement is "particularly important for [ELL children with] limited English proficiency . . . precisely because of potential differences in values and beliefs about the role of teachers, literacy, education, and schools held by parents" and teachers (Ernst-Slavit, Han, & Wenger, 2001, p. 200). For example, one teacher discovered that Chinese parents, when asked to participate in a Read-at-Home project, felt that the teacher was shirking her responsibilities as a teacher (Ernst-Slavit et al., 2001). They had never read aloud to their child, nor had they ever participated in this activity in their own childhoods. In their experience, education was achieved through rote learning. When their child, Tong-Bing, brought home a book to be read at home, the parents required him to copy the entire book in a special notebook. Through conversations with the community expert, the teacher was able to help the parents understand the importance of and goals for reading books aloud at home, and she modified instructional activities to capitalize on Tong-Bing's custom of copying to learn.

Considering Culture When Talking about Books

Children from diverse cultures are likely to have widely differing cultural practices related to listening to stories read aloud or told. In the culture that dominates in most classrooms, when teachers read a book aloud, children are expected to sit still, listen, and answer questions only when they are invited to do so or when they signal their desire to talk by raising their hands. When children make spontaneous comments about books, teachers sanction children by gently reminding them to raise their hands. In any case, children's comments are expected to be tightly related to the content of the story (Ballenger,1999). In contrast, native Hawaiian children value collaborative performance over listening. During a "talk story" (Au, 1980) a child may begin telling a story, but other children soon join in (and overlapping talk is acceptable) until the story ends with a particularly skillful child's taking over the story to its end. In contrast, Native American children are expected to be attentive during storytelling and not to interrupt (Diamond & Moore, 1995). Haitian children use books as springboards to talk about issues of personal concern and interest. Their comments seem to interrupt book reading and to be unrelated to the story content. They seem to ignore teachers' gentle reminders to look at the book and listen to the story or teachers' attempts to steer conversations around the story events (Ballenger, 1999).

All three communicative styles—Hawaiian, Native American, and Haitian—as well as those of children from many other diverse cultures reflect children's worldviews about books and literacy. Culturally responsive teachers carefully reflect on the nature of conversation and behavior of their children during these important classroom activities and consider ways to adjust their own book reading and conversations to be more compatible with children's communicative styles. Teachers have found that as they craft unique, culturally responsive conversations to be more like children's familiar communicative patterns, children can also move toward conversational patterns considered more mainstream (Ballenger, 1999).

Multicultural literature provides especially fruitful material for engaging children in culturally responsive conversations. Multicultural literature includes books "by and about members of groups considered outside the socio-political mainstream of the United States" (Bishop, 1992, p. 32), such as African Americans, Latinos, and Native Americans. It also includes books about people of color from outside the United States, including folktales, fiction, and informational books. Multicultural books selected for classroom use should be culturally authentic. Culturally authentic books have characters, settings, and events that a member of that cultural group would recognize as real and accurate (Sims, 1982). Multicultural literature dispels stereotypes and allows children to discover the elements of life common across cultures as well as unique customs shaped by individual families within cultural groups. Table 5.1 provides a list of examples of multicultural books appropriate for prekindergarten and kindergarten children, books that are useful in stimulating culturally responsive conversations.

BRIDGING THE GAP BETWEEN SPOKEN AND WRITTEN LANGUAGE

It is no accident that speaking, listening, reading, and writing are all called language arts. All four call upon competent use of language. In speaking and listening, children display spoken language competence. In reading and writing, children display written language competence. Young children, even 3-year olds, are already started on the road to literacy development by virtue of being spoken-language users. Children know from using talk in their interactions with others that language is essentially a communication process; it has meaning. Language makers construct meanings and share them with one another, whether the concrete meanings of the sentence "Joey hit me!" or the abstract meanings of "I like red." Likewise, children know how to exploit the power of language to effect

TABLE 5.1. Culturally Authentic Books[a] for Prekindergarten and Kindergarten Children

Caron Lee Cohen. *The mud pony.* 1992. Scholastic.

Niki Daly, *Jamela's dress.* 1999. Farrar, Straus Giroux.

Kristyn Rehling Estes. *Manuela's gift.* 1999. Chronicle.

Carmen Lomas Garza. *Cuadros de familia/Family pictures.* 1993. Children's Book Press.

Lucia M. Gonzalez. *The bossy Gallito/El gallito bossy.* 1999. Scholastic.

Francisco Jimenez. *La mariposa.* 2000. Houghton Mifflin.

Tony Johnston. *Uncle rain cloud.* 2001. Charlesbridge.

Lenore Look. 2001. *Henry's first-moon birthday.* 2001. Simon & Schuster/Atheneum.

Margaret Read MacDonald. *Mabela the clever.* 2001. Albert Whitman.

Pat Mora. *Tomas and the library lady.* 1997. Knopf.

S. D. Nelson. *Gift horse: A Lakota story.* 1999. Abrams.

Jose-Luis Orozco. *Diez deditos/Ten little fingers and other play rhymes and action songs from Latin America.* 1997. Dutton.

Allen Say. *Tea with milk.* 1999. Houghton Mifflin.

Cynthia Leitich Smith. *Jingle Dancer.* 2000. Morrow.

Gary Soto. *Too many tamales.* 1996. Scott Foresman.

Margaret Holloway Tsubakiyama. *Mei-Mei loves the morning.* 1999. Albert Whitman.

Janet S. Wong. *This next New Year.* 2000. Frances Foster Books.

Rosalma Zubizarretta. *La mujer que brillaba aun mas que el sol/The woman who outshone the sun.* 1994. Scott Foresman.

[a]Realistic fiction or folk tales about underrepresented cultural groups in the United States.

changes in their everyday lives, to make things happen, whether directly with the sentence "Gimme a cookie" or indirectly with the sentence "Let's color." An important consideration for teachers is what else children need to learn, aside from what they already know about spoken language, in order to learn to read and write. In this section of the chapter we describe how spoken language is similar to, but also different from, written language. We discuss the new language strategies that children need to develop through early experiences with written language that is read aloud to them.

Strategies for Understanding Spoken Language

All children are advantaged in many ways as they embark on the process of language acquisition; they have unconscious, inborn knowledge of many of the structural characteristics of human languages (Gleason, 2001). Still, parents and other caregivers have important roles to play in this process—they engage children in routine activities and conversations. Routines—by repeatedly providing, across several months, the same actions, language, participants, and objects—give children what they need to participate in and gradually to understand the language. They are helped in this by the strategies of looking, listening, and connecting. Children look at what their parents hold or point to, they listen to what their parents are saying, and they make connections between spoken words, actions, and objects.

The strategies of looking, listening, and connecting work because parents and children share the same context. They are at the same place, at the same time, looking at the same things. In addition, parents check to make sure they understand what their children are intending to say; parents and children ask and answer questions to clarify their understandings. Being in the same context, using information from that context, and asking clarifying questions allow children to be understood in conversations, but they also allow children to acquire new vocabulary and try out more sophisticated syntax. This kind of language is called *contextualized* because it draws upon the resources offered by two or more speakers talking about a common and often routine context or event in which they are participating.

Children continue to use strategies for understanding contextualized language as they enter preschool. They use the common, shared context of preschool routines to understand new words their teachers use as a part of those routines. The objects, people, and activities of the routines help children understand the words. ELL children are especially dependent on contextualized language strategies when their teachers speak a language they are just learning. When teachers point to particular portions of pictures or hold up real objects as they talk, they are helping these children to use contextualized language strategies to connect meanings to the spoken English words.

Strategies for Understanding Written Language

Written language has many of the same properties that spoken language has. Therefore, children can sometimes use their already developed contextualized language strategies for understanding written language that is read aloud, for example, when especially rich illustrations in a picture book provide supportive context for the words of the text that the teacher reads. However, written language is also different from spoken language, requiring children to learn new strategies in order to thoroughly understand its messages. As we will show, contextualized language strategies only partially help children understand the messages conveyed through the language found in books. Unlike in conversations, storybooks and informational books convey meaning primarily through words. The language found in printed texts is called *decontextualized* language because it must be understood outside of any real-life context. During reading, the context of the story must be constructed in a child's mind through the words of the text without observation of a real-world here and now. Understanding unfamiliar words presented in a book must usually be accomplished by listening to other words; there is no help from the ongoing actions of others in a shared context. Illustrations in picture books do help bridge the gap between being in a shared context and only having words. Still, children must learn to listen more to the words of a text and use the limited information provided in the illustrations to construct an understanding of words and their meanings.

Fortunately, pretend play helps children learn to understand decontextualized language. The language in pretend play works in ways similar to the language of books. It is the words, and only the words, that make a cardboard box into a rocket when a child says, "Let's play astronaut. This will be the rocket."

Nonetheless, constructing an understanding of the meaning communicated in a book is ultimately different from constructing an understanding of the meaning communicated in an everyday conversation. Compared to everyday conversations, where speakers can ask one another questions for clarification, readers are relatively on their own in trying to understand a book. In Chapter 6 we will see that talking about the events and characters in books as they are read aloud is one way that teachers help children prepare for the usually somewhat solitary meaning making of reading. Young children are able to ask questions and make comments as their teachers read aloud, much like they would in a conversation. Talking together about a book helps children make the transition from using contextualized language strategies to using decontextualized language strategies.

Functions Served by Spoken and Written Language

Spoken language does more than allow speakers to convey a meaning; it also allows speakers to accomplish a purpose. One of the first things children learn as they begin talking is that language is useful. Children use language to control the actions of others ("Up now") and to satisfy their wants ("Cookie!"). Written language functions in many of the same ways as spoken language, but it also serves unique functions. Children must learn to adapt for reading and writing the familiar purposes of spoken language, that is, how language helps them to accomplish everyday tasks. In addition, they must learn to use written language for its unique purposes.

Halliday (1975, 2002) identified seven purposes behind the spoken language of his young son, and these same seven functions have been observed in the language of other children and of adults. Written language (e.g., a story, a telephone book, or an invitation) can serve these same purposes. Knowing about the various functions of language allows teachers to plan activities to help children become more effective users of both spoken and written language. Halliday's functions are

- *Instrumental.* Satisfying needs and wants. For example, in speech, "Gimme that!" and in writing, a birthday present wish list.
- *Regulatory.* Controlling others. For example, in speech, "Stop that!" and in writing, a KEEP OUT sign.
- *Interactional.* Facilitating interaction with others. For example, in speech, "Let's jump rope" and in writing, a party invitation.
- *Personal.* Expressing opinions and other personal thoughts. For example, in speech, "I like to climb" and in writing, a kindergartner's written journal entry, *The chick is EGSOKDiD NOW thAt tehchcick is ReDDy TO fly* (The chick is exhausted now that the chick is ready to fly) (Richgels, 2003).
- *Heuristic.* Seeking information. For example, in speech, "Why?" and in writing, a classroom poster asking children to write *yes* or *no* to the written question *Did you lose a tooth?*
- *Imaginative.* Creating the world of make-believe. For example, in speech, "This

can be our castle" and, in writing, one of children's favorite storybooks, *There Was an Old Lady Who Swallowed a Fly* (Taback, 1997).

- *Informative or representational.* Conveying information. For example, in speech, "Today is my birthday" and in writing, the informational book *From Egg to Robin* (Canizares & Chessen, 1998).

Good teachers are aware of how frequently their language serves one of the seven functions. They also know which functions dominate their children's talk and which are rare or missing. They know which functions they need more consciously to model and promote. For example, a teacher might interject a comment during an informational book reading such as "This page will tell you something I bet you didn't know before" that makes explicit the informational purpose of reading such a book together. (In the discussion in Chapter 6 of shared writing, we discuss more about making the purposes of writing and reading more explicit.)

Unique Functions Served Only by Written Language

The purposes of printed text go beyond those of spoken language; written language can accomplish things that spoken language cannot. Among these are communicating across distance and time. For example, we can write a letter to relatives who live in a different state or read a novel written in the 19th century. Another function that only written language can serve is creating a record. We know that we have paid our credit card bills because we have the canceled checks. Written language, unlike spoken language, is more effective in allowing us to examine our own thoughts and clarify our expression of them. We know better what we think of the governor's veto of a controversial bill after we put our thoughts on paper and, especially, after we revise that writing before sending it to the local newspaper for the "Letters to the Editor" column.

Good teachers are conscious of the unique functions that written language serves and plan activities that explicitly demonstrate these new uses. They also make explicit comments about such uses. When a teacher writes a note for a child to take home, he or she might say, "I want you to take this note home and give it to your mom and dad. I can't go with you to talk to them, but they can read this note and know what I want to say to them. Here, I'll read what it says . . ." This makes explicit that written language allows others to communicate across distances. When teachers read a storybook, occasionally they can note the publication date and say, "Oh look. Dr. Seuss wrote this book in 1963. That was before you were born! But we still have it and we can read it today and enjoy his story today." This makes explicit that written language allows us to communicate across time.

The Teacher's Role in Spoken and Written Language Development

This chapter has described many ways that teachers can accelerate children's spoken language development, including modeling the use of sophisticated language, engaging children in one-on-one conversations, improving the quality of whole-group conversations, and embedding conversations within instruction. We have also explained how teachers can accelerate children's written language development. That is, even before children can read and write in a conventional sense, they must begin to develop strategies for understanding and communicating through language that is written. This can only happen if teachers read books aloud and if they demonstrate different purposes for writing. This head start on developing strategies for dealing with the language of books is important and often overlooked. Children who have had frequent opportunities to engage in writing and reading activities in their homes come to preschool with a head start on knowing how to use reading and writing. They also have in place some strategies that allow them to understand the decontextualized language found in books. However, for the at-risk children for whom this book is written, teachers must recognize opportunities for helping them discover written language's purposes and to develop strategies for understanding its messages. The next chapter provides more information on developing children's written language competence.

CHAPTER SUMMARY

Conversations among children as well as between the teacher and children are considered an integral part of the classroom environment as well as an effective instructional activity. Conversations are especially critical for the language development of children who are English-language learners. Classroom environments are enhanced when teachers engage children in high-quality, whole-group conversations and frequently seek out children for one-on-one and small-group conversations. Teachers can use information from parents and other community experts to personalize conversations with children and provide instruction that is more compatible with children's current level of literacy knowledge and culturally accepted ways of interacting with literacy. Teachers can carefully select culturally authentic literature and include it as a critical component of their literacy program. Finally, teachers need to be aware of the ways in which spoken language competence can be used to build bridges to reading and writing. They can help children develop decontextualized language strategies and make the functions of spoken and written language explicit during literacy activities.

CHAPTER 6

Classroom Activities That Expand Children's Vocabulary and Comprehension

The purpose of this chapter is to describe four instructional activities that are highly effective in helping children develop strategies for comprehending the written language of books and other printed texts. These activities strengthen children's awareness of how language and literacy are used, extend their vocabularies and syntax, and introduce children to new concepts and knowledge related to science and social studies content. The activities introduced in this chapter are reading books aloud, telling and dramatizing books, providing real experiences such as experiments and projects, and using shared writing.

READING BOOKS ALOUD

As we described in Chapter 5, young children are experienced at using the contextualized strategies of looking around a shared context, listening, and connecting to figure out meanings communicated through spoken language. They rely on the give and take of conversation with others and on a shared context to obtain clues for understanding the message and the meaning of any new words. Therefore, the most effective way to read aloud to children is to intersperse conversation with the reading, not just to read straight through the book. We call this *interactive reading* (Whitehurst, Arnold, et al., 1994; Whitehurst, Epstein, et al., 1994; Whitehurst et al., 1999) because it includes a great deal of interactive conversation between children and their teacher.

Interactive Read-Alouds

During interactive read-alouds, the teacher and children make comments, ask and answer questions, and make predictions. In the following interactive read-aloud, Cindy (a preschool teacher) and Jeremie read and discuss the pop-up book *Dinnertime* (Pienkowski, 1980). In this story a series of animals (illustrated with large pop-up mouths) announce they will eat another animal (shown on the previous page of the story). The conversation (with the text from the book presented in *italics*) is in both Haitian Creole (Jeremie's home language) and English (Ballenger, 1999, p. 62).

MS. CINDY: (reads first double spread of text) *One day a frog . . .*

JEREMIE: He got mouth?

MS. CINDY: *. . . was sitting on a log catching flies when down came a vulture.*

JEREMIE: Cindy, he got mouth.

MS. CINDY: Yes, they all have mouths (reads second double spread of text) *Vulture said to frog "I'm going to eat you for my dinner* [pointing to vulture] m pral manje ou (I'm gonna eat you) *and that's what he did.*

JEREMIE: Li di li pral manje moun? (he said he will eat people?)

MS. CINDY: Non, li mem, li di, "m pral manje ou" (no, that one he said, "I will eat you.")

JEREMIE: Manje on frog (eat a frog?)

MS. CINDY: Yeah, li pral manje on frog (he will eat a frog)

In this interactive read-aloud Jeremie commented twice on the pop-up mouths. Cindy only briefly acknowledged the mouths, then quickly returned to reading the text. She alternated between reading the text in English and repeating the essence of the text in Haitian Creole. Jeremie signaled by asking a question ("he said he will eat people?") that he was confused about who the vulture was going to eat. It is not surprising that Jeremie is confused. The text referred only indirectly to the frog, which is not illustrated on this page. In order to understand the story, children must infer that the vulture is going to eat the frog (the text only says "I'm going to eat *you* for my dinner"). Jeremie's question shows that he incorrectly inferred that the vulture will eat people, probably based on his prior knowledge about dangerous animals. To clarify this misunderstanding, Cindy pointed to the animals in illustrations and made explicit which animal is going to do the eating and which animal is going to be eaten. Then, Jeremie asked another question, which served to confirm his understanding that the frog will get eaten, and Cindy's response provided feedback that he was correct. Cindy intentionally expanded Jeremie's language by recasting some of his language ("he got mouth?" and "eat a frog?") into a more conventional response ("they all have mouths" and "he will eat a frog").

The Teacher's Role during Interactive Read-Alouds

The teacher's role in interactive read-alouds has five purposes:

- To prompt children's active involvement in constructing a book's meaning
- To clarify and extend children's understandings about the meaning of the book
- To expand and extend the language of children's responses
- To explain the meanings of some vocabulary included in the book
- To prompt children to use new vocabulary in their responses

Interactive read-alouds allow children to construct more complete and accurate understandings of the book being read. Teachers help them do this by making comments, asking questions, and encouraging children to ask questions and make comments. Teachers listen carefully to children's questions and comments so they can provide clarifying information. Questions and comments that are particularly effective in prompting children's participation in interactive read-alouds are presented in Table 6.1.

Prompting Deeper Understanding and Interpretation

Teachers are careful not to make interactive book reading merely a question–answer activity in which teachers read and ask questions about the story content and children answer questions (McGee, 1998). Instead, the purpose of asking questions is to provide opportunities for children to take an active role in trying to understand the story, which is important because good readers are not passive. They do not merely read through the words of a book. Instead, as they read they engage in many mental activities, such as calling up prior knowledge about the events and objects included in the book, making inferences about why characters act as they do, predicting what will happen next, and monitoring whether their predictions were accurate, whether their inferences have

TABLE 6.1. Types of Questions and Comments Used in an Interactive Read-Aloud

Questions

Completion: A comment with a pause for children to fill in the blank: "Rosie the hen went for a walk across the "

Recall Questions: "Where were some places that Rosie went on her walk?"

Open-Ended Questions (without right or wrong answers): "Does Rosie know the fox is behind her?" "Who has something they would like to say about this page?"

"Who, What, Where, and Why" Questions: "Who do you think will get stung?" "What does the fox step on?" "Where is Rosie going next?" "Why doesn't the fox ever get Rosie?"

"Did You Ever?" Questions: "Did you ever visit a farm?" "Did you ever read another story about a fox?"

Prompts for Prediction: "What do you think will happen next?"

Comments

I notice: "I notice that Rosie never looks behind her."

I wonder: "I wonder why the fox keeps tripping up." "I'm wondering if Rosie is scared."

This reminds me of: "This reminds of me Coyote and the Roadrunner cartoon."

I'm thinking: "I'm thinking this is a very dumb fox."

I remember: "I remember this time when a dog chased me. I didn't run; I just kept on walking so the dog wouldn't jump up on me and bite me."

Note. Adapted from Whitehurst, Arnold, et al. (1994) for *Rosie's Walk* (Hutchins, 1968).

proven to be true, and whether the text is making sense. For most good readers, these mental activities occur almost unconsciously—readers just seem to naturally make sense of what they read. But in the beginning, before children can actually read on their own, they need prompting to begin using these mental activities so that they will become automatic later when they do read.

Therefore, another of the teacher's roles in interactive book reading is to make sure children engage in mental activities. This is accomplished by selecting four or five places in the story to stop and ask one or two questions or invite predictions. This stopping to talk requires children to think, infer, predict, and reason. The places that teachers choose to stop and talk should be carefully selected. Teachers need to consider the overall meaning of the story or informational book. For example, *The Three Billy Goats Gruff* is a tale about greed and trickery. The troll would simply have eaten the first Billy Goat if he was merely hungry rather than greedy. The clever Billy Goats use the troll's greed to trick him into letting the two smaller Billy Goats cross the bridge safely. A teacher can help children think about the theme of greed by asking, "If he was so hungry, why did the Troll let the first Billy Goat cross the bridge?"

Another favorite folktale, *The Three Little Kittens*, explores the themes of children's desire to please their mother and a mother's use of punishment and reward to prompt good behavior. It includes the concepts of clean versus dirty and lost versus found. During an interactive read-aloud of *The Three Little Kittens*, teachers can draw attention to these concepts when they make comments such as "Oh dear, they've lost their mittens." They can pantomime being a kitten by frantically looking all around to locate the lost mittens. Teachers can invite children to put on pretend mittens, lose them, and then exclaim, "Oh, no. I've lost my mittens." They can invite children to make personal connections to the story by saying "I wonder where they lost their mittens? Where is a place you might lose your mittens?" or by asking "What do you think your mother will say when you tell her you've lost your mittens? What did Mother Cat in the story do to punish her kittens for being careless with their mittens?"

Effective interactive read-alouds arise from a mixture of child-initiated and -directed conversation and teacher-initiated and -directed conversation. Sometimes conversations do not go as teachers have planned. Children's comments and questions may propel interactive read-alouds in unexpected directions. For example, one teacher was reading *Goodnight Moon* (Brown, 1947) to a group of kindergartners. She had read this book every year of her teaching career and had a very good idea of the nature of conversation she expected. But this time, the conversation took an unexpected turn. These kindergartners noticed that Mother Bunny was having trouble putting all the babies (including the kittens on the rug) to sleep, not just the little bunny. These children argued that Little Bunny was the only baby being good—he was in bed, but the kittens would not settle down to sleep. Rather than interrupt her children's unexpected interpretation of the story and redirect their attention back to her planned questions, this teacher respected the children's thinking and followed their lead throughout the reading. She asked them to support their interpretations by using details from the illustrations and making connections to their own experiences.

Building Vocabulary and Extending Language

Introducing and prompting children to use new vocabulary is also a critical component of interactive read-alouds (Cornell, Senechal, & Brodo, 1988; Hargrave & Senchal, 2000). Before reading a book aloud, teachers can select 8–10 vocabulary words or phrases to highlight during reading. The words and phrases selected should be those critical for understanding the story, those that children are likely to encounter in other books, or those that are more sophisticated labels for everyday objects and events. For example, a prekindergarten teacher selected the words and phrases *owling, woods, feet crunched, Great Horned Owl, silent, clearing, echo, pumped its wings,* and *forest* to highlight when she read *Owl Moon* (Yolen, 1987) with her 4-year-olds. As she read the book, she read the words and phrases in the text, then turned to look at the children to give in a few words a short definition or explanation, and then turned back to the text and read the sentence with the target word or phrase again. As she made comments and asked questions, she included target words and phrases ("I remember a time when my feet crunched in the snow") and prompted children to use them in their responses ("Who can remember what kind of owl they saw?") Children acquire new vocabulary when their definitions are highlighted, when teachers repeat them either during reading or in their conversation, and—most importantly—when they use the words themselves to talk about the book (Robbins & Ehri, 1994; Senechal, 1997).

Selecting Books for Interactive Read-Alouds

The most important step in interactive read-alouds is selecting an appropriate book. With today's large and ever-growing number of good children's books, both fictional and informational, on any topic, there is no reason to read anything but high-quality books. Good teachers take the time to preview, evaluate, and select before reading to children. They also read their selections ahead of time, so that their interactive reading can be fluent, understandable, engaging, and entertaining, and so that they know ahead of time when best to stop for conversation.

High-quality children's books are distinguished by richness of vocabulary, compliance with story grammar, congruence with children's world knowledge, and interplay of text and illustrations. These qualities provide opportunities to prompt conversation by saying "*Quivering.* That's a good word! Why do you suppose he was quivering when he saw the giant?" or "Oh dear! She has to get to the other side. How do you suppose she will solve that problem?" or "Have you ever heard of a *tchotchke*? What do you think that might be?" or "I wonder why he's hiding from Tony? What do we already know about Tony?" or "I think there's a clue in the picture. What do you see in the picture that tells you why she 'jumped for joy'?"

Books that are particularly appropriate for younger preschoolers include characters and activities that are familiar to children, texts with few words, and illustrations with direct relationship to the story line. However, any high-quality book can be shared with younger children if teachers adjust their reading. Beautifully illustrated storybooks with too much text can be told rather than read (see "Interactive" Storytelling section in this chapter). Books about unfamiliar activities or different time periods can also be shared with young children when teachers consider how to connect the unfamiliar locations or events to activities and people that are familiar to children. Teachers should not automatically assume that books with rare or unusual vocabulary, books about technical topics, or stories unfamiliar to children's everyday lives are uninteresting to young children (*The Tale of Peter Rabbit* written by Beatrix Potter in 1902 continues to be a favorite of children, including children living in inner cities!). However, children also need multiple opportunities to experience books that accurately reflect their culture as well as opportunities to experience books about the culture of others (Barrera, Ligouri, & Salas, 1992). Some books in the read-aloud program need to be carefully selected for their cultural relevance and authenticity (see Table 5.1 for a list of culturally authentic books).

Using Read-Alouds to Develop Concept about Stories

In Chapter 2 we described the concepts that preschoolers and kindergartners develop about stories (see Table 2.1 for a description of all the components of a concept about story included in a story grammar). Through listening to stories read aloud to them, children gradually acquire concepts about stories. Young children pay most attention to characters' actions in stories and less attention to the settings or internal thoughts and motivations of characters. Teachers can strengthen children's awareness of the components in stories by deliberately planning activities that draw attention to particular story concepts (Fitzgerald, 1989), including

- A story has a beginning, a middle, and an end.
- Stories have characters.
- A story has a setting that tells where the story takes place.
- The main character has a problem that needs to be solved.
- The main character takes action to solve the problem. (adapted from McGee & Richgels, 2000; McGee & Tompkins, 1981; Tompkins & McGee, 1989)

Teachers can introduce the concept of beginnings, middles, and ends of stories by rereading a favorite story, emphasizing each portion of the story as they read. Then they can invite children to retell what happened at each of those parts of a story. Children can arrange pictures of story events (cut from an extra copy of the book) in sequence (see "Preparing Props for Book Acting" later in this chapter), identifying which pictures go with the story's beginning, middle, and end. Teachers can introduce the idea of main characters and their problems by reading several books about favorite characters. Children love to read series books about the Berenstain Bears, Franklin, Arthur and D. W., and Henry and Mudge. Each book of a series introduces the familiar character facing new problems. Many of the books of a series are set in a familiar story locations, but each book also introduces a new setting. Teachers can draw children's attention to story problems by introducing stories in which characters have a problem with other characters versus stories in which characters have a problem within themselves. For example, *Thunder Cake* (Polacco, 1990) tells of the story of girl who is frightened by a thunderstorm. Her Grandma helps her conquer her fear by keeping her busy making a cake. In contrast, *Timothy Goes to School* (Wells, 1981) tells of the rivalry between two characters, Timothy and Claude. In this story, Timothy discovers a new best friend, Violet, who helps him ignore Claude's rudeness.

Interactive Read-Alouds of Informational Books

Teachers naturally seem to select stories to share with young children, and most classroom libraries have fewer informational books than stories (Duke, 2000). However, today many high-quality informational books are being published, even for very young children. These books have little text and engaging illustrations and photographs on topics of interest to children. Some informational books are available in big-book format as well.

Reading informational books is a powerful source for introducing children, particularly children at risk for reading failure, to new knowledge and vocabulary. Unlike most middle-class children, many at-risk children have had little exposure to experiences that allow them to acquire knowledge or vocabulary about the scientific and technical world around them (Duke, 2000). Reading informational books seems to support especially rich discussion and thinking (Pappas & Barry, 1997; Richgels, 2002; Smolkin & Donovan, 2002). Children naturally ask questions and seek information from these books. Their curiosity extends their willingness to listen to more difficult books.

Teachers have many options for how to present informational books in interactive read-alouds. They can be read through, or teachers can read only portions of them. One preschool teacher we know begins informational book read-alouds by inviting children to say what they know about the book's topic. Then she shows the illustrations on each page in the book, inviting the children to make comments by saying "Do you have something to say about this?" Finally, she reads the book as an interactive read-aloud. The way teachers share informational books with young children will depend on the age and experience of the children.

Informational books provide many opportunities to discuss the meanings of new vocabulary and to encourage children to use these words as they talk about the book. Because informational books are full of technical vocabulary, effective teachers are careful to select a few of these words, the ones central to understanding the concepts presented in the book, for attention. During reading, teachers can stop to define a term briefly and then reinforce the meaning of the technical word by saying "This part of the text tells me the meaning of this word. Let me read it to you slowly."

Many informational books explain phenomena—why a volcano erupts or how a spider captures its prey. Embedded in such explanations are events linked by cause and effect. Effective teachers make explicit how the ideas in a text are linked together (Smolkin & Donovan, 2002), using words or phrases such as *as a result of, because of,* and *that causes.* With informational books, teachers may pause frequently to summarize, to link new information with information that has previously been read, and to connect information to children's experiences.

Children's knowledge and vocabulary can be further extended by reading three or four informational books on a common topic over the course of several days. Reading several informational books on the same topic is easier now because of the many series of informational books published for young children. Often the books in a series are leveled: That is, the publisher identifies whether the book is intended for very young or slightly older children, based on the amount and complexity of its content. Thus, teachers can find many different books about spiders, for example, on a variety of different levels. Some of these books will be intended for very young children; they will include detailed photographs but very little exposition because the text is so short. Other books will be intended for older preschool and kindergarten children; they will include many photographs and some other visual aids such as labeled drawings and will have more text with a few technical words. Still other books will be intended for elementary-age children; they will include a variety of illustrations, including labeled drawings, graphs, charts, tables, and indexes. These books will have a considerable amount of text with many technical words. Teachers are often surprised to find that young children enjoy browsing through all three levels of informational books. The most technical books are not appropriate for reading aloud in the preschool or kindergarten, but they do provide teachers with invaluable information about a topic. As teachers read aloud books on a simpler level, they can respond to children's questions using the technical information found in higher-level books (Casbergue & Plauché, 2003). Teachers can sometimes read aloud a section of a more technical book on occasions when its information is needed. Table 6.2 presents a list of leveled informational book series appropriate for preschool and kindergarten children.

As with all interactive read-alouds, informational books should be placed in the book center for children's independent exploration after they have been read aloud. Arranging informational books on a shelf along with a few props encourages children to visit the Book center and use the props to retell information from the books. For example, one teacher put a copy of the book *See How They Grow: Penguins* (Fletcher, 1993) along with several sizes of plastic eggs and stuffed penguins in a special basket she uses to display books in the Book center. Browsing through the books and props in the book basket is a popular center activity in this classroom.

TABLE 6.2. Leveled Informational Book Series for Young Children

Social Studies Emergent Readers, Scholastic	See How They Grow, Dorling Kindersley
Science Emergent Readers, Scholastic	Animal Close-Ups, Charlesbridge
Scholastic Science Readers, Scholastic	The Dominie World of Animals, Dominie Press
First Discovery Books, Scholastic	Viking Science Easy-to-Read Books, Penguin
All About Series, Scholastic	Rookie Read-About Science, Children's Press
Eyewitness Junior Series, Dorling Kindersley	Sunshine Science Series, The Wright Group
Eyewitness Readers, Dorling Kindersley	Animals Keeping (Clean, Cool, Safe, Warm), Random House
Look Inside Cross-Sections, Dorling Kindersley	Let's-Read-and-Find-Out Science Books, HarperCollins
Mighty Machines, Dorling Kindersley	

Before and after Interactive Read-Alouds: Extending Activities

In addition to conversation during reading, interactive read-alouds include conversation before and after reading of the book. Before beginning an interactive read-aloud, teachers can show the book's cover, initiating conversation about its illustration, the title, and perhaps the author and illustrator, especially if either is familiar from a book previously read. This prereading conversation can prompt children to think what the book may be about, so that they are using their prior experiences and are beginning to make predictions that the teacher and they can reference in conversation during reading of the book. Conversation after a book reading can be about key parts, favorite parts, favorite words, surprising plot developments, connections to children's lives, or connections to other books or other classroom activities.

Good books are well loved; children want to hear them read again and again. Teachers plan so that children can experience the joy of listening to a favorite book on multiple occasions. Teachers, aides, and volunteers should be available to read to small groups of children in the Book center when children request this activity. Good books also suggest many extension activities: children's browsing through the book on their own at the Book or Library center, the teacher's demonstrating for the whole class a science experiment that was described in an informational book, or children's examining seashells under magnifying glasses after reading several books about the ocean. Effective teachers connect art, music, movement, and science activities to books. After reading *Snowballs* (Ehlert,1995), young children love to use the hole puncher to construct snowflakes, and after reading *The Legend of the Indian Paintbrush* (dePaola, 1988), they enjoy using watercolors to create the evening sky at sunset. Children enjoy making up movements for each animal in the book *In the Tall, Tall Grass* (Fleming, 1991) and singing through *The Wheels on the Bus* (Kovalski, 1987). They are eager to collect leaves and compare them after reading *Autumn Leaves* (Robbins, 1998). These activities prompt rich conversation about the information in books, giving teachers many opportunities to encourage children to use new vocabulary and try out more sophisticated syntax.

Shared Reading

Shared reading is a form of reading-aloud to children, and usually occurs as teachers read *big books* or charts with enlarged versions of poems, songs, or stories. The purpose of shared reading, like all read-alouds, is for children to enjoy a good book or poem. However, shared reading's purpose is also for children to see that teachers are reading from printed text, to learn to follow the text as it is read, and to match the printed words with the words spoken by the teacher (see Chapter 7 for more information about using shared reading to develop concepts about print). The first step in shared reading is an interactive read-aloud. The enlarged text or big book is read aloud using the techniques used in any interactive read aloud. In fact, we have found that interactive read-alouds are often more successful with big books, especially for younger children. Their enlarged illustrations allow children to see the smallest details, which they are eager to discuss. Big books can be left on the easel during center time for children's further independent explorations.

Reading to Large and Small Groups

The most effective interactive read-alouds for preschoolers take place in small groups of four to eight children (Morrow & Smith, 1990; Whitehurst, Arnold, et al., 1994). Groups of this size allow each child to make many contributions and teachers to listen to and respond to individual children. However, this does not mean that teachers should never read aloud to a whole group of preschoolers. Rereading familiar poems or songs written on large charts or a favorite big book is appropriate for large groups. Reading a new book for the first time to older preschool and kindergarten children in large groups is also appropriate. However, ELL children with fewer experiences with books, or those with language difficulties need additional frequent opportunities to share books with their teachers in small groups. Children most at risk of reading failure need more than one interactive read-aloud each day. Effective teachers arrange their schedules, call upon community and parent volunteers, and supervise their aides so that all children have many daily experiences with books, including in large and small groups and one on one.

Teachers also help parents learn how to read to their children more effectively and frequently. A take-home book program is a must for children who have access to only a few books at home. Teachers can place appropriate books in sturdy cloth bags and organize a simple check-out procedure to keep track of the book bags and their circulation (Richgels & Wold, 1998). Sharing tips with parents on how to read and talk about books with their children should be an important part of most parent meetings. Even more effective is making home visits, where teachers or other professionals demonstrate for parents how to read books with their children.

Books for take-home programs should be sturdily bound and accompanied by stuffed animals or retelling props (see the next section in this chapter). At-home reading programs are most successful when two or three related books are placed in the book bag. Appropriate selections for a take-home book program include alphabet books, books with rhyming words or alliteration, books read in school, and books composed by the children.

RETELLING AND DRAMA

Studies show that some teachers do not read aloud to their students frequently enough (Dickinson & Sprague, 2001), but teachers tell stories even less frequently. Teachers who tell stories provide important models for children to become storytellers. Engaging children in retelling or dramatizing stories or telling and then dramatizing their own stories are some of the most effective instructional techniques for increasing children's comprehension, vocabulary, and syntax.

Interactive Storytelling: The First Step

In storytelling, rather than reading a book, teachers tell the story by learning its plot and some of its key language, especially important dialogue. Teachers who can read a storybook with expression can just as well tell a story entertainingly and understandably. They can differentiate character's voices with adjustments in volume, pitch, and speed of delivery without being dialect experts; they probably do so during a read-aloud without even realizing it.

The important thing in storytelling is to make the telling sound natural. This comes from a bit of practice, not so that teachers have all the words memorized, but so that they know the story well enough to make its delivery smooth. Sometimes teachers like to use minor props or easily changed costume elements (a hat or a stick-on mustache, not a full costume). Having a few key plot elements or vocabulary words posted on a chart in sequence for reference during storytelling keeps the story flowing. Many teachers begin storytelling using the book to support their storytelling. They hold up the book and turn its pages as if they were reading the story, but actually tell the story rather than read the text.

Selecting books for storytelling depends on the children's age, experience with storytelling, and classroom curriculum. Younger preschool children benefit from simple versions of familiar folktales or short sections of informational books with few characters and events. Older children enjoy stories that include more events and well-developed characters. Effective teachers will be sure to tell stories from many different cultures, including stories familiar to children. Parents are often the best storytellers, and many are eager to share their heritage through telling stories handed down in their families.

It is important that after the first telling children become participants in storytelling. In the interactive portion of storytelling, teachers tell the story but prompt children to join in at selected places. Children can repeat words when a story uses repetition (such as the words "trip, trap, trip, trap" in the *Three Billy Goats* tale) or speak the repeated dialogue of a character (such as the wolf's "I'm going to huff and puff and blow your house down" in the *Three Little Pigs* tale). Children will ask for many repetitions of interactive storytelling, especially when teachers are clever enough to put storytelling props in every child's hands (McGee, 2003).

Guided Book Acting: The Second Step

The next step after interactive storytelling is to guide children as they retell or dramatize the entire story. While retelling and drama are not precisely the same thing, the two can be effectively blended together into Book Acting (McGee, 2003) through the use of props. Distributing retelling props among children naturally assigns them a portion of the story to retell or act out. First, the teacher prepares children to retell or dramatize the story in Book Acting.

Preparing to Retell or Dramatize in Book Acting

Book acting is most successful when children remember the story in great detail. Teachers help children recall the events in the story, reviewing the entire story using the illustrations as support. They begin by asking children to tell what happened first in the story. After children respond, teachers ask either clarifying questions or leading questions. They might ask for explanations or provide explanations themselves. Teachers help children recall the major events in sequence and the gist of characters' dialogue. Effective teachers ask questions about characters' intentions ("Why did the Troll let the first Billy Goat cross the bridge?") and feelings ("How do you suppose that first Billy Goat felt as he crossed over the bridge right next to that Troll?") (Clarke-Stewart & Beck, 1999). This review of the story need not take long, but provides valuable support for later activities, when children will be occupied with holding and using storytelling props.

Preparing Props for Book Acting

The best props for book acting are those that can be easily obtained or made and are simple for children to manipulate. Props include pictures cut from an extra copy of a book, small objects, items of clothing, puppets, and masks. Pictures can be hung on either a story clothesline or a storytelling stick. A story clothesline is constructed by tying a length of clothesline between two sturdy pieces of furniture, such as the teacher's chair and an easel. The best pictures to use on a story clothesline are approximately 6 inches square or larger. A storytelling stick is constructed from a yardstick with several small squares of self-stick Velcro attached to its length. Pictures used on the story stick need to be smaller, but large enough for children to see.

Small objects that represent the characters and important events are easy to obtain. For example, three small bears, three sizes of spoons, three sizes of paper cups (for chairs), and three sizes of cloth (for beds) can be used to tell *The Three Bears* tale. *Mirandy and Brother Wind* (McKissack, 1988) is easily told using a jacket, several scarves, an old blouse, an apron, a small quilt, a peppermill, and a tablecloth. Masks are also easy book acting props to make. We recommend using paper plates with the entire inside section cut out. The outside of the plate can be decorated to represent the character using construction paper or yarn. Straw puppets are also effective book acting props. They are easily constructed by stapling pictures of characters to plastic drinking straws.

When book acting is done with large or small groups, teachers will need to gather enough props for each child to participate. Just a few simple props work best. For example, when teachers tell *The Three Little Kittens* tale, each child could have a plastic bag of props, including a short section of clothesline, clothespins, a tin pie plate, and two mittens sewn from inexpensive material.

Guiding Children during Book Acting

As teachers retell a story, they invite children to use their props and model how to use them. At first teachers do most of the narrating and dialogue until children become more familiar with the props. Then children are invited to chime in during repetitive portions of dialogue. Eventually individual children are invited to improvise their own dialogue. Teachers can insert some of the book's literary language in their own dialogue, expand on children's dialogue, and make suggestions for more effective handling of the props.

Book acting is especially beneficial for ELL children. The props help them to visualize the meaning of the story; the repetitive dialogue is more easily managed because it is so easily memorized; and acting out the book in groups provides a natural support for children whose language is not yet well developed. Teachers have found that having a parent or other volunteer read the story in the children's home language and help children retell the story in that language supports their later retelling in English (Carger, 1993).

While book acting can be a fun whole-group activity, its effectiveness is strengthened when it is accompanied by small-group practice. For example, there are many fine picture book versions of *The Three Little Pigs* and other favorite tales. Teachers might read different versions of the tale to different small groups of children, continuing to use the same props for retelling the story. Teachers can use small groups to discuss how to use the story props in the Book Acting center. This center would include several copies of books recently retold along with the appropriate retelling props. Teachers model how to use particular props to retell stories in the Book Acting center. Experience has shown that children have difficulty sharing props and selecting portions of the story to tell, so teachers will need to model several ways to solve this problem.

Independent Book Acting: The Third Step

The final step in book acting is to provide opportunities for children to engage in book acting on their own during center activities. While many of children's dramatizations in the Book Acting center will include events from favorite stories told in whole and small groups, mixed in with these actual story events may be many child-composed innovations. Children should be encouraged to reuse props to construct new stories or add improvised events to favorite stories. Helping children retell new stories that include the events from familiar stories with new twists and characters provides enormous challenges for language and comprehension (Meier, 2000). Children should also be encouraged to select and make their own book acting props. In order to select objects to represent characters, children must determine qualities that define a character (Rowe, 1998). Thus, allowing children to collect or construct their own props may be more intellectually challenging than providing them.

Pretend and Memorized Reading

Pretend reading is very similar to retelling favorite stories or informational books. *Pretend reading* does not include props; instead, children look at the book's illustrations and pretend to read. This means they attempt to retell what they remember about the book. Teachers can engage children in this activity by demonstrating pretending to read and assuring children they need not actually read. They are just remembering what was in the story. At first children describe events in the pictures rather than attempt to retell or pretend-read (Sulzby, 1985); their attempts sound more like everyday conversation than like a text being read aloud. Gradually, as children acquire practice in pretend reading and as they become more familiar with a book, their attempts at pretend reading sound more like written language. That is, children begin to retell stories using past tense and are able to include some of the words and phrases of the story text. In pretending to read informational books, children's retellings may include a timeless present tense and some of the technical vocabulary included in the informational book text (Duke & Kays, 1998; Pappas, 1991). When children's pretend readings include some of the words of the text, it is called *memorized reading*. The ability to memorize bits of text, as we will show later in the chapter, is an important step on the way toward conventional reading and writing.

Dramatizing Children's Original Stories: Story Playing

Another way to use storytelling in the classroom is to dramatize original stories that children compose. The *story playing* technique (Paley, 1990) has four elements: One child is invited to tell a story, and the teacher writes the child's story. The teacher reads the story aloud and other children make comments, ask questions, or suggest elaborations. Finally, the child acts out the story, inviting other children to join in the story play to take on any needed roles. One way to organize story playing is to invite a few children to tell a story as they enter the classroom. As the teacher writes a child's story, he or she rereads what the child has said so that the child can see the connection between the talk and the written words. The teacher allows the storyteller to make corrections, additions, and deletions to the written story. The children know that this written copy of the story will be used for their later acting out of the story. During the school day, the storyteller may continue to elaborate on the story. As children become accustomed to the technique, they anticipate the end-of-the school day performance by including elements of the story in their dramatic play in play centers. Finally, at the end of the day, the children act out the story as the teacher reads the current written version of the story. Some children are in the cast (they are chosen by the original storyteller), some in the audience (they are free to contribute to the ever-evolving story with comments and suggestions). In this way, story playing demonstrates revision, a process children will later use their own writing. Its importance for the preschool and kindergarten child, however, is that it is on-the-spot meaning making; it has immediate connections to the classroom lives of the students, which at this age should include many play opportunities.

PROJECTS, EXPERIMENTS, AND OTHER REAL EXPERIENCES: THE ROLE OF KNOWLEDGE ACQUISITION IN LITERACY DEVELOPMENT

Most of this book has been about the development *of* literacy (Neuman, 2001). We have described what kind of literacy concepts children develop, how they learn these concepts, and what teachers can do to accelerate this learning. However, children also learn *through* literacy. They use literacy as tools for developing insights about the natural world. Children learn about animals, space, oceans, and rocks by reading books about these topics. Of course, children also learn about these topics by watching television, visiting zoos, going to the beach, and collecting rocks in nearby streams and rivers. However, as children get older they learn the most about topics in science and social studies through books, hands-on experiments, and participating in projects. These experiences are intended to build children's higher-level thinking skills. They are aimed at helping children pose and answer questions, make inferences about cause-and-effect relationships, and think critically. We have already described how reading informational books aloud is a critical component of a high-quality literacy program because it does support children's higher-level thinking. However, informational book reading needs to be extended and supplemented through carefully thought-out units of study that include experiments and projects.

Experiments are a natural part of discovery science and are particularly useful in helping children understand scientific concepts and develop process skills of investigation (Harlan & Rivkin, 2000). As a part of experiments, young children observe, classify, measure, predict, infer, and construct explanations. They use the basic steps of the scientific method, including becoming aware of a problem by asking, "What will happen if . . . ?", hypothesizing or predicting an answer or solution by stating "I think this will happen," finding out by trying out a prediction, and sharing the results with others by telling what happened. These steps are easy to implement, even with young preschool children. Imagine three children standing on a playground in the late afternoon. One child notices his shadow. The teacher urges the child to ask *What if?* questions: "What will my shadow look like if I put my hands over my head?" or "What will my shadow look like if my friend Eddy stands right next to me real close?", or, "What will my shadow look like if I sit down?" Each of these questions can be accompanied by a prediction, for example, "I predict my shadow will get smaller if I sit down," and an experiment (actually sitting down to see what happens to the shadow). The results of these experiments can be communicated to all the children later in the day or the next day during circle time. As children share their discoveries and experiments, other children will become interested in pursuing experiments. Teachers should encourage all children to repeat experiments again and again as long as their interest and curiosity are aroused.

There are many resources that teachers can use for finding science experiments that are appropriate for young children, including the Internet. However, teachers on tight budgets can use everyday objects to engage children in investigations. For example, grapefruit and orange halves float when they are hollowed out. Teachers can gather small objects from around the house to use with the grapefruit and orange hollows in a sinking and floating experiment. How many spoons will sink a grapefruit? How many pennies? How many buttons?

The project approach, like discovery science, is another curriculum idea that engages children in posing and answering questions. Projects are generally child-made constructions that they have created after extensive study and observation. For example, children have constructed a veterinary clinic, a dispatch office for school buses, a garden tiller, a bulldozer, an automobile, firefighting equipment, and a fire truck (Helm & Katz, 2001). Before construction, children visit actual sites or observe machines and tools in use. They draw pictures and diagrams, compose lists of materials that will be needed, and make plans for initial construction. During construction, children articulate prob-lems that arise and brainstorm solutions. After constructions are complete, they commu-nicate their project results by drawing and dictating or writing. Children dictate lists of things they learned, construct a big book with photographs and dictated captions, or draw the step-by-step sequence followed to produce their construction.

SHARED WRITING

Composing written messages is another classroom activity that provides many opportu-nities for children to extend their understanding of the functions of language and stretch vocabulary and syntax. We describe how to use shared writing to compose messages. Then we discuss a variety of texts that can be composed during shared writing, includ-ing pattern innovations from literature, charts and graphs, reports of science observa-tions or class activities, and correspondence.

Using Shared Writing

Shared writing is the joint creation of a text by teacher and students; the students provide many, if not all, of the ideas, and the teacher does the actual writing, usually on a large piece of chart paper or marker board where all the children can see it (Payne & Schulman, 1998). Shared writing was earlier known as Language Experience Approach (van Allen & van Allen, 1982) because it often begins with a shared experience such as going to an apple orchard to pick apples. After extensive conversation about the experi-ence, teachers make explicit the purpose for the writing. They tell children that they are writing a summary of what happened on the trip to the orchard to help everyone always remember the great time they had on the trip. Teachers ask children to contribute a word (for example, to a list of the kinds of apples they saw on the trip), a phrase (listing the activities they enjoyed at the orchard), or a sentence (describing in sequence what they did). Then, teachers write those contributions verbatim on a chart or marker board. The teacher and the children read and reread the resulting text several times together. For example, they may read it later in the day just to celebrate everyone's contribution, or they may read it the next day to be sure they remember all or most of it.

Shared writing of this type helps children connect spoken words with written words. The words they say (even when the syntax is unconventional) are written and reread. However, sometimes teachers want the product of shared writing to be more con-ventional (such as when it is a thank you letter to be sent to a beekeeper for visiting the classroom). In this case, teachers listen to children's ideas about what to say, but take a more active role in the actual composition of the message. Teachers can help children compose together a letter to parents about a special visitor or event. They may write together a record of a science experiment. Or they might write together directions to be posted at a new center.

Shared writing experiences with younger preschoolers need not be as frequent as those with older preschoolers or kindergartners. Many teachers have found that with young children it is easier to compose lists than more complex text. After reading *Yuck Soup* (Cowley, 1989), one group of 3- and 4-year-olds dictated a list of the ingredients found in yuck soup. Another group of 4- and 5-year-olds compiled a list of animals found in *Over in the Meadow* (Wadsworth, 1992). After writing the lists during shared writing, the teachers hung the lists in the Art center, and the children were invited to draw or paint pictures of the animals or yucky ingredients. Later, the shared writing charts decorated by cut-outs of children's art were placed in the preschool hall where parents picked up their children.

Making Shared Writing a Daily Activity

To be effective, especially with kindergartners, shared writing should occur daily. Many teachers have used *Morning Message* (Payne & Schulman, 1998) to accomplish the daily writing goal. Morning message is sometimes called daily news or class message because it is usually written early in the morning, and topics that are written include the date, a greeting, upcoming school events, or anticipated activities. Many teachers have a rotation schedule so they select two or three children who dictate the morning message each day. Most teachers use one or two phrases that are repeated daily and then invite children to add additional sentences. Teachers help children remember the repeated message included in the news every day. Then they either help the selected child compose a sentence or guide children as they compose a message together. A typical morning message may include the following:

> Good morning kindergartners!
>
> Today is Tuesday.
>
> Marie is going to her grandmother's house.
>
> Josef is going fishing with his uncle.

Another way to incorporate daily shared writing, one we actually recommend over daily message, is to compose texts for a class *memory book*. Teachers can take photographs of important classroom events or have children draw pictures—such as a picture of the sorting room children visited on their trip to the apple orchard. Then teachers can help children compose messages to accompany the photographs or pictures. For example, a teacher might help children compose the caption: 'Our apple orchard field trip.' Then they would remind children of the purpose for writing: "That will help me remember that you drew these pictures after our field trip to the apple orchard. Oh, look, here's Mark's picture of the sorting room. Mark, what shall we write under your picture so people will remember the sorting room?" The children already know that the memory book displays their pictures of the apple orchard, and they may even recognize Mark's picture, but this teacher talk reinforces the record keeping function of written language

Making Shared Writing Purposeful

Shared writing offers many opportunities to share with children the many kinds of printed texts we read and write. It allows teachers to make explicit the nature of language used in particular kinds of texts and their purpose. For example, want ads in the newspaper and birthday present wish lists serve the instrumental purpose of satisfying needs and wants. All children enjoy composing lists for hoped-for birthday presents, but they are also interested in how people use want ads: to obtain help for yard work or to locate a jersey worn by a favorite hockey player.

Teachers can seize opportunities to use shared writing to read and then compose texts that serve real purposes. For example, they can read aloud several of their own letters to relatives and then help children compose a letter to a classmate who has moved away or to a distant grandparent. When a child is absent from school, teachers could have on hand several get well cards to read as models. Then they can help children compose their own card. Teachers can extend experiences with get well cards by placing them in the Writing center along with specially cut paper and envelopes for children's pretend writing.

Teachers can introduce children to yard sale signs, party invitations, grocery lists, telephone books, maps, and directions in order to enrich play in the Home Living center. They bring in examples they have gathered from their homes or found in their neighborhoods, share them with children, and then place them in the center. Each of these print items can become a shared writing activity or an activity for the writing center.

Teachers can capitalize on opportunities to demonstrate using writing purposefully as they arise during classroom activities. When children have completed an especially complicated structure from blocks, teachers may invite children to dictate a DO NOT DISTURB sign. Later, the teacher would read the sign to the children and talk about what it means. Leaving the sign and block construction in place for a day or two emphasizes its regulatory purpose. Later, teachers can photograph the children, their block construction, and the sign and add it to the class memory book, using this as still another opportunity for shared writing.

Using Shared Writing to Display Information

Shared writing can be used to collect and display information gathered during a social studies or science unit. During a unit on plants, children can dictate for a whole-class science journal their daily observations of a sweet potato's growth in a glass jar. Later, teachers can help children compose a list of things they have learned about plants. *Venn diagrams* (two circles drawn so that they overlap) or *comparison charts* can be used to compare information about similar objects or events. For example, teachers can help children compare a maple leaf to an oak leaf and then use the information from their discussion to compose a Venn diagram.

Another way to use shared writing to display information is by constructing surveys. Classroom events suggest many topics for surveys, which can be answered with the words *yes* or *no* or by having children write their signatures under columns labeled *Yes* and *No*. A child who recently went on a trip spurred the survey for "Have you been to Disney World?" A child who came to school one day with a cast over a broken bone helped to construct the survey for "Have you ever had a cast?" A rainy day sparked the survey "Did you wear boots today?" The answers to even simple questions such as "Do you like red?" provide many opportunities for displaying information. Once a survey is completed, teachers can help children compose summary statements such as "Three children wore boots today. Twelve children did not." After learning how to take surveys, many children enjoy creating their own during center time. To encourage survey taking, teaches can stock a Writing center with a few clipboards and pencils.

Using Shared Writing to Compose Pattern Innovations

One of the most popular activities for shared writing is to compose a *pattern innovation*. A pattern innovation borrows the repetitive words and phrases from a *pattern book*, a book that includes repeated actions and words, but adds new content. Using the illustrations in the book, children easily memorize the repeated words in a book's pattern. Once they have the pattern memorized, children can use it to construct their own original new story by adding new words into the pattern. For example, a group of 4-year-olds constructed the following pattern innovation for the book *Brown Bear, Brown Bear, What Do You See?* (Martin, 1967): "Orange pumpkin, orange pumpkin, what do you see? I see a white ghost looking at me."

Because pattern books often have highly complex sentence patterns, they provide especially rich opportunities for children to practice using more sophisticated syntax than they use in their everyday speech. In fact, young children seem to revel in mastering complicated patterns and repeating them often. We observed two 4-year-olds who were enrolled in a prekindergarten for at-risk children browsing through the book *It Didn't Frighten Me!* (Harste & Goss, 1993) and repeating the entire book from memory, including: "One pitch black, very dark night, right after mom turned off the light, I looked out my window only to see a purple witch! But . . . that purple witch didn't frighten me!"

CHAPTER SUMMARY

In this chapter we have described four instructional activities that extend children's comprehension and vocabularies: interactive read-alouds, retelling and dramatizing books, projects and experiments, and shared writing. Interactive read-alouds are especially effective at helping children use decontextualized language strategies. The best interactive read-alouds include both the children's questions and comments and the teacher's thoughtful questions and clarifications. Effective teachers plan interactive read-alouds carefully, noting a story's theme and the organization of content in an informational book. Interactive read-alouds can be accompanied by explicit study of story elements and book extension projects. Teachers can plan frequent interactive read-alouds of information books tied to themes and units in science or social studies. Experiments and projects extend interactive read-alouds of informational books. Retelling and drama are also effective instructional activities for bolstering children's language use and vocabulary development. Teachers can sometimes tell stories and guide children as they attempt to retell or dramatize books. Finally, teachers can demonstrate the variety of purposes for writing through shared writing. Teachers can help children compose get well cards, surveys, Venn diagrams, signs, and pattern innovations. Through all these activities, teachers create daily opportunities to accelerate children's spoken and written language development.

CHAPTER 7

Classroom Activities to Develop Children's Concepts about Print and Alphabet Letter Recognition

In this chapter and the next, we describe instructional activities that are designed to help children acquire print processing skills. First, we address several issues that influence the nature of classroom activities designed to promote children's print processing skills. We discuss whether instruction should be embedded or separate, and to what extend instruction needs to be systematic and explicit. Finally, we describe research-based activities that are effective in developing 3-, 4-, and 5-year-olds' concepts about print and increasing their ability to recognize alphabet letters.

WHAT TEACHERS NEED TO KNOW

No instruction is more hotly debated than instruction focused on developing young children's print processing skills. Teachers need to be aware of the issues surrounding print-focused instruction and be prepared to discuss their instructional decisions.

Embedded versus Separate

Early childhood teachers are protective of children, in many cases for good reason. They are concerned that play will disappear from preschool and kindergarten to be replaced by instruction delivered exclusively to whole groups. They worry that children will be required to complete worksheets, forced to sit at desks or tables for most of the day, and required to learn isolated facts. For that reason, NAEYC produced a statement describing developmentally appropriate instruction for preschool and kindergarten, and joined with IRA to produce a statement titled *Learning to Read and Write: Developmentally Appropriate Practices for Young Children,* which describes developmentally appropriate literacy instruction (Neuman, Copple, & Bredekamp, 2000). This statement reviews evidence from research and concludes that play is an important way that children learn about literacy. Instruction recommended in this statement can be described as *embedded*. Embedded instruction occurs as children are involved in a reading or writing activity focused on meaning (for example, when teachers read a book aloud for children to enjoy its story). During these activities, embedded within their larger purpose, teachers also attend to print and demonstrate how children can use print processing skills.

There is an important reason why these experts recommend that print and alphabetic principle instruction be embedded in meaningful activities. Even as children learn about print concepts and sound–letter relationships, they must never be misled into thinking that knowing about those concepts is what reading and writing are all about. Print concepts are necessary but not sufficient for becoming effective readers and writers. Readers and writers do not use print concepts alone without also employing concepts about the functions of written language and deciphering its meaning. For this reason, instructional activities designed to help children focus on print, attend to sounds, and match sounds to letters should frequently take place in meaningful and functional contexts, with texts that can make sense to and serve evident purposes for the children. There is ample research documenting that children who have acquired many concepts about print and knowledge about how print functions from embedded literacy experiences acquire more conventional skills associated with beginning reading and writing instruction more easily, quickly, and successfully (Purcell-Gates & Dahl, 1991).

On the other hand, many experts recommend that print processing skills are best developed through systemic, explicit instruction. For example, the authors of *Preventing Reading Difficulties in Young Children* (Snow et al., 1998) described effective programs at the preschool and kindergarten level as providing children with ample opportunities to learn within a "joyful, playful atmosphere around literacy activities" (p. 171). This statement seems to support the effectiveness of embedded literacy activities, although the authors' suggestions imply a more deliberate approach that would guarantee children's acquisition of key literacy concepts. However, they took a slightly different stance when recommending instruction in phonological awareness; they stated that "phonological awareness can be successfully enhanced through *training* in young children who are not yet very advanced in metaphonological skill" (p. 154). The word *training* suggests that instruction ought to be isolated, separate from rather than embedded in meaningful reading or writing activities. The authors of the National Reading Panel (2000) Report take the next step. They directly state that preschoolers and kindergartners need explicit and systematic instruction in phonemic awareness and phonics.

What should the answer be? Embedded or separate instruction? We recommend that teachers take a deliberate, systematic approach to all instruction, including embedded instruction, and that occasionally, when the need arises, engage children in separate instruction that is more explicit so long as that instruction is playful and connected to other ongoing reading and writing activities. This will be especially true for kindergartners.

By deliberate we mean that teachers will know the various literacy milestones that children can be expected to develop related to print processing skills (see Chapter 2).

They will plan activities that will allow children to use their current print concepts, but will provide support for children to take the "next step" in acquiring new knowledge, knowledge that moves children toward more conventional skills. Teachers will make print processing concepts explicit during demonstrations of reading and writing. They will name the concept, define it, demonstrate it, and state why it is useful in reading and writing. For example, when reading books with many rhyming words, teachers will state, "These words are called rhyming words, and rhyming words sound alike at the end, like in the words *hat, sat, rat, cat*. Knowing rhyming words helps readers remember words when they read and can help writers find words they want to write."

By systematic, we mean that teachers will use ongoing monitoring assessments to keep track of each child's literacy development. When children seem to be stuck—not developing more sophisticated understandings—teachers will consider whether to provide instruction that is more direct rather than embedded. By explicit we mean that teachers will draw children's attention to salient concepts both inside the reading and writing context and outside it. In this way, teachers will provide instruction that highlights print concepts as they are embedded in meaningful activities. However, sometimes teachers will plan instruction that supplements, but is separate from, meaningful reading and writing. For example, teachers can prepare alphabet puzzles to draw attention to specific letters that children are confusing or construct phonological-awareness games using pictures of rhyming words, some of which are related to rhyming words found in familiar poems and books and some of which are not. As teachers play alphabet letter puzzles or rhyming games with children, they will make explicit connections between letters or rhymes children are learning in the game and letters and rhymes in other reading and writing activities, like remarking "There's that L, like in Lakisha" when playing an alphabet puzzle game or "Mittens, kittens, those were rhyming words in *Goodnight Moon*," when playing a rhyming game.

Raising Children's Consciousness

Aside from whether instruction is embedded or separate, instruction focusing on print and alphabetic principle concepts does need to differ from instruction focusing on meaning and language. Print processing skills differ in an important way from strategies that children use in constructing the meaning of written language. Print concepts and sound–letter correspondences are aspects only of written-language competence, not of spoken-language ability. Most spoken-language knowledge is unconscious, that is, we know without being conscious that we know. Consider, for example, the sentence *Joe fell down the stairs*. We can easily make that into a question, *Did Joe fall down the stairs?* Now, consider how we came up with the word *did* in the beginning of the question. It was not in the original sentence; we automatically supplied it without being conscious of the need to do so. However, reading and writing calls upon conscious, rather than unconscious knowing. One of the greatest hurdles for beginning readers and writers is the new necessity of becoming conscious about language. In other words, written language, at least for beginners, requires a great deal of conscious language knowledge that is unnecessary for spoken language.

Much of what teachers do to help children acquire print processing skills is to make children consciously aware of the need to pay attention to these aspects about print. This consciousness raising can occur for many children during embedded activities, when teachers make remarks about alphabet letters or words, point to where they will start reading, or bracket a familiar word. But to be truly effective in using embedded instruction with all children, teachers have to be experts at three things. First, they must know literacy development very well. Second, they must know the literacy development of each and every child in their classroom. Finally, they must be masters at knowing just the right teachable moment for a particular child or a small group of children to insert a comment about print processing within ongoing classroom routines and center activities. Knowing literacy development very well allows teachers to plan, in general, for the levels of print processing skills children could be expected to exhibit (see Table 2.2, for examples). Knowing each child's developmental level allows teachers to be systematic, to fine-tune their plans to take into account children who have more or less developed print skills. Being masters at knowing the "teachable moment" for children means they can draw a child's attention to a new print concept when that child is ready to learn it. (Chapter 10 describes a teacher who has a high level of knowledge about literacy and exceptional teaching craft. The chapter demonstrates how she uses daily routines to provide powerful, deliberate, embedded literacy instruction.)

Not all teachers have this level of knowledge or craft, yet, it represents the most effective kind of literacy teaching. Probably because many teachers do not have this level of knowledge and craft, policymakers often call for teachers to use commercial programs to teach print processing skills (to develop phonemic awareness or phonics, for example), in which activities are sequenced and teachers are provided with directions of what to say and do with children. This chapter provides a middle ground between assuming teachers have already developed highly effective embedded literacy instruction and assuming teachers know so little that they must rely on commercial programs. Effective teachers, even when they are required to use commercial programs, make decisions about how to use and supplement materials. In each section of this chapter and the next we discuss developmental levels of print processing skills teachers can expect in general. Then we describe how teachers can make embedded instruction more deliberate and explicit by attending to those levels of print concepts. Finally, we describe some activities that can supplement embedded instruction.

CONCEPTS ABOUT PRINT

The first step in planning embedded instruction is to consider the nature of concepts about print that can be expected of children in preschool and kindergarten. Teachers can use the benchmarks presented in Table 2.2 as a guide.

Considering Developmental Levels

Children learn to distinguish print from pictures, recognize that the print is read, discover linearity and directionality, learn book orientation, and eventually begin to track print. They point to written words and try to match these with spoken words in fingerpoint reading, locate words that are the same, distinguish between alphabet letters and words, and eventually acquire a few sight words. Children only gradually become aware of written words. At first they focus instead on alphabet letters, lines of text, and the size and shape of the entire text. Teachers can use these benchmark concepts and their knowledge of children's development to plan the kinds of concepts they will talk about during instruction.

Embedded Concepts about Print Instruction

Two instructional activities, in particular, provide many opportunities to develop concepts about print—shared writing and shared reading of enlarged charts of poems, stories, or other printed texts. During shared reading, effective teachers model book handling and make deliberate comments about left and right and top and bottom and beginning, middle, and end. They point to the first word of a text and say, "All right, I'm going to start reading here where I'm pointing. Put your eyes up here on the first word." When they write a sentence during a shared writing activity, they say, "I'm going to start writing here at the top of the page on this side. Watch while I make the first letter" and "Look, before I start the next word, I'm going to move my marker over and leave a space." When they converse with children about their writing in the Writing center, they use such words as *sound, letter, word, beginning, middle, end, first,* and *last.* They say, "You want to write *tired*? OK, let's start with the first sound in that word. What sound do you hear at the beginning of *t-tired*?"

There are some simple means for directing children's attention to the forms of written language. When teachers display a text (a poem on an easel for children's study as part of What Can You Show Us? which is discussed later in this chapter, a shared writing text, or a teacher-made poster to accompany a science display), they can highlight organization and repeated words by using color. Mrs. Poremba, the teacher we feature in Chapter 10, writes the lines of a displayed text in two alternating colors so that it is easier for children to focus on one line at a time and to know which line to look at when she or classmates talk about a particular letter, word, phrase, or line of the poem (Richgels, Poremba, & McGee, 1996). The same word appearing frequently in a poem, a recipe, or a page of a big book makes reading easier and provides a natural opportunity to develop tracking and careful attention to printed words.

After examining the poem in Figure 7.1 displayed on the easel, students will usually notice the repetition of the word *Running.* "There it is again!" they will say. If they do not, the teacher may point to its first appearance and say, "Where else do you see this word?" or "How many other times do you see this word?" or "Do you see any other words in more than one place?"

Sometimes children find particular letters especially interesting or significant. Often these are letters in the children's names ("That's mine"). Sometimes they have favorite words, often because they are among the first words a child learns to read or write, usually simple words (e.g., recognizing the word *on* or *no,* Richgels, 2003). They will easily find and remark about these letters and words in a displayed text. Good teachers will celebrate these discoveries and make these connections explicit in order to reinforce the

Running

Running in the rain.
Running through the snow.
Running on the beach.
Rrrrr-rrrr-rrrr!
That's how I like to go.
Running up and down.
Running all around.
Running in and out.
Rrrrr-rrrr-rrrr!
That's the way I sound
When I'm on the go.
Running!

FIGURE 7.1. Running poem.

discoverer's learning and to prompt classmates' learning. They may say, "Yes, there's one of your favorite words, *on*. I've noticed that you use that word *on* in your writing. Do you see it again anywhere else in the poem? Point to it. Boys and girls, look where he is pointing to the word *on*: *o-n*. That's how you spell *on*."

Concepts about print activities may be a casual part of reading aloud to 3-year-olds, more deliberate with 4-year-olds, and intensive for kindergartners. Three-year-olds are more likely to develop book orientation concepts and the beginnings of directionality through one-on-one read-alouds with classroom aides, parents, or volunteers. As teachers or others write their dictated captions for artwork, these younger children see that print corresponds to spoken words. With 4- and 5-years olds, teachers can plan additional activities to develop concepts about print. These include Write Ons, What Can You Show Us? activity, and fingerpoint reading.

Write Ons

Write Ons are used as a follow-up to a teacher's writing during shared writing. After teachers have completed their writing, they switch from attending to the message to attending to the print. For example, they can invite children to come to the easel on which the shared writing is hung and point to and identify an alphabet letter, point to two words that are the same, or find a word that has three letters. Some teachers have children use one color of marker to circle all of the same alphabet letters or words. At the end of a Write On activity, the teacher invites each child to write something on the chart. For many preschool children, this can be an alphabet writing opportunity. The teacher invites a child to point to a letter, name it (teachers can help when needed), and then write it. When needed, teachers first model writing the letter to support the child's attempt. When completed, the Write On chart can be hung in the Writing center for further writing during center time (Figure 9.2 presents an example of a preschool Write On chart). More experienced kindergarten writers can be invited to locate, read, and write words on the Write On chart.

What Can You Show Us?

Stepping up to the chart, pointing out letters or words, and commenting on them is a part of the *What Can You Show Us?* activity as well. However, teachers use the What Can You Show Us? activity *before* children read an enlarged chart that will later be used in shared reading. Mrs. Poremba uses imaginary friends, Aunt Edith and Uncle Wally, to write letters to her kindergartners several times during the year. These letters are handwritten on large charts and include some rebus pictures. The familiar format of a friendly letter, over time, helps the children notice many concepts about print. When a new letter arrives, the teacher places it on the easel and announces that she will read it later in the morning. First, she invites children to step up to the easel and show something they notice. Children point to alphabet letters that are in their names, words they know (such as *Dear Kindergartners* or *Love, Uncle Wally*), word parts they notice, and words they think they can read; they even attempt to read the entire message (Richgels et al., 1996).

The What Can You Show Us? activity may continue over the several days that children reread the same text for shared reading. They can be invited again to show what they know before any of these later rereadings; their talk will show increased literacy knowledge as they have more such experiences with the same printed text. The teacher uses her shared reading of the text to emphasize left-to-right and word-by-word reading. By the end of 3 or 4 days, many children have memorized the letter. The teacher may put a copy of the letter in the Book center and encourage children to read it during center time using fingerpoint reading.

Fingerpoint Reading

Fingerpoint reading is used to help older preschoolers and kindergartners to learn directionality, to track print word by word, and, eventually, to recognize some sight words. Fingerpoint reading follows an interactive read-aloud of a big book or an enlarged chart. While children do enjoy tracking the print found in both big books and on charts, we recommend that teachers use pocket charts for fingerpoint reading. The text of big books is not always large enough for groups of children to see the words adequately, the word spaces may not be prominent enough, or the text may be too long for the kind of memorization work children need to do in fingerpoint reading. Even charts of poems may be too long for preschoolers, but may be appropriate later when kindergartners have more practice with fingerpoint reading.

The first step in fingerpoint reading is to familiarize children with the story or poem. Good books are always presented in interactive read-alouds so their meanings are thoroughly explored. The initial reading of the text is followed by several shared readings in which children chime in and say any repeated words or dialogue. If teachers are using a big book or enlarged chart of a poem, they point across the lines of text with a hand or a pointer as the children chant along.

Next teachers select a portion of the text (usually 10-15 words in length) to use in fingerpoint reading. The text selected should make sense; therefore, many teachers select the first sentence or a sentence that is repeated. Shorter text allows children to quickly memorize it and focus their attention on the print, rather than spend time learning to say the text words exactly. Teachers copy the text on sentence strips using larger-than-normal word spaces. For example, one teacher used the text from the *The Three Little Kittens* tale and reproduced it in three lines of text:

> Three little kittens
>
> they lost their mittens
>
> and they began to cry.

Teachers need to make additional copies of each of the words in the text for matching activities. They also need to construct *word masks* in a variety of sizes (see Figure 7.2).

To introduce the pocket chart text, teachers refer back to the book and read the text selected for the pocket chart. Then they tell children they have copied this sentence on the pocket chart, and read it aloud to children, pointing to each word on the pocket chart. (We do not recommend that teachers use long pointers during fingerpoint reading because younger children have a difficult time holding and controlling the pointer to isolate words one by one. Instead, teachers can use a shorter sticks, pencils, 12-inch rulers, or specially made fingers cut from construction paper and taped to a plastic drinking straw.) Teachers and children read and reread the pocket chart, pointing to each word one at a time. In order to develop print concepts, children must have the text memorized so that as they are saying a word, the teacher can help them point to that word. As all the children chant the text, individual children are invited to fingerpoint-read, and teachers help them point to each word as it is chanted.

There are many activities that teachers can use to draw careful attention to print.

FIGURE 7.2. Word masks.

Teachers will select activities depending on the knowledge and experience of the children. Teachers can have children match words written on cards to words in the text. They can demonstrate checking whether two words match by comparing the letters in each word from left to right. Then teachers can mask a word and have children select from among three word cards the word that is masked. Teachers can hold up a word card and invite children to identify it by fingerpoint rereading until they reach that word. Teachers can challenge children to find a word that has just two alphabet letters, three letters, and so on. They can ask children to find words that begin with a target alphabet letter or match words from the fingerpoint reading text to words in the big book or chart.

Teachers will want to place the fingerpoint reading pocket chart, pointer, word cards, and masks in a center for children to use independently. Teachers can open a special Pocket Chart center, or put them in a Letter and Word center. Observing children as they independently fingerpoint-read and locate words will provide teachers with a good insight on children's literacy development and suggest next steps for instruction.

As children become familiar with fingerpoint reading, teachers can use text that is longer and text that is deliberately selected to include several high-frequency words, some words that are in familiar word families that can be used to build new words, and some words that can be used to draw attention to beginning or ending letter–sound correspondences. The Running poem appearing in Figure 7.2 is a perfect choice for children who have had experience with fingerpoint reading, have developed many concepts about print, and are beginning to learn letter–sound correspondences. Teachers will prepare this text by writing each word on a card and placing it in the pocket chart. Teachers should expect that children will be more accurate with their tracking, and only need help when they misjudge two- or three-syllable words, such as *running*. Teachers can take advantage of children's growing knowledge of letters and sounds as well. They can cover up several words in the text with blank word cards. As children reread the familiar text, they predict which word is under the word cover and guess the beginning letter of that word. Teachers pull off the cover and confirm children's guesses. Another activity that helps children use letter–sound correspondences during reading is to make the text into a cloze activity. Here, several word cards are removed from the text leaving blank, cloze spaces. Again, children reread to figure out which word would go in the cloze space and then use letter–sound correspondences to select the target word from all the word cards taken out of the text.

Teachers can draw even more attention to the print in the text by having children build new words using one or two familiar words from poem. For example, children can find the word *way*, and teachers can write it on a white board. Then teachers can say, "This word is *way*, but what if I wanted to read the word *day*. How would I have to change this word to make it *day*?" Children could use their own whiteboards to write several other words, including *bay, hay, may, pay,* and *say.* Later, children will enjoy playing with these materials during center time. Having whiteboards, the pocket chart poem, and cover-up cards encourages children to reread the chart and to write their own words.

ALPHABET LETTER LEARNING

Learning to recognize the alphabet letters is one of the hallmarks of preschool and kin-dergarten literacy instruction. Yet, just as with concepts about print, much that must be learned about alphabet letters is too often taken for granted.

Considering Developmental Levels

Much about alphabet recognition is learning what to pay attention to and what to ignore. For example, children have to ignore the following: how alphabet letters written in one font or type style differ from letters in other fonts or styles; how print in commer-cial signs, in logos, on television screens, and on magazine covers or displayed at the supermarket differs from print in books or magazines; how published print in books and newspapers differs from print that is handwritten; and how one person's handwriting differs from another's. Gradually children learn that the letter *M* is the letter *M* whether it appears on a *McDonald's* sign or on their teacher's handwritten words *Good morning*.

On the other hand, children need to learn to pay attention to letter features in a way that is different from how they have learned to think about other objects and pictures. For example, a dog or even a picture of a dog is a dog whether it is facing right or left. But not alphabet letters; lower-case *d* could be conceived of as facing left, whereas the lower-case *b* could be conceived of as facing right. With alphabet letters, these differ-ences are critical. However, children have learned to ignore such differences because in the real world they do not matter (for chairs, cats, or cars it does not matter which way they are oriented because they are still considered chairs, cats, or cars) (Schickedanz, 1998). Therefore, raising children's consciousness about features that matter in alphabet recognition is an important part of alphabet learning. Children can only learn to attach the letter's name to the letter when they perceive that letter as unique.

At first children learn only a few alphabet letters that are uniquely important to them. The letters in their names are for many children some of the first letters learned. Gradually, children distinguish among more alphabet letters and learn the names of many letters. Children at first recognize more upper-case letters than lower-case letters. Effective teachers expect that 3-year-olds will be interested in recognizing and distin-guishing their names from the names of other children in the classroom. They may be interested in alphabet puzzles and writing letters. Four-year-olds are interested in learn-ing to write their names, recognizing many letters by name, playing alphabet letter games, and learning to write the names of other children. Five-year-olds continue to enjoy alphabet letter games and learning to write the names of other children. Many 5-year-olds have developed sufficient literacy skills to use their letter knowledge in fingerpoint reading and to invent spellings.

Embedded Alphabet Instruction

For preschoolers and kindergartners, we do not suggest that alphabet letters be taught through direct instruction and isolated practice in any particular handwriting method.

Children need to experiment with and discover the features of each letter's formation. They only gradually master the visual–motor and fine-motor control necessary for forming all upper- and lower-case letters of the alphabet (McGee & Richgels, 1989). For many children, the opportunity for learning about letter features occurs simply through learning to write their names, participating in What Can You Show Us? and Write On activities, and engaging in pretend reading. Sometimes as teachers demonstrate writing letters in these activities, they can describe the letters' features as they write them.

Good teachers will always use a consistent and legible manuscript style of handwriting in their own writing; they may comment during shared writing about how they are forming letters; and they may give advice and provide models when they join children at the Writing center. But they do not insist that preschool or kindergarten children practice in handwriting books or worksheets. When children notice that their letters do not look like they want them to look (e.g., in Chapter 4 Kristen wanted to write a letter *K* but knew her attempts did not match her expectations for what that letter ought to look like), teachers can provide explicit feedback.

Reversals are expected in the writing of preschoolers and kindergartners. Commenting about them or correcting them usually is not helpful; children often ignore such input. The more they write and see the writing of others (watching the handwriting process when others write and reading the products in texts of all kinds, especially in books), the more conventional and legible children's handwriting will become. When children notice their letters are reversed, then teachers can provide help for getting the letter started in the right direction. Only occasionally do idiosyncrasies that interfere with legibility persist into the elementary school years, when direct remedial handwriting instruction becomes appropriate.

The Sign-In Procedure and Name Writing Activity

The *sign-in procedure* involves having children write their names as a daily attendance activity (Harste, Burke, & Woodward, 1983). Teachers prepare cards with children's names printed on them (for 3-year-olds the name can be accompanied by a photograph). As the children enter the classroom, they locate and remove their name card (from a special name board), sign in on paper specially cut for this purpose, and put the paper in the attendance basket. Some teachers prepare a sign-in sheet with the names of four or five children. Figure 7.3 presents a sign-in sheet used in a prekindergarten classroom. The teacher in this classroom used different colors for the sign-in sheets, and they were placed in special locations in the classroom. As the children entered the classroom, they put away their belongings and then went to their sign-in sheet and wrote their names.

Over time and without direct instruction, most children's names begin to appear more conventional. Figure 7.4 presents Kimberly's signature at sign-in and how it changed over 3 months. At the end of 3 months, although Kimberly's signature is still not completely conventional, it has developed from a scribble, into a few recognizable letters, into a form that includes a letter or mock letter for every letter in her name. In kindergarten the sign-in procedure can become even more complex. Children can be asked to sign in, answer a question with yes or no, and then use the sign-in sheet to

FIGURE 7.3. Prekindergarten sign-in sheet.

write any words of interest to them as they occur during morning routines (see the sign-in sheets presented in Chapter 10, Figures 10.3 and 10.5).

Another activity that draws attention to alphabet letter features is having children learn to write their classmates' names (Cunningham, 2000). Each day a child's name is selected, and the teacher prepares a name-learning sheet. The child's name is written at the top and at the bottom of the sheet; at the bottom each letter in the name is enclosed in a box. Children cut out the letters in boxes. During cutting, the teacher and children

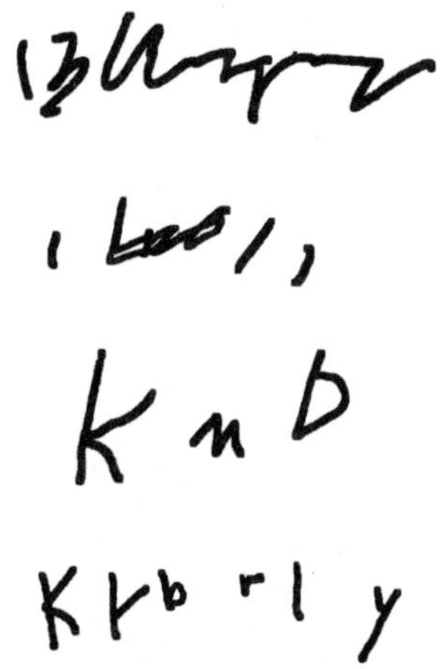

FIGURE 7.4. Kimberly's signature (first signature in November, second signature in December, third signature in January, last signature 1 week later in January).

talk about the letters and their features. Then children arrange the letters to spell the child's name, and the teacher can play "show me" games ("Show me the capital *E*, show me the *d*"). Then on a large chart the teacher can demonstrate writing the child's name. Children write the letters left to right across the page as many times as they wish. The papers are gathered up and stapled together, and the named child gets to take the resulting name book home.

Figure 7.5 presents four preschool children's attempts at writing Eldric's name. As shown in this figure, the 4-year-olds in this class have a range of letter-writing abilities. Some children demonstrate a good grasp of linearity and directionality as well as knowledge of how to form letters. Other children have only begun to develop the concepts about print and motor control for writing letters in names.

Many children continue name writing during center time. Teachers can encourage children to use clipboards on which they might invite other children to write their names. Or they can use name cards available in the Letter and Word center to write as many names as they find interesting. Teachers can extend name learning in the Letter and Word center by preparing a letter matching game for each child. Each child's name is

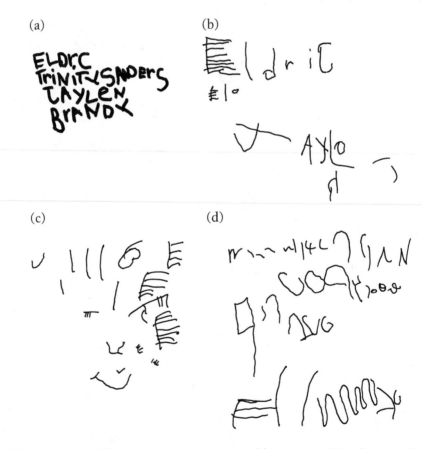

FIGURE 7.5. Four children's attempts at writing Eldric's name. 7.5a. Trinity writes Eldric. 7.5b. Jayla writes Eldric. 7.5c. Kaitlyn writes Eldric. 7.5d. Jimmy writes Eldric.

printed on a card (along with a picture of the child) and enclosed in a plastic sandwich bag. Plastic letters that spell the name are also enclosed in the bag for children to arrange in the spelling of the name.

Alphabet Books, Games, and Puzzles

Alphabet books provide many opportunities for children to learn the name of alphabet letters and hear the phonemes associated with them. The best kind of alphabet books for helping children learn the letter names and for hearing phonemes are those in which the alphabet letter is prominently printed in isolation, and each page includes only a few familiar objects and printed words. Pictures of unfamiliar animals or foods are not particularly helpful in allowing children to discover the relationship between letters and phonemes (for example, on an *O* page one child continually called the opposum a mouse, and so he read the page "*O* is for mouse" (Yaden, Smolkin, & Conlon, 1989). Many appropriate alphabet books have simple texts like "*A* is for apple" or "*M* is for mouse." As teachers read these books, they can make more prominent the connection between the alphabet letter name and its phoneme. After reading the text, teachers can say, for example, "M tells your mouth to say mmm at the beginning mmm-mouse" (Murray, Stahl, & Ivey, 1996, p. 311). In addition to alphabet books, many publishers have produced letter books. Letter books come in sets, with one book for each letter of the alphabet. These books are generally only a few pages long and have colorful photographs or illustrations. Each page of a letter book presents one object, its word, and the letter. At the end of some letter books is a poem or riddle that features alliteration.

After teachers read alphabet and letter books, they can be added to the Letter and Word center. Teachers can use extra copies of the book to cut pictures for alphabet matching games. Children can match laminated pictures to pages in the alphabet book. Alternatively, teachers can prepare alphabet letters created with many different fonts for children to match to pages in an alphabet book.

Teachers can construct many kinds of alphabet puzzles and games. One we recommend is writing a series of letters on a sheet and having children match letter tiles or plastic letters to each of the letters on the sheet. We recommend that the letters spell significant words, such as the children's names in the classroom or words related to theme study. When commonly confused letters are selected as answers for puzzles, teachers or aides will need to be available to provide children with feedback on their matching of the alphabet tiles to the letters on the board (Schickedanz, 1998). Another effective alphabet game is played with the teacher and a small group of children. The teacher begins to write a letter, perhaps by writing a vertical line. The children guess which letter the teacher will make. As children guess inappropriately, the teacher can also write that letter and show how it differs from what has already been written (Schickedanz, 1998).

A Final Word about Alphabet Learning

Most of what is important about alphabet letter learning takes us beyond just the letters themselves. In fact, the print processing skills that we describe in this chapter are intertwined during development. At first children may think that letters by themselves have an almost magical power to communicate. They write random strings of letters that they intend to convey a message (see Figure 3.3). However, these letter strings have nothing to do with spelling because their letters bear no relationship to the sounds in the words they are intended to spell. Eventually, children do generate theories about how to combine letters in some systematic relation to sounds they hear in words. This is the beginning of invented spelling and conscious use of letter–sound correspondences. When children begin to realize that syllables are composed of several individual sounds, they use more than one letter to spell the syllable; they move toward fully phonemic spelling, often using letter–sound correspondences more consistently than in conventional spelling. In order to do this, they need conscious awareness of phonemes.

CHAPTER SUMMARY

In this chapter we have defined deliberate and systematic instruction, and we have distinguished between embedded and separate, more explicit instruction. Instruction in print processing skills is embedded when it occurs during reading and writing for a meaningful purpose. More explicit instruction outside such a context can occur when teachers prepare games or other instructional activities that focus on a single literacy concept, but even then instruction can be playful and connected to other ongoing reading and writing activities. Deliberate and systematic instruction is based on close observation of children's literacy development in order to plan activities that precisely match what children currently can do and what they might do next. Teachers use demonstrations and explanations to make instruction explicit. Shared reading and writing provide many opportunities for teachers to demonstrate a variety of concepts about print. Write On and What Can You Show US? activities and fingerpoint reading further support children's development of concepts about print. Alphabet learning also occurs during shared reading and writing but can be extended through the sign-in procedure, name games, and other alphabet puzzles and games.

CHAPTER 8

Classroom Activities to Develop Phonological Awareness and the Alphabetic Principle

In this chapter we continue to describe instructional activities that help children develop print processing skills, including phonological awareness, the alphabetic principle, and sound–letter correspondences. We address the role of phonological awareness in children's literacy development and draw implications from research for instruction for 3-, 4-, and 5-year-olds. Finally, we discuss helping children discover the alphabetic principle and extending their knowledge of sound–letter correspondences. This chapter, along with Chapters 5, 6, and 7, provides information about instruction included in a well-balanced literacy program focusing on all critical areas of literacy development.

PHONOLOGICAL AWARENESS

Phonological awareness is highly complex and requires children to attend consciously to the sounds in words rather than to their meanings. It is one of the necessary ingredients, along with alphabet letter recognition, that children must grasp in order to discover the alphabetic principle. Phonemic awareness is at the highest level of phonological awareness and involves the ability to detect each phoneme in a spoken word, to blend phonemes into words, and to segment words into phonemes. While we know that children acquire some level of phonological awareness before learning to read and write in a conventional sense, the exact level that any one child must achieve before beginning to read is not known. Still, research is clear that children need to begin learning about phonemes and other sound units before reading instruction begins. We know further that a few children as young as 3 years old have begun to acquire the ability to detect rhyme and alliteration.

Considering Developmental Levels

Unlike other aspects of children's literacy development, we have little information about children's natural development of phonemic awareness. We do know that very young children play with sounds in words and engage in word play. We also know that some young children invent spellings before receiving any instruction in either phonemic awareness or in letter–sound correspondences (e.g., Bissex, 1980). Inventing a spelling indicates that children have developed on their own the ability to identify, isolate, and segment phonemes and relate them to alphabet letters. However, there is a large gap between being able to play with the sounds of language in word play and demonstrating phonemic awareness and letter–sound knowledge in invented spellings. We assume that children's experiences with hearing rhyming words in poems, nursery rhymes, and books helps them acquire phonological awareness of onsets and rimes. Furthermore, we assume that learning alphabet letters and reading alphabet books helps them acquire phonemic awareness of individual phonemes and their relationships to alphabet letters. For some children, these assumptions must be true—they do invent spellings even before kindergarten entry. But for other children who do not invent spellings even after a full year of kindergarten instruction, we cannot assume that experiences with nursery rhymes and alphabet books are enough.

We do know something about the development of phonemic awareness from research. Researchers have administered several phonological assessments to children as young as 2 years old, and from the results of children's performances on these isolated assessments have drawn conclusions about the sequence of children's phonological development. In general, children first are able to match pictures by rhyme and beginning phonemes, then children can blend onsets (/d/) with rimes (/og/) spoken by the teacher into words, especially when presented with several pictures or objects from which to select as part of the blending activity. They can also segment and say in isolation the beginning (and ending) phoneme from a word. Next (usually not until kindergarten and even first grade) children can segment words into onsets and rimes and finally into phonemes (National Reading Panel, 2000). Children's phonemic awareness is strengthened by learning to read conventionally; many children learn to segment a word into all of its phonemes only after beginning to read simple texts.

We also know from research that children acquire phonemic awareness best when spoken and picture activities are accompanied with instruction about alphabet letters. In fact, phonemic awareness training is useless until children can recognize at least a few alphabet letters (Johnston, Anderson, & Holligan, 1996; Stahl & Murray, 1994). However, phonemic awareness activities that involve children's matching pictures with the same beginning phonemes and matching these to alphabet letters are not strictly phonemic awareness activities. Instead, these kinds of activities involve phonics instruction (where letters are related to phonemes). For kindergartners especially, the most effective phonemic awareness training is embedded in phonics instruction (National Reading Panel, 2000).

A Word about Research-Based
Phonemic Awareness Programs

Many researchers have designed and tested phonological awareness programs. They have found that young children do develop the beginnings of phonemic awareness using these programs, and it does give them a head start in their later being able to decode words during reading (children's comprehension during reading is not as much affected by phonemic awareness training as is their decoding skill). In general, the training programs follow a similar sequence, use similar activities, and have similar outcomes as their goals, although the goals differ from preschool to kindergarten.

Many programs for phonological awareness instruction begin with helping children notice rhyme, using activities the researchers assume move from easier to more difficult (e.g., Adams, Foorman, Lundberg, & Beeler, 1998). In one program teachers read nursery rhymes aloud, pausing for children to supply the rhyming words. Other activities include having children generate (say) a third rhyming word to go with a presented pair of rhyming words or tell which of four words does not belong in a group because it does not rhyme with the other three (Brady, Fowler, Stone, & Winbury, 1994). Another program begins rhyming word activities by reading a rhyming book or poem that contains at least 10 rhyme pairs and that matches a topic of ongoing class interest (van Kleck, Gillam, & McFadden, 1998). After reading the poem, the teacher makes picture cards for the rhyming words and for nonrhyming word pairs as foils to use in rhyming games. The games involve rhyme recognition (repeating rhyming words as the teacher displays and names the rhyming word pictures), rhyme identification (finding another rhyming word picture when one of a pair is presented), rhyme judgment (telling whether or not two words presented on picture cards rhyme), and rhyme generation (thinking of a new word that rhymes with a pictured rhyming pair).

The next phase of phonological training usually targets beginning phonemes (Brady et al., 1994; Lindamood & Lindamood, 1975). In many programs children are taught to articulate phonemes, and teachers describe phonemes according to their articulatory features, for example, about the *p* sound and the *b* sound that they are "lip poppers—and that the *B* sound is the 'noisy brother' and the *P* sound the 'quiet brother' " (Brady et al., 1994, p. 36). Teachers provide demonstrations of articulating the phoneme in isolation and emphasizing its presence in spoken words ("listen carefully to this word /b/—/bark/; /bark/ starts with the sound /b/"; van Kleck, Gillam, & McFadden, 1998, p. 71). Next children are taught to identify or categorize phonemes by selecting pictures of words that can be grouped together because they have the same initial phoneme. Children are also taught to segment and isolate phonemes, for example, to "say a little bit" (just the beginning phoneme) of a word. Some programs teach children to identify, group, and isolate ending phonemes after learning beginning phonemes.

Most programs do not attempt to teach children all 44 phonemes, but rather select some consonant phonemes found in many words along with a few short vowel sounds. Research has shown that once children learn to identify and segment some phonemes, they automatically—without training—can identify and segment other phonemes (Byrne & Fielding-Barnsley, 1991). Most phonological awareness programs for 4-year-olds include rhyming and beginning phoneme activities. Letter–sound matching, blending, and segmenting activities are added to phonemic awareness programs for kindergartners.

Embedded Phonemic Awareness Instruction

As we have shown, many of the research-based phonological awareness programs begin with books or poems. First, teachers read aloud nursery rhymes, poetry, or books with alliteration (see Table 8.1 for a list of books that include rhyme or alliteration). Then teachers select words from the poems or books to use in follow-up games. Teachers can easily adapt these activities to help children pay attention to words as units of written language and to the sounds within those words. They can play rhyming games and direct children's attention to rhyming words in poems. With experience, many kindergartners can hear the similarity and the difference in rhyming words when they see them in a text such as a poem enlarged on a chart for shared reading. They come to see that the only difference in how rhyming words look is their first letters. Hearing and seeing these differences can be the start of associating sounds and letters.

TABLE 8.1. Books with Alliteration and Rhyme

Alliteration

The B Book (B), Phyllis McGinley

Dinorella: A Prehistoric Fairy Tale (D), Pamela Duncan Edwards

Four Fur Feet (F), Margaret Brown

Some Smug Slug (S), Pamela Duncan

Sheep on a Ship (SH), Nancy Shaw

Watch William Walk (W), Ann Jonas

Rhyme

Big Fat Hen, Keith Baker

One Duck Stuck, Phyllis Root

Mouse Mess, Linnea Riley

In the Small, Small Pond, Denise Fleming

Barnyard Banter, Denise Fleming

Jamberry, Bruce Degen

Boo to a Goose, Mem Fox

Puffins Climb, Penguins Rhyme, Bruce McMillan

1. 2., Buckle My Shoe, Liz Loveless

Silly Sally, Audrey Wood

Who Said Moo?, Harriet Ziefert

Mrs. McNosh Hangs Up Her Wash, Sarah Weeks

Guess Who's Coming, Jesse Bear, Bruce Degen

We suggest drawing attention to rhyme and alliteration as part of conversation about the text of a big book rather than as an isolated training activity. Of course, this requires that teachers be very familiar with potential activities and watch for the best times to use them, and even plan for times when they are likely to be usable. At least one research study has shown that children do acquire phonological awareness when instruction is embedded in shared reading activities (Ukrainetz, Cooney, Dyer, Kysar,& Harris, 2000) as is described in the following paragraph.

Reading sessions in the *PA [phonemic awareness] through Shared Reading* approach begin with the reading of a storybook chosen for its rhymes or alliteration and interest to the children. "The [teachers] read a portion of the book, then start a *sound talk* episode by identifying rhyming or alliterative words, then move into one or more of the four target skills" (Ukrainetz et al., 2000, p. 339). The target skills are initial sound identification, final sound identification, and sound segmentation (breaking a word into its component phonemes, while extending one finger per sound from a closed fist). For example, when children noticed the rhyming words *Fred* and *bed* and supplied a third, *shed*, the teacher said, "Yes, all those words rhyme. *Fred-bed-shed*. Let's count the sounds in *Fred*. Put our fingers out for each sound. /F-r-e-d/. 4 sounds! How many in *bed*? /B-e-d/. 3 sounds. Now *shed*. /sh-e-d/. 3 sounds. Which one is longest? Yeah, *Fred* has four sounds" (p. 340).

Writing sessions begin with the teacher and students drawing pictures about a previous day's book. Then they do a shared writing about the teacher's picture. Finally, the children write about their own pictures using scribble writing, strings of letters, or invented spellings. Again, the writing is accompanied by conversation. "The talk focus[es] on identification of sounds and aligning the number of letters written with the number of sounds in the words. The instructors have the children identify the sounds, count the number of sounds, provide a matching number of letters, and use their best guess of the specific letter involved" (p. 340). For example, when a student dictates, "I went to the zoo today," the teacher says, "I w-e-n-t [sounds said slowly]. Whew, four sounds in that word, that's lots to write" (McFadden, 1998, p. 11).

Books appropriate for use in the PA through Shared Reading approach include patterned books with repetitive words and phrases, Dr. Seuss books, poetry, and nursery rhymes. For example, during a reading of *The Cat in the Hat* (Dr. Seuss, 1957) the following exchange occurred between the teacher and Sarah:

TEACHER: Okay, listen for the rhyming words when I read this time. [Reading] The sun did not shine. It was too wet to *play*. So we sat in the house all that cold, cold, wet *day*.

SARA: Cold, cold.

TEACHER: We repeated the word "cold" but listen again for rhyming words, those words that sound like music together [repeats reading, stressing and pausing before rhyming words].

SARA: Play, day. (p. 10)

Later in the same episode, when another student notices the rhyming words *to* and *do*, the teacher asks, "What do you do to make the word *to* into the word *do*? Sarah says, "Take off the /t/ and put on a /d/!" (p. 10).

Books used to develop phonological awareness can be placed in a specially developed Sound center. Teachers can place audiotapes and copies of the books for children's listening and make picture cards for matching games. Observing children as they play with the materials in the Sound center will provide teachers with opportunities to assess how well children have grasped concepts being demonstrated in small-group lessons.

Conceptual Development, Not Skill Practice

The best instruction in phonological awareness is thoughtful and based on careful observation of what children can do rather than following a preplanned sequence of lessons. Teachers need to keep in mind that phonological awareness is a concept that children must acquire rather than a skill that can be developed through drill and practice (Adams, 2001). Consider Justin and Duran, two boys who are entering kindergarten. When assessed by their teachers prior to school entry, Justin could not match pictures using rhyme or beginning phonemes. In fact, when shown some of the pictures he began singing the "Itsy Bitsy Spider" song and matched a picture of a sun and rain. In contrast, Duran stated that he had never heard of rhyming words. His teacher followed the directions on the assessment, but she could tell Duran was unsure of the concept. He matched four out of eight rhyming pairs. However, the teacher noticed that Duran was attempting to match using a sound strategy (he elongated the words just as she had demonstrated). He was unsuccessful selecting one rhyming pair because he thought the picture of a *pan* was a *pot*. Therefore, he selected the picture of a *top* rather than a *can* to go with the picture of a *pot* despite the teacher's reminding him that the picture was of a *pan*. After school began, the teacher was curious to see if Duran had developed better rhyming word skills—2 weeks later he correctly matched all eight sets of pictures.

What is the difference between Justin and Duran? Justin likely has not developed any *metalinguistic* skills, whereas Duran has. Metalinguistic skills include any ability to pay attention to a word aside from its meaning. They involve being able to pay attention to the length of a word, its letters, and its sounds. What Duran lacked was not metalinguistic skills. Rather, he lacked an insight into what rhyming words were; once he became conscious of rhyming words, he quickly acquired the concept, most likely because he had already acquired some metalinguistic skill. Justin, on the other hand, clearly focused on the words' meanings in the rhyming and beginning phoneme activities. He will need many experiences drawing his attention away from a word's meaning to its visual and sound properties. His teacher might begin with conscious attention to syllables—which are very easy to detect. Therefore, Justin might acquire the beginnings of metalinguistic skills as he learns to tap out a word's syllables. This will provide the foundation for his later learning about rhyming words and beginning phonemes.

This explains why we do *not* recommend leading the whole class in meaningless chants about sounds and letters that are part of some programs for teaching phonemic awareness. Those chants go something like this: "Let me hear you say *cat*. Everybody—" "Cat!"

"Let me hear you clap *cat*. Everybody—"

"Cuh (clap)-aaah (clap)-tuh (clap)."

"Yes! That's *cat*. Cuh-aaah-tuh. *C-A-T*. Everybody—"

"*Cat*. Cuh-aaah-tuh. *C-A-T*."

And so on with *hat* and *cut* and *cab* for 10 minutes of whole-class time. This is not the best use of class time precisely because it teaches phonemes as if they can be learned through rote practice rather than through thoughtful interactions between children and their teacher.

Because phonological and phonemic awareness have been the focus of so much attention, teachers may be pressured to adopt a phonemic awareness training program that has been demonstrated as effective through research. The best research programs (including those we mentioned in this chapter) are short (research suggests that a total of from 8 to 18 hours of instruction overall is plenty of time for children to develop phonological awareness). They engage small groups of children in short (as few as 10 minutes) game-like activities. No studies have included 3-year-olds. We argue that 3-year-olds should have lots of opportunities to enjoy books with rhyme and alliteration without teachers deliberately trying to teach them what these are. Four-year-olds who are also learning to recognize alphabet letters can enjoy rhyming and alliteration activities and blending games. Kindergartners need more deliberate attention to all aspects of phonological awareness. However, this should still be accompanied by many purposeful reading and writing activities.

DEVELOPING THE ALPHABETIC PRINCIPLE

As children have more and more experience with classroom print and environmental print, they build personal repertoires of letters they can name, letters they can write legibly, and words they can read without hesitation (sight words). Even a small repertoire of such knowledge can serve as the foundation for building another kind of knowledge, knowledge of sound–letter correspondences. It certainly need not include knowledge of and ability to form all the letters of the alphabet. Children can begin to discover the alphabetic principle and to explore how sounds and letters work together in our writing system when they know only a handful of letters.

Embedded Sound–Letter Correspondence Instruction

The best instruction for helping children discover and use the alphabetic principle is teachers' demonstrations during writing and their feedback to individual children's attempts at writing. Good teachers of sound–letter correspondences know what they are teaching: That is, before they teach phonemic awareness, they know what a phoneme is, and before they teach sound–letter correspondences, they know the ins and outs of *phonics* better than their students ever will need to know them (see Appendix A for more information about phonics and phonemes). Phonics is far more complex than simply learning one phoneme attached to one letter. For example, some letters (such as the letter *c*) correspond with more than one sound (consider *candy* and *city*). Some sounds correspond with no single letter (such as the sound at the beginning of *shake*). Good teachers of letter-sound correspondences find out what their students know and build on that (see assessments from Chapter 3). They find out by providing abundant opportunities for children to write and then watching what they do, participating in what they do, conversing with them about what they do. Good teachers of letter–sound correspondences model and talk about what they want their students to learn. Finally, good teachers of letter–sound correspondences provide meaningful opportunities for students to learn and apply what they learn, usually in writing but increasingly so in fingerpoint reading (see Chapter 7).

Teachers can take advantage of letter books, alphabet books, and alphabet book writing to help children learn letter–sound correspondences. Kindergarten teachers can read several alphabet books and use shared writing to keep lists of words that begin with letters of interest. Children may use environmental print items from environmental print bulletin boards (see Chapter 4) to locate words with target alphabet letters. Kindergarten teachers may help their children construct an alphabet wall of environmental print. Children can glue environmental print items on large chart paper divided into 26 squares, each labeled with an alphabet letter. When they are writing at the Writing center, many kindergarten children can use *alphabet charts* on which all of the alphabet letters are printed along with a picture for each letter. Teachers can make an enlarged copy of the alphabet chart for shared reading.

Kindergarten teachers will want to use frequent assessment to make sure the children are making progress in learning to recognize alphabet letter names and to associate phonemes with them (especially the consonant letters). This can happen informally when teachers place materials in a Letter and Word center for children's use. When indicated, teachers can provide small groups of children with additional practice in identifying letters and associating sounds with them. We recommend that this practice occur in small-group lessons of the sort we have already described. Teachers can play short letter–sound games with children, who sort toys and other objects into groups associated with letters. Teachers can read alphabet books to small groups of children and have them compose lists of words that begin with a particular letter. They can sit with a small group of children to support them during journal writing, perhaps demonstrating spelling words using letter boxes (discussed later in this chapter).

From Shared to Interactive Writing

Shared writing offers many opportunities for teachers to demonstrate for children how to slowly say words, emphasize phonemes, and match letters with those phonemes. Effective teachers will recognize when it is enough to demonstrate spelling only a few words and then only their first sounds (with 4-year-olds, for example) or when they need to demonstrate spelling several words, trying to capture a beginning, ending, and perhaps middle phoneme (with kindergartners, when appropriate). These decisions will be based on their knowledge of children's current level of phonological awareness, knowledge of sound–letter correspondences, and ability to orchestrate these during spelling.

For example, a teacher might write a list of the day's schedule, saying "I'm going to write *music* here so that you know we have music class today. I hear *mmm* at the beginning of *music*. When I just start to say *music*, I say *mmm*. Do you hear the *mmm*, like in our friend Maria's name, and like in our calendar word *Monday*? *Mmmusic. Mmmaria. Mmmonday.* Maria uses an *m* to write her name, don't you, Maria? And I see an *m* here at the beginning of *Monday*. So I'm going to start writing *music* with an *m*." This teacher's sound talk relates the phoneme /m/ to several words the children know (one of their classmate's names and the name of a day of the week). The teacher draws attention to the printed letter in those words (demonstrating for children a strategy they might use in their own writing) and uses that letter to spell the new word *music*. This kind of talk does not start out asking children to name the letter that corresponds to the phoneme. Instead, the teacher demonstrates how children can think and discover for themselves how to link letters in words they know with sounds they want to write.

A form of shared writing in which children write portions of the message with the teacher's help is called *interactive writing* or *shared pen writing*. Once the topic and purpose of writing are established, the first step in interactive writing is to negotiate a sentence. The teacher and children make suggestions about what a sentence might say. The teacher helps children keep the exact words of the sentence in mind by slowly repeating the sentence and holding up a finger (from left to right) for each word in the sentence as they say them. Then children repeat the sentence as the teacher again holds up a finger for each word. Some teachers draw lines on the chart paper from left to right to show where each word of the sentence will be written. The lines help children keep track of the message and its words as they are writing. When the children have the sentence clearly in mind, the second step is initiated: recalling a word and slowly stretching it out and saying its sounds. Next, the teacher shares the pen and selects a student to write letters associated with the sounds in the word. The teacher helps this child articulate the first sound and write a letter. After the first letter is written, the teacher may decide to write the remainder of the word him- or herself because of its length or the complexity of its spelling, or children may contribute other letters to the word's spelling. Next, the teacher rereads the sentence by pointing to the words that have been written and helps children recall which word comes next. Then that word is stretched, and another child may be selected to share the pen and write a letter or several letters in the word.

The spelling on an interactive writing chart is usually conventional because the chart is intended to be read and reread by the children or others (for example, when it is placed in the hallway for other children, teachers, and parents to read). However, teachers may elect not to help children spell the words conventionally. Instead, they may demonstrate writing words with a few letters and emphasizing that those letters do capture sounds in the word. The decision of whether the words are to be spelled conventionally or with invented spellings should be based on the purpose and use of the writing. It should also be clear to children whether they are using grown-up spellings so that others can read it, or whether they are using kid spellings so that children can do all the writing. Figure 8.1 presents a kindergartner's response to *The Grouchy Lady Bug* (Carle, 1986) using the technique of composing a message, counting the words and drawing a line for each word, and then listening to the phonemes in each word to produce a spelling.

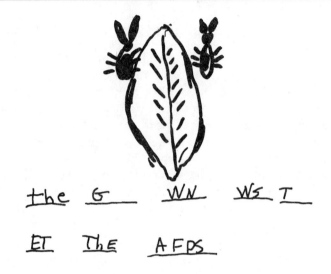

FIGURE 8.1. Response to *The Grouchy Lady Bug* (Carle, 1986): "The grouchy one wants to eat the aphids."

Because of the complexity of sharing a pen with several children, reading and rereading the sentence, and taking time to stretch out the sounds of words, interactive writing usually only comprises a sentence. Small groups or even one-on-one are best for this activity so that every child has a chance to participate. In addition, small groups can be selected so that children with similar needs (such as listening to the ends of words, or learning to hear the beginning sound) are included in the lesson.

Responding to Children's Writing

Helping children write independently is the most effective way of extending children's concepts about the alphabetic principle. Each time teachers help a child spell, they have opportunities to increase the child's awareness of sound–letter correspondences and to teach a new problem-solving strategy that children can use for creating more sophisticated spellings on their own. A teacher's first goal when responding to children's attempts to use sound–letter correspondences in writing is to help them to write comfortably at their current stages of development and with their existing strategies. A teacher may gently nudge students to the next stages or more sophisticated strategies, but only when she is present to give guidance (within the zone of proximal development) and with her assurance that they may fall back on what they are now most comfortable doing.

Not all children need to be encouraged to attempt to spell words using invented spelling (and knowledge of sound–letter correspondences). However, if a teacher observes, for example, that a young writer uses one letter per word and that the letter usually corresponds with a sound in the letter's name, then she might provide feedback about the effectiveness of this strategy to the student: "I see you wrote *fun* with this *f*.

That works; I can hear *fff* in *fffun* and *fff* in *efff*." Later, when that same writer asks how to write *roller coaster*, the teacher can say, "Wow, that's a hard one! Let's see, what sounds do you hear in *roller coaster, rrrroller coaster*?" The student may identify the *rrr* sound and choose the letter *r*, and the teacher may with similar talk help the student to hear the long *o* sound and choose the letter *o*. The teacher may encourage even more segmenting and spelling—"What else do you hear in *rolllller coaster*?" If the student then answers, "*Rrr* again" and says, "That's all," then the teacher accepts and celebrates *ror* as a spelling of *roller coaster*. "Yes! I can read that: 'Roller coaster!' Can you read your whole story to me?" Such an interaction, short though it is, can help a writer move from spelling with just one letter to hearing more than one sound and spelling with three letters.

Using Letter Boxes

An activity that helps stretch children's phonemic awareness and strengthens their understanding of the alphabetic principle is using *letter boxes*. Letter boxes are small squares written on a whiteboard (or affixed to the board with tape). Teachers use letter boxes to show children how to listen to each phoneme in a word and then match it with an alphabet letter or letters. For example, a teacher might use letter boxes to help a small group of children who need instruction in phonemic awareness to isolate phonemes in a word. The teacher might introduce the word he or she will spell in the letter boxes with a meaning clue about the word ("When I take off my shoes and socks, you can see my _____"). Next, the teacher demonstrates sliding up the tokens (with the letters *f, e*, and *t*) into the letter boxes, one for each phoneme, saying "*ffff-eeeee-ttttt*." Then he moves his finger from left to right under the letters and reads, "*Ffff-eeeee-ttttt, feet!*" Last, he reads to the small group a short, funny poem about feet. The teacher may choose to demonstrate segmenting and blending other words, such as *seat, beat,* or *meet*. As the children in the group say the words, segment them, and push up tokens, the teacher provides feedback and further demonstrations.

What is important for this lesson is not the correct spellings of the words (that will come later, in first grade). Rather, for kindergartners the focus is on segmenting words into each of their phonemes and attaching a letter to each phoneme. Research has shown that children's ability to hear, segment, and spell final phonemes, and then middle phonemes is important for their using the alphabetic principle. Effective teachers are careful to make sure children actually need this kind of instruction before they provide it. For example, if one child spells *pickle* as *pekl*, the teacher will recognize the very sophisticated phonemic awareness and sound–letter knowledge demonstrated through that spelling. He will know that this child does not need phonemic awareness teaching, although another child, who spells *pickle* and every other word she wants to write with a random string of letters, does need such teaching.

Supporting Children's Early Attempts at Invented Spelling

Teachers are always pleased to see children make the transition from writing with a randomly selected string of letters to writing with letters that have a systematic relationship to the phonemes in a word. Although we do not want to overemphasize the importance of being able to invent spellings (especially for preschoolers and beginning-of-the-year kindergartners), first invented spellings are a milestone in every child's literacy development. For some children this milestone is achieved without adult support before they enter kindergarten. For other children, even after several months of demonstrations in shared writing and small-group lessons in phonemic awareness and sound–letter correspondences, an adult's guidance is necessary for them to begin inventing spellings.

One reason some children have difficulty inventing spellings independently is related to the messages they want to write. Some children seem to know that it is OK to write only a word or two. For them, hearing sounds in those one or two words is relatively easy. Other children have trouble composing a message that they can keep in their memory. Their long sentences change as they try to write them. In the jumble of a sentence in which words change over time, many young writers give up on the attempt to listen to sounds in words. It is as if the words will not sit still long enough for the writer to hear any sounds in them.

There are three ways teachers can help with the message problem. One is by having children draw a picture of anything interesting to them. Then the teacher helps the child select just a few or only one word to write about that picture. Another way teachers can help students compose shorter messages is to select writing prompts that call for only one-word responses. For example, the pattern in the book *Goodnight Moon* (Brown, 1947) includes the phrases "goodnight, kittens; goodnight mittens." The pattern of *goodnight* _____ is a good prompt for helping children attempt an invented spelling. Teachers can read the book, establish the pattern, and prepare a *Goodnight Moon* response booklet with the word *goodnight* written on each page. Then they can demonstrate how to think up words to write in the goodnight pattern. As a group, children can remember phrases from the book or make up their own responses ("goodnight lamp, goodnight shoes, goodnight bed"). Then teachers can demonstrate saying the words slowly, listening for sounds, and selecting letters to use to spell the sound.

Figure 8.2 presents two children's writing as a part of this lesson. Eduardo clearly was able to use phonemic awareness and sound–letter correspondence knowledge in order to produce a spelling; Robert was not. The children's responses to this activity provided their teacher with clear indications of the kinds of instruction and activities each child needed next. Eduardo needs to be encouraged to write (perhaps in a daily journal), but Robert needs more demonstrations in shared writing, some phonemic awareness activities, and perhaps more opportunities to write alphabet letters. He will enjoy writing in a dramatic play center rather than in a daily journal.

The third way that teachers can help children keep their messages firmly in mind as they write is to use the *magic line* (adapted from Feldgus & Cardonick, 1999). As children compose their sentences they write a magic line for each word (as teachers have demonstrated in interactive writing). Then children go back to the first word, say it slowly, and write the letters they hear on the line. If they cannot hear any sounds, then the magic line will say the word. For many children, the magic line frees them to attempt writing because they know when all else fails the line can do the work! Figure 8.3 pres-

(a)   (b)

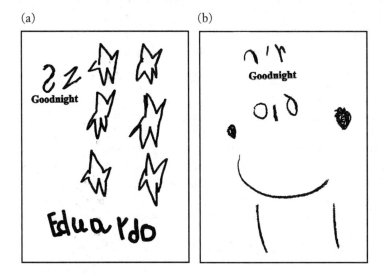

FIGURE 8.2. Invented spellings for *Goodnight Moon* (Brown, 1947). 8.2a. Edwardo spells *stars*. 8.2b. Robert's writing.

ents a kindergartner's journal response. She used one letter string (*ci* to spell *he*), the magic line (to spell *eats*), invented spelling (*cs* to spell *cookies*), and a place holder—a letter without any sound–letter relationship (*L* to spell *now*) to compose her message.

This child's use of the magic line is another example of a problem-solving strategy. That is, instead of teaching this child to use, for example, the letter *h* to spell *he* and the letters *e* or *t* to spell *eats*, her teacher taught her to use what she did know to solve the problem of composing a message and spelling its words. With the magic line, Natasha was able to signal her entire message and to spell at least one word, *cookies,* with its initial and final sounds. Effective teachers teach problem-solving strategies that will allow children to do a task with more success the next time they attempt it.

From Fingerpoint Reading to Guided Reading

A few children may demonstrate levels of reading and writing knowledge that indicate they can benefit from guided reading instruction. Most kindergartners will not reach this

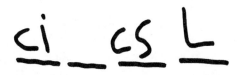

FIGURE 8.3. Kindergartner's journal entry: "He eats cookies now."

TABLE 8.2. Literacy Behaviors That Indicate the Onset of Early Reading

The child . . .

1. Recognizes nearly all alphabet letters fluently.
2. Demonstrates phonological awareness by tapping syllables, producing rhyming words, sorting words by beginning phoneme, isolating beginning phonemes, and blending single-consonant onsets with rimes.
3. Demonstrates knowledge of consonant letter–sound relationships.
4. Spells words with boundary phonemes included on some words.
5. During fingerpoint reading, memorizes text and tracks print with nearly one-on-one correspondence.
6. Corrects tracking during fingerpoint reading using concept of word and letter–sound checking.
7. Attempts independent reading of familiar text using memorization, fingerpoint reading, known words, and letter–sound cross-checking.
8. Retells important events from stories and main details from informational text with some literary and technical vocabulary.

level of literacy knowledge, but some children will. Table 8.2 presents a list of indicators that suggest the onset of Early Reading, indicating that children can benefit from conventional reading instruction usually provided in guided reading instruction. Teachers may use books that have been leveled for difficulty to select appropriate easy text for beginning conventional reading instruction. There are several ways that books have been leveled. One way is through Reading Recovery, which levels books from 1 to 20, with levels 1–3 considered kindergarten; 4–14, first grade; and 15–20, second grade. Irene Fountas and Gay Su Pinnell (*Guided Reading: Good First Teaching*, 1996) use alphabet letters to indicate levels, with A–C considered kindergarten level, D–I considered first grade, and J–M second grade (adapted from Schulman & Payne, 2000, p. 175). Many commercial companies also publish leveled books with their first level of text usually on the primer level.

We do not expect that many kindergartners will benefit from guided reading instruction. However, teachers can adapt fingerpoint reading to the first, kindergarten, levels of easy-reading books. Books at levels 1–3 or A–C are highly predictable; they are patterned books with many repeated words in predictable sentence patterns. Teachers can use fingerpoint reading strategies and activities (see Chapter 7) with these books, but have children fingerpoint-read in the little leveled books rather than on a pocket chart. Many kindergarten teachers prepare a basket of books for each child in their classroom. These are copies of poems used in fingerpoint reading, familiar pattern books, and letter books that children can read independently. By the end of kindergarten many children pretend to read, other children fingerpoint-read, and a few children can read by using a few sight words, tracking and memory, and decoding.

A FINAL WORD OF CAUTION

We began this book with the intention of describing high-quality early literacy programs that would prevent reading and writing failure before it ever had a chance to begin. We emphasized that the nature of these programs would not differ from programs for children who are "on the fast track" of literacy development. Throughout the book we stressed what we currently know about children's literacy development as a guide for instruction. We emphasized that it is "appropriate to teach young children about the alphabet [and other literacy concepts], although teachers must be careful to use practices that are effective [and appropriate] in achieving this goal" (Schickedanz, 1998, p. 35). We stressed the need for authentic reading and writing activities within a well-balanced program that maintains the joyful, playful atmosphere found in the best preschools and kindergartens. We also integrated into our recommendations findings from research, especially related to developing children's print processing skills.

We are very aware that current conceptions about early literacy clearly privilege certain kinds of decontextualized and school-like literacy behaviors and knowledge over the more contextualized and functional knowledge about literacy that all young children possess (Neuman & Celano, 2001). We acknowledge that we have implied that all young children can reach high standards in literacy development. We believe this can happen when teachers capitalize on all children's funds of knowledge. The instruction that we describe in this book can provide all children with rich experiences that address a broad array of a child's developmental needs. They address a balance of literacy activities at the same time recognizing, valuing, and extending children's diverse home literacies.

CHAPTER SUMMARY

In this chapter we have described ways teachers can embed instruction that supports children's development of phonemic awareness as a part of reading poems and books with alliteration and rhyme. In PA through Shared Reading, teachers can draw children's attention to sound features of words, help children detect rhyme and alliteration, and even segment words into phonemes. Children also enjoy playing games with rhyming words and words with the same beginning phonemes. Teachers can capitalize on alphabet letter activities to help children learn letter–sound correspondences; using letter boxes to show children how to segment words into phonemes and associate them with letters is one way of doing this. Shared writing demonstrations can be crafted to help children discover more about letter–sound correspondences and the alphabetic principle. Teachers can also extend children's understandings of these concepts when they help children write. Finally, when children can orchestrate a sufficient amount of literacy knowledge, they begin fingerpoint reading little, leveled books.

CHAPTER 9

Prekindergarten in Action

This chapter describes how to develop a prekindergarten curriculum that integrates reading and writing activities within a themed unit designed to meet national social studies standards. While the teacher we describe in this chapter is not real, the setting of the classroom does exist and many of the activities we describe have been developed in our numerous professional contacts with preschool teachers. The samples we use in the chapter were gathered from various preschool settings. This chapter is written to provide information about how to plan a curriculum at a level where teachers are often not provided with state-mandated standards or guidelines.

INTRODUCTION

Ms. Simpson and her aide teach 18 4-year-olds in a preschool for low-income families funded by the state Office of School Readiness. Her classroom is located in an old refurbished high school that also houses several Head Start, Even Start, and adult education classrooms. Because some of the programs in this building are funded in part by Title I monies through the local school system, Ms. Simpson has access to many services, including transportation and professional development. Although her program does not include a music, art, or physical education teacher, Ms. Simpson works closely with the kindergarten teachers in the local school system and uses the services of a reading specialist and a speech and language pathologist. The school system is located in a rural part of the state where many parents are only occasionally employed or hold minimum-wage jobs. Despite the fact that nearby communities provide numerous cultural, educational, and sporting events, many of Ms. Simpson's children have not had extensive experiences beyond their local community. Most children have never been to the small community library and most do not own more than a few children's books.

THE PRESCHOOL CURRICULUM

In the past, Ms. Simpson's preschool curriculum was not different from that found in many preschools. She typically focused on several broad themes such as Fall, Families, Plants, The Farm, Wild Animals, Floating and Sinking, and Favorite Story Characters. These themes allowed her to cover many content standards related to mathematics, science, and social studies that she felt were appropriate for preschool children (e.g., National Committee on Science Education Standards and Assessment, 1994; National Council for the Social Studies, 1994). She integrated reading and writing as part of these themes by reading related stories and informational books aloud to her children daily, adding theme-related books to theme centers and the Book center, and using shared writing to record information dictated by the children. Her classroom was organized around six permanent centers: Book, Art, Writing, Home Living, Blocks, and Math/ manipulatives. She added new activities to each of the centers frequently and often added a new center related to the current theme. She has a large carpeted space for whole-group activities and small tables where children eat snacks or work on projects. There is a large playground area which has age-appropriate equipment, including a climbing structure, large sandbox, and playhouse. In addition, the children have access to balls, jump ropes, tricycles, and other outside equipment and toys.

Literacy and the Preschool Curriculum

Ms. Simpson has recently made several changes in her curriculum especially related to literacy development. She made these changes in response to a growing concern over her children's lack of progress once they began attending elementary school. Because of Ms. Simpson's concerns, she and the school district reading specialist began to meet to discuss the progress of her children from kindergarten through first grade. They discovered that on the state-mandated assessment at the end of kindergarten and first grade, many of the children performed in the bottom fourth of the class despite their active involvement in the preschool program. Ms. Simpson and the reading specialist looked carefully at the children's performance on literacy assessments and discovered that at the end of preschool many children, but not all, could write their names with many recognizable letters, recognize some alphabet letters—especially the letters in their names—match some rhyming words, and retell some portions of a favorite story. Ms. Simpson was surprised that several children recognized only one or two alphabet letters and could not match pictures by rhyming sounds. Still, by the end of kindergarten a majority of the children who had attended the preschool recognized nearly all of the alphabet letters, matched pictures with the same beginning sounds, and could match some letters with sounds. Again, several of the children did not display this level of literacy knowledge. In addition, many of the children at kindergarten's end did not invent spellings independently and did not consistently track words one-on-one in fingerpoint reading activities. Many of these children struggled to learn to read, and only a few children from the preschool read above the primer level at the end of first grade.

Ms. Simpson was concerned by these results and asked the reading specialist to help her look at the entering kindergarten performance of other children who had success-fully learned to read by the end of first grade. They discovered that these children entered kindergarten writing their first names fluently, recognizing most upper- and lower-case alphabet letters, and matching pictures with the same beginning sounds. Ms. Simpson decided to rethink her preschool curriculum to provide more focused opportu-nities for children to develop higher levels of literacy knowledge like those displayed by the more successful children. She realized that there had been many opportunities for children to informally acquire literacy concepts in her classroom—through rhyming word chants and songs, playing with alphabet puzzles, pretending to write in the Home Living center, and listening to stories in the Book center. However, children were allowed to select these activities, and Ms. Simpson suspected that many children had not chosen these activities frequently enough to extend their literacy knowledge.

Ms. Simpson decided to take a more deliberate approach toward literacy in her cur-riculum. She would continue to use themes and centers as the central part of her curric-ulum. However, she would add a few literacy-focused activities to her classroom rou-tines so that all children would engage in reading and writing daily. With the reading specialist's help, Ms. Simpson decided to add the sign-in procedure (see Chapter 7) to her routine for children's arrival. This routine would ensure that each child wrote daily and would provide numerous opportunities for her to interact with children as they were writing. She also decided to add more retelling activities to her read-aloud pro-gram—she would model and guide children's retelling of at least two books per theme (see Chapter 6). Retelling would allow children many opportunities to use the vocabu-lary found in the books she read aloud and to extend their comprehension. She also wanted to try out the Write On procedure that she had learned about at a recent profes-sional development conference. She thought that Write On activities would increase the children's concepts about print and the number of alphabet letters they would recognize and develop their fine-motor skills. To help reinforce alphabet letter recognition, Ms. Simpson and the reading specialist decided to try a modification of the Write On activity in—what they would later call Alphabet Write On. In this activity, Ms. Simpson would model writing two or three alphabet letters that were the focus of her theme in upper- and lower-case form on a large chart. Then she would place the chart in the Writing cen-ter and invite children to practice writing the letter during center time. She also decided to be more deliberate during shared writing in talking about concepts about print and alphabet letters.

Selecting Themes

Although Ms. Simpson was concerned about providing her children with opportunities to develop the levels of literacy knowledge that would enable them to become successful readers and writers, she was also concerned that preschool continue to preserve chil-dren's natural curiosity about the world in which they lived. She had become increas-ingly aware that the themes she selected to guide the curriculum were often unrelated to children's real experiences. Many activities that she planned in the past had seemed arti-ficial. She had read about the project approach (Helm, Beneke, & Steinheimer, 1998;

Helm & Katz, 2001) in which children investigate a topic by finding answers to questions they helped to pose. Resources for answering questions are brought into the classroom by children, parents, community members, or the teacher. Children seek information from visits to community sites, and they demonstrate their knowledge through drawing, building, or constructing.

Although Ms. Simpson admired many aspects of the project approach, she was unprepared to adopt it outright. Instead she decided that the part of the project approach which would be most beneficial to her children would be having them gather information from their home and community experiences. She would plan activities in which she and the children would collect information and then construct a way to display the information in the classroom. These displays would provide authentic opportunities for writing as the children categorized and labeled information. She also decided to try to help her children conduct surveys.

While Ms. Simpson was excited about trying out her new curriculum ideas, she decided to begin the school year with the Home and School theme that she had used in the past. However, she modified her daily schedule slightly to accommodate the new literacy activities (see Figure 9.1). During this theme children began the new sign-in procedure as they entered the classroom after breakfast. They collected information through surveys and constructed graphs showing their favorite toys and food at home and school. They read, discussed, and retold *The Runaway Bunny* (Brown, 1942) and *Rosie's Walk* (Hutchins, 1968). During shared writing, they dictated lists of *places Rosie went on her walk* and *things Little Bunny turned into*. The children brought photographs of people who lived in their homes and graphed how many people lived there. Because of the children's interest in the photographs of different family members, Ms. Simpson read *Two Eyes a Nose and a Mouth* (Intrater, 1995). After reading the book the children dictated a shared writing list of features found on faces, and Ms. Simpson introduced the Write On procedure. Each child selected a letter on the list that he or she wanted to write. Then

8:00–8:30	Breakfast, sign-in, table games, and puzzles
8:30–9:00	Whole-group calendar, music, shared reading, ABC, phonological awareness, art demonstrations
9:00–10:00	Centers
10:00–10:45	Snack, outdoors
10:45–11:15	Read-aloud, shared writing, Write On, retelling/drama (narrative)
11:15–11:45	Lunch, bathroom, book selection
11:45–12:30	Rest, book browse
12:30–1:30	Centers
1:30–2:00	Read-aloud, project activities, cooking (nonfiction)
2:00–2:40	Outdoors
2:50	Dismissal

FIGURE 9.1. Ms. Simpson's daily schedule.

Ms. Simpson hung the chart in the Writing center, and some children added additional letters. Figure 9.2 presents the *Face* shared writing and Write On.

Although she was happy with the way the new literacy activities seemed to be working, Ms. Simpson still wanted to develop themes that would be more interesting to the children and provide more opportunities for investigation. One afternoon an idea for a new theme occurred to her as she supervised her children's boarding the school buses and being picked up by parents for their trips home from school. She decided to plan a theme around automobiles—the most frequent form of personal transportation. In the past she had used Transportation to focus on all forms of travel by land, water, and air. However, she realized that the theme Automobiles was far more related to the children's lives and potentially offered more opportunities for investigation than the more generic Transportation theme.

Developing the Theme

To prepare for the theme, Ms. Simpson researched automobiles using the Internet. She found information about the history and significance of the Model T and other models of automobiles, including the 1949 Ford Coupe and the Mustang. She located information on current makes and models of automobiles, and she took a virtual tour of the Henry Ford and Rolls Royce Museums and viewed photographs of old cars rebuilt by collectors. She found many Internet sites devoted to restoring antique cars and to car

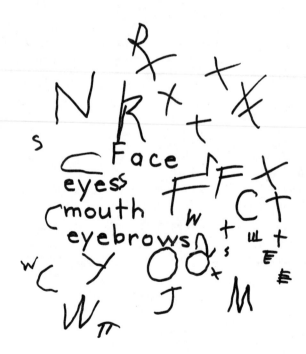

FIGURE 9.2. Shared writing and Write On for Face.

clubs. As she studied the information on these Internet sites, Ms. Simpson became keenly aware of how the automobile had not only changed the way goods are produced and sold, but also the very nature of society. However, she realized many of these abstract ideas were not appropriate for her young children. She did think that her children would be highly motivated by the topic and could learn a great deal about history as a part of this theme.

Ms. Simpson visited the local library to locate children's books related to automobiles, using keyword searches. She also used online bookstores to locate more resources for the theme. By using the library, buying a few new books, and using a few books from her previous transportation theme, Ms. Simpson pulled together nearly 25 books she could use for the Automobile theme (see the list of books in Figure 9.3). She quickly read the books, jotting down the major ideas presented in each book. From a friend, she borrowed a *Wee Sing in the Car* (Beall, 2001) book and CD, which included several songs about traveling in cars. She planned to use the songs on the CD for music activities. She realized that none of the books she selected for the theme came in big book format. However, she noted that several of the books she found included rhyming phrases. She decided to copy portions of *Duck in the Truck* (Alborough, 2001) and *Pigs in the Mud in the Middle of the Rud* (Plourde, 1997) on large charts to use for shared reading and a smaller portion of those texts for fingerpoint reading.

Using a Theme Planning Web

Ms. Simpson realized that she needed a better way to plan theme activities that would help her identify content standards, books for read-alouds, songs and chants, books for retelling, projects that would lead to information displays, activities for cooking and art, and center adjustments. She decided to arrange her ideas on a web. The *Theme Planning Web* would include learning outcomes for the children as well as cooking, art, retelling, center, and project activities. Ms. Simpson would also add activities for phonological awareness and alphabet recognition to the Planning Web (see Figure 9.3 for a completed Theme Planning Web).

After reading all the books she selected for the unit and browsing the Internet sites, Ms. Simpson was ready to begin the Theme Planning Web. She thought about the major concepts and vocabulary she might help her young children learn. She decided that several major ideas were appropriate learning outcomes for 4-year-olds. They could learn that there are many makes (manufacturers) and models of automobiles; automobiles have many parts—some designed for safety and some mechanical; automobiles have changed over time; automobiles influence the way we live; automobiles are manufactured from raw materials such as steel, sold at businesses called car dealerships, bought by families, and repaired at service stations; and families have to balance their needs with their wants when they purchase an automobile. Next, she consulted the standards set forth by the National Council for the Social Studies (1994) because the theme seemed better suited to learning outcomes related to social studies than to science. She used the standards along with her major ideas to formulate the major learning outcomes for the theme (see Learning Outcomes in Figure 9.3). She wrote these outcomes on her Theme Planning Web.

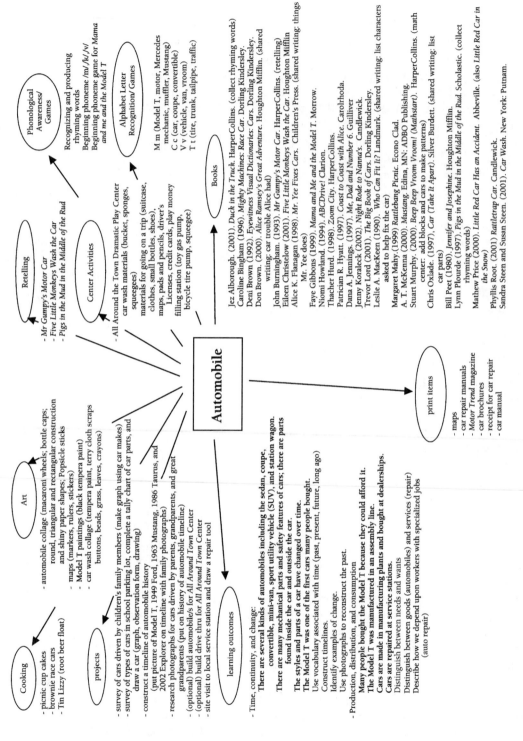

FIGURE 9.3. Automobile Theme Planning Web.

140

Finally, she made decisions about the phonological awareness and alphabet recognition skills that she would highlight during the theme. She selected four alphabet letters (*m, c, v*, and *t*) for special focus because these letters appeared in several words important to the theme. (Her earlier theme on Home and School had focused on the letters *h, s*, and *f*). Ms. Simpson continued to focus on rhyming words that she had initiated in the Home and School theme. Several of the books she selected for the unit included many examples of rhyming words that would be useful in reinforcing this skill. However, she also wanted to initiate children's awareness of beginning phonemes, so she decided to focus on the phonemes /m/, /k /, and /v/ because she knew these phonemes were in many vocabulary words in the theme. She located several objects with those beginning phonemes and gathered at least five pictures of objects that began with each phoneme to use in games.

Planning Theme Activities

Now Ms. Simpson was ready to add other activities to her Theme Planning Web. First, she thought about the activities she might use to address the learning outcomes. She decided she would need to gather old photographs from her family (ones in which the family car was also included), pictures from the Internet on the history of Ford (Model T, 1949 Coupe, Mustang, and Taurus), and several copies of brochures from several car dealers. She knew her children could not go on long field trips, so she decided to visit the nearby Mercedes manufacturing plant and take photographs of the assembly line. She gathered old photographs of automobiles from the Internet and asked her father for back issues of *Motor Trend* magazine. Finally, she gathered miniature cars for the Block center. She would use these artifacts, photographs, and toys to initiate conversations with her children about their knowledge of automobiles and to develop new concepts about the makes, models, and parts of automobiles. These resources would also provide a visual introduction to the manufacturing of automobiles and how they have changed over time.

Then she brainstormed cooking and art activities and thought about projects that children could do to collect data for graphs, charts, and other displays. She planned a special dramatic play theme center (All around Town) in which children could pretend to wash cars, go on car trips, order fast-food at a drive through, and buy gas or get a car fixed at the gas station. She thought about the props she would need to gather for the All around Town center. She selected three books that would be appropriate for retelling and considered props to use in this activity.

INVOLVING PARENTS AND THE COMMUNITY

All preschools in Ms. Simpson's building host parent meetings once a month. Ms. Simpson decided to write a letter to parents about the Automobile theme prior to the upcoming meeting. She wanted parents to visit the preschool with their cars. She stressed that having a variety of cars for children to explore would be especially fun. She also invited parents to bring in car repair tools and old car parts. Because two of her children spoke Spanish at home, Ms. Simpson asked the elementary home-school liaison to write the letter in Spanish for those parents. At the parent meeting she described the theme and talked about ways parents could support it at home. She stressed the importance of using lots of vocabulary words related to cars. The parents brainstormed a list of over 50 words related to automobiles. Ms. Simpson shared with parents the importance of using these words in their everyday conversations with children. One parent asked how to help her daughter learn to write her name better. Ms. Simpson showed the parents the sign-in procedure and spent a few minutes talking about having paper and markers available for children to use. She assured parents that their children would learn to write their names and they did not have to worry about having perfect signatures at this age. She discussed how to talk with children about alphabet letters when they were trying to write their names and discouraged parents from holding children's hands as they wrote or making children trace over letters. As they left the meeting several parents made commitments to bring their cars to school.

Ms. Simpson also visited a service station that was located near the school to find out whether the children could come to observe a car being repaired. She convinced the mechanic (who had worked on her previous car) that her children would like to see him roll under a car, change the oil, and fix a flat tire. She discussed safety issues and set the day and time for the visit.

TEACHING THE AUTOMOBILE THEME

Ms. Simpson was ready to make weekly plans for teaching the Automobile theme. Over the years she had found it more convenient to make weekly rather than daily plans. Because the children's interest in projects, books, songs, and activities was often unpredictable, weekly plans allowed her to be more flexible in extending activities when children's interest was high and to move ahead to new activities when children were uninterested. In her weekly plan, Ms Simpson listed books for read-alouds, other print items that could be read for information or introduced for center activities, resources to use in theme activities, books for retelling or drama, art and cooking activities, music, and the text used for shared reading. She identified ideas for shared writing and the Write On procedure and jotted down additions to center activities she would need to make.

Introducing the Theme

Ms. Simpson began her theme by introducing the children to the miniature cars she brought for the Block center. The children talked about their toy cars at home, their families' cars, and favorite cars. She discussed the word *automobile*, wrote it on a strip of poster paper, and placed it in the Writing center. She also showed children the copies of *Motor Trend* magazine she had found and placed some of these in the Writing center, some in the Art center, and some in the Home Living center. She encouraged children to write about or draw automobiles during center time that day.

Finally, Ms. Simpson read *Beep Beep, Vroom Vroom!* (Murphy, 2000) aloud. In this story a little sister tries three times to arrange her big brother's miniature cars in the same pattern that her brother uses. As she read, Ms. Simpson commented on the story, and many children talked about their miniature cars, brother–sister relationships, and hating to be "too little" to play with good toys. After reading, Ms. Simpson turned to the page in the book with the cars lined up in a pattern and asked the children to describe the pattern. She gave each child a plastic sandwich bag containing small squares of construction paper for making the pattern of red, blue, yellow, red, blue, yellow. For shared writing, Ms. Simpson wrote the colors of the pattern in a list, using colored magic markers. She named each letter as she wrote it. Ms. Simpson reread the chart several times, inviting the children to join her. Then the children were invited up to the chart to identify an alphabet letter they would like to Write On the shared writing chart. Ms. Simpson hung the chart in the Writing center and reminded the children that they could write more letters or words on the chart during center time. She encouraged children to bring their miniature cars to school to use in the Block center. As she collected the bags of construction paper and placed them in the Math center, she suggested visiting this center to make more patterns. She reminded children they could make patterns with the paper, blocks, or any other manipulatives in that center. As the children selected their centers, Ms. Simpson realized that the activities she had planned for the remainder of the week would likely extend into the next week because of the children's enthusiasm for the topic.

Theme Activities

Ms. Simpson planned to read portions of the new car brochures the next day. This would make a good transition between toy cars and real automobiles. It would introduce children to the concept of the difference between make and model of cars and start a discussion about the parts of cars. Later in the week she would show a picture of herself and her current car and three pictures she had found of cars her mother, father, and grandfather had previously owned. One of these photographs showed her grandfather's 1949 Ford. This would begin the study of automobile history and serve as a springboard into one of the projects: finding family photographs that included cars!

As the theme unfolded, Ms. Simpson's children acquired much information about automobiles and their history. They learned the difference between the make of a car and model. In one shared writing experience, children listed the three most popular makes of cars and wrote on alphabet letters of interest. Children also collected information about the parts of cars. Figure 9.4 presents Jamaica's tally of car parts she found when she observed and drew a picture of Ms. Simpson's car in the parking lot (adapted from Helm & Katz, 2001). They learned vocabulary words such as *vehicle, automobile, Tin Lizzy, Model T, sedan, coupe, convertible, SUV, bumper, windshield, wipers, glove box, hood, tailpipe, muffler, chrome, steering wheel, dashboard, gearshift, upholstery, tachometer, odometer, oil gauge, gasoline, highway, overpass, tunnel, intersection, pedestrian, traffic, passenger, license tag, Ford, Chevrolet, Toyota, BMW, Mercedes, Mustang, Corvette, Viper, motor, manufacturer, assembly line, dealership, service station, repair, wrench, mechanic, motorcar,*

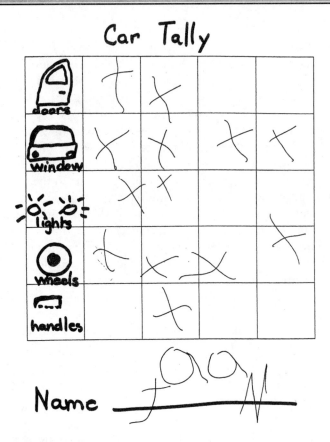

FIGURE 9.4. Jamica's tally of car parts.

running boards, starter, and *pedal.* They collected family photographs showing cars from the past and used them along with pictures they found on the Internet to construct a 100-year timeline from 1902 to 2002. Several children built three automobiles for the All around Town dramatic play center out of cardboard boxes and other household items. They learned new songs and enjoyed making and eating cupcakes and deviled eggs.

The children also engaged in many reading and writing activities as part of the theme. Ms. Simpson guided the children as they retold *Mr. Gumpy's Motor Car* (Burningham, 1993) using a flannelboard and *Pigs in the Mud in the Middle of the Rud* (Plourde, 1997) using laminated construction paper animals and characters attached with Velcro to a storystick (yardstick to which squares of self-stick Velcro have been attached). All of the children visited the Book center and retold these stories numerous times. They constructed street signs for roadways that they built in the Block center. They listened to and discussed an alphabet book about cars, stories that took place in cars, fictionalized accounts of real automobile adventures, and informational books about cars. As part of these book experiences, children talked about automobiles from the past and the stereotype of girls not being allowed to drive cars. They recalled rhyming words they heard in *Duck in the Truck* (Alborough, 2001) and then played rhyming word games with picture cards.

During the theme, Ms. Simpson introduced three phonemes (/m/, /v/, and /k/) by modeling and talking about how to articulate each phoneme. Children practiced articulating a phoneme and deciding whether a spoken word had that phoneme. They matched pictures that had the target phoneme and sorted pictures according to beginning phonemes. They played a game based on *Mama and Me and the Model T* (Gibbons, 1999) in which children drove a Model T around the game board by matching pictures with the same beginning phoneme. Some children cut pictures of objects and made phoneme charts as part of a center activity. Ms. Simpson modeled writing the alphabet letters *Mm, Vv, Cc, and Tt* on Alphabet Write Ons, and all the children wrote dozens of alphabet letters on the Write Ons during center activities. They cut words from the newspaper and circled the letters *m, v, c,* or *t* (Figure 9.5 presents a portion of the Alphabet Write On for *m* and the letter cutting from the newspaper). The children wrote checks for food (see Figure 9.6), ordered food at a pretend drive through (a puppet stage converted to a "Burger barn") and wrote speeding tickets. They read maps as they played in the All

FIGURE 9.5. Alphabet Write On for *m* and letter cutting.

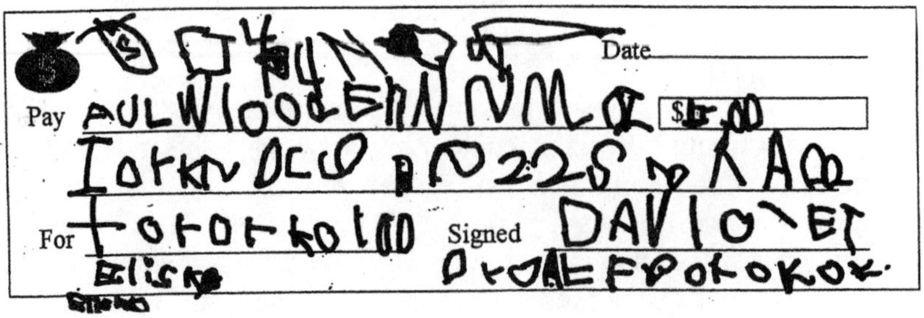

FIGURE 9.6. Check for a drive through order.

around Town dramatic play center and made maps in the Art center. They sang songs and fingerpoint-read favorite parts of stories, including the repetitive phrase from *Pigs in the Mud in the Middle of the Rud* (Plourde, 1997).

CHAPTER SUMMARY

Ms. Simpson reflected on the success of the Automobile theme as it began to draw to a close. Her 4-year-olds seemed to thoroughly enjoy learning more about cars, the history of automobiles, and the many makes and models of cars. Near the end of the theme the reading specialist visited the classroom and commented on how many children chose to read and write during center time. She especially noted how skillfully Ms. Simpson's aide was able to reread books to small groups of children when she visited the Book center, and how well she was able to model more sophisticated language as she joined children in play in the All around Town dramatic play center. Already Ms. Simpson and the reading specialist noticed that many children had made progress in being able to write their names and recognize alphabet letters. They noted that several children pretended to read books to themselves in the Book center, often choosing books with rhyming words. Most children pretended to write as they played in the dramatic play center or in the Writing center. They were talking more during book reading and were beginning to notice more print in their homes. The children's parents commented on how much the children talked about cars as they traveled. Ms. Simpson was sure that these children were well on their way to being prepared to enter kindergarten and be successful readers and writers.

CHAPTER 10

Kindergarten in Action

This chapter describes the actual classroom learning events that occurred during several days in Mrs. Karla Poremba's kindergarten. The information described in this chapter was gathered by Donald J. Richgels when he spent 164 of 1 year's 175 school days in Mrs. Poremba's class. He wrote field notes, collected writing samples, conversed with students, occasionally assisted with instruction, and made 43 hours of videotape recordings and nearly continuous audiotape recordings (for a detailed account of that year, see Richgels, 2003). The kindergarten context described in this chapter includes planned themes and units and greater attention than in preschool to developing alphabet knowledge, phonemic awareness, and understandings of sound–letter correspondences.

ROUTINES

Conversation, instruction, and learning in Mrs. Poremba's classroom frequently occurred in the context of such routines as signing-in, opening of the day, Words for Today, What Can You Show Us? activities, interactive read-aloud, shared writing, Writing center writing, and journal writing. A classroom routine can best be thought of as long-term scaffolding. Over several months, sometimes the whole course of the school year, the predictable, repeated actions, props, people, and language of the routine provide a structure within which learning occurs (Richgels, 1995).

First, the teacher and students learn together how the routine will work, that is, what roles, actions, and language the actors in the routine will enact. In the early weeks and months of the lifetime of the routine, the teacher does most of its work, modeling what to say and do and how to use the props. As the routine is repeated over many months, the teacher gradually withdraws and students take over more and more of the work, especially as they show greater competence, so that in the end they have mastered the actions and language that they at first depended on the teacher to do. In the end, the students can use the language independently of the routine; their acting appropriately, that is, in ways that demonstrate understanding, no longer depends on the repetition and scaffolding of the routine.

Words for Today routine is an example of such a routine (Richgels, 2003). At the beginning of the year, Mrs. Poremba posted an 8½-by-11-inch sheet of paper on which to write weather words in addition to those permanently displayed (*sunny, cloudy, windy, rainy,* and *snowy*) on the weather report chart that was used for daily opening-of-the-day activities. The sheet of paper bore the heading More Weather Words. A recorder asked students for suggestions of more weather words and wrote them on the paper, calling attention to sounds in words and sound–letter correspondences and modeling other spelling strategies. At the beginning of the year, Mrs. Poremba was the recorder.

The language of the routine included Mrs. Poremba's questions when asking for new words (e.g., "Do you have a weather word for us?"), her modeling talk and questioning as she wrote the new word (e.g., "*Muddy!* Oh my gosh, that's a great weather word. I'm going to write that word right here on our 'More Weather Words.' *Muddy.* What does it start with?"), and the new weather words themselves (e.g., *muddy*) (Richgels, 2003). The props were the More Weather Words sheet of paper posted on the opening-of-the-day activities bulletin board and the marker stored above the bulletin board. The roles were recorder and word suppliers. The actions were announcing the beginning of the activity, retrieving the marker, soliciting words, writing words, and rereading the completed list of words.

At the beginning of the year, the students functioned comfortably within the routine by supplying many of the same words day after day and allowing Mrs. Poremba to do the writing and reading work. She was patient with this, accepting, for example, the word *muddy* sometimes even when the weather was not wet. Gradually, the students' contributions became more sophisticated. Eventually, they suggested so many non-weather words that Mrs. Poremba changed the heading on the sheet of paper to "Words for Today." Finally, the students took over the role of recorder, so that one of the two helpers of the day led the class through the routine and Mrs. Poremba sat on the side to provide help only when requested (and even then, she often turned the request back on the students).

One day in May, not all the suggestions for Words for Today were even single words. With the whole class's help and using a variety of strategies including copying, sounding out, using sight words knowledge, and looking words up in a picture dictionary, Ian wrote three classmates' suggestions, the first a word, the second a phrase, and the third a complete sentence: *breeze* (BeZA, with a backwards Z), *Tri-City Soccer* (tRy SIty SACR), and *The world is our home* (the WORld Is OUR HOMe) (Richgels, 2003).

THEMATIC UNITS

Routines were not the only source of student-centered structure in Mrs. Poremba's class. Units of study were another source. A thematic unit is a coordinated series of activities around a theme or topic over an extended period of time, usually from 3 to 5 weeks. It allows for integrated teaching and learning of all the traditional subject areas: reading, writing, speaking, and listening from language arts, social studies, science, math, music, art, and even physical education. Unit topics can come from a school district's prescribed curriculum, usually in social studies and science, and from students' own interests. Mrs. Poremba's environmental awareness unit, for example, was a part of her school district's social studies curriculum.

A BEAR UNIT

At the beginning of the year, Mrs. Poremba designed and implemented a unit around a topic she knew would be fun and interesting for 5-year-olds: bears. Among the activities and subtopics in this bear unit were reading and distinguishing between factual and fictional books about bears, writing (by dictation) about bear art projects, researching for and shared writing of a Bear Facts poster, doing What Can You Show Us? activities with big books about bears and with a Brown Bear Bread recipe, and interactive reading of the big books and the recipe, making Brown Bear Bread from the recipe and eating it at snack time, sign-in writing and Writing center writing about bears, reading and comparing of several versions of the Three Bears story, reading of other bear storybooks, and having a Teddy Bear picnic.

Reading *Ten Little Bears*

In preparation for the bear unit, Mrs. Poremba collected fictional and nonfictional books about bears. On the first day of the bear unit, Mrs. Poremba and her students did an interactive reading of a big book edition of *Ten Little Bears* (Ruwe, 1989). In this story 10 bears lose one of their group and then another as each goes on a ride—in a sailboat, in a tractor, in a moving van, and so on—until only one bear is left. This is a pattern book. The text changes from page to page only by the reduced number of bears and the naming of a different vehicle.

Mrs. Poremba directs the children's attention to the book on the easel and gets them to make predictions. She says, "I want you to look at this book, and I want you to turn and talk to a friend about what you think this story could be about."

Many children whisper, "Bears." The cover shows 10 bears holding hands. This leads to a discussion of the game Crack the Whip.

Mrs. Poremba summarizes, "So about bears holding hands, playing—"

"—Crack the Whip!" finish many kindergartners together.

After further discussion about how to play Crack the Whip, Mrs. Poremba again gets the children to focus on the book, this time on important print: "Now if I wanted to find out the name of this story, where would I have to look?"

"The title page!" replies Zack, and his answer is taken up by several other kindergartners. But Mrs. Poremba wants them to look at the print that is already visible, without opening the book. "The title page is one good idea. Where else could I look?"

"The words!" answer several kindergartners together.

"I could look at the words right up here." And Mrs. Poremba points to the title on the cover of the book. "Let me read them to you. . . . The name of our story is *Ten—Little—*"

"—*Bears*," finish several kindergartners together.

"*Bears*," Mrs. Poremba repeats. "Good reading, kindergartners." She reads the author's and the illustrator's names and notes that two people worked together to make this book. She opens the book to the title page and reads the title and author and illustrator information again.

On the first page of the story, Eric D. thinks he sees a dog. Others think it is one of the 10 bears. Mrs. Poremba again directs the children's attention to the print and lets them know that the text is the final authority. "How about if I read the words?" she asks. "We'll see if those words help us to know." She reads, " 'Ten little bears were sitting at home. They wanted something to do.' " She rereads the page, and comments, "Look at them! They look bored to tears." But, because today is the 10th day of school, the kindergartners are especially interested in the number *10*. At Freddy's suggestion they count the bears, and at Nathan's suggestion, Mrs. Poremba writes a *10* on an erasable marker board. Then Mrs. Poremba initiates talk about an important concept, one that will drive the action of the story. "Well, let's read about these 10 bears. Look at them! How do you think they're feeling right now?"

"Bored," answers a kindergartner, using Mrs. Poremba's word from a minute ago. Other kindergartners contribute: "Sad." "Mad." "Bad."

Mrs. Poremba celebrates the kindergartners' words. "There's a good word." And she invites the children to show with their faces how the bears feel.

This inspires one kindergartner's suggestion of a new word: "Angry!"

Then Mrs. Poremba and the class read the rest of the book, each page ending with "Then _____ little bears were left at home." They count the bears on each page, and soon individuals are reading by using the pattern, each page's illustration of a new vehicle and the descending numbers. By the end of the story all the kindergartners are joining in the reading. They notice the page number on page 10, and when five bears are left, one kindergartner remarks that she is 5 years old. "There's that word *home* again," Mrs. Poremba says, pointing to the word that ends each page.

Reading *The Three Bears*

The next day, Mrs. Poremba reads *The Three Bears*, a version of Goldilocks and the Three Bears by Paul Galdone (1972). The text is more complex and less patterned than the text of *Ten Little Bears* (Ruwe, 1989), and although it too is a big book, its print is smaller. Therefore Mrs. Poremba plans a less interactive reading; she will tell the class, "I probably won't stop to talk to you during the story." But first she involves them in making connections to yesterday's reading and to the unit topic, and again, like yesterday, she elicits predictions and directs students' attention to print. "Yesterday we read a story called *Ten Little*—"

"—*Bears*," finish a few kindergartners. . . .

"Since we read a story called *Ten Little Bears*, and because I know kindergartners are always interested in bears, I found another story to read to you. . . . I want you to look at the book to get your ideas . . . turn and tell a friend."

The kindergartners whisper to one another.

"Some of you know something about the story already. Zachary, what do you know about the story?"

"Goldilocks," answers Zack, and others pick this up.

When Mrs. Poremba asks for other ideas, Jeff combines yesterday's book title with today's: "There's three little bears."

Mrs. Poremba confirms this by referring to the picture and then asks, "Where could I look to find the name of this story?"

"Title!" suggests Zack.

Mrs. Poremba reads the title from the cover: "The title for this book is right here. It says, '*The Three Bears* by Paul Galdone.' " She turns to the title page and points out that Paul Galdone wrote the words *and* drew the pictures. She asks how many people worked on this book.

"One!" shouts Meagan.

"That's kind of different [from yesterday's book]," Mrs. Poremba comments. Even though she reads the story with less interaction by the students, she directs the kindergartners to listen carefully and to think while she reads. She points with a ruler to the words as she reads them, inviting the kindergartners' attention to the print. The children laugh in appreciation of Mrs. Porebma's different voices for the three bears, and they are free to comment. For example, Freddy says, while Mrs. Poremba is still reading about Goldilocks' sitting down on the little chair, "Then it broke." Ian comments, "She's not a smart girl at all." They finish Mrs. Poremba's "just—" with their "—right" and add a chorus of "Oh-oh!" when Goldilocks falls asleep. They supply "—voice" when Mrs. Poremba does stop after "great big—" and "middle sized—" and "little wee—."

Mrs. Poremba does stop when Goldilocks wakes up to see three bears looking at her. "Turn and tell a friend what you think will happen next," she directs.

Most kindergartners whisper, "She's gonna run away," and when Mrs. Poremba shows the next page, they shout to one another, "I'm right!"

After the reading Jason says, "Teacher, this is funny." While the other kindergartners begin their free-choice activities, he demonstrates how closely he had been paying attention to the illustrations. He finds a page early in the story on which the three bears are shown reading books. With a very serious expression on his face and making his arms pass over one another, he explains to Mrs. Poremba that the littlest bear has the biggest book and the biggest bear the littlest book, that the books go from left to right for biggest to littlest while the bears go from right to left for biggest to littlest.

Another Version of *The Three Bears*

The next day, the school's principal, Mrs. L., comes to Mrs. Poremba's room and reads Jan Brett's (1987) version of the Goldilocks and the Three Bears story. Mrs. L. explains that she will be reading the same story the children had heard the day before, but in a different telling, and she calls attention to Jan Brett's distinctive illustration style, which includes decorative frames around each page. Mrs. L. reads, and as they did the day before, the kindergartners finish some predictable phrases and interject comments about remarkable events. As Mrs. L. reads Jan Brett's words about "a great huge bear," a kindergartner remarks, "I thought it was 'great big bear.' "

"That was another version," explains Mrs. L. "Just like some people might say 'Hi,' and some other people might say 'Hello.' "

When Mrs. L. has finished reading and returned to her office, Mrs. Poremba asks the kindergartners what they like about Jan Brett's version.

"The pictures," answers one kindergartner.

"And the flowers," answers another.

"When the girl jumped out of the window," answers Zack.

"She landed on the house," says a kindergartner.

"She landed on the house roof?" asks Mrs. Poremba. "Is that what it says?"

"No," answers a kindergartner. This leads to comparing the two books.

Comparing Two Versions of *The Three Bears*

"You know, I'm thinking about Jan Brett and how, at the end of the story, Goldilocks jumped out of the window." The kindergartners stop checking, for now, whether both versions have Goldilocks landing on a first floor roof, but we will see that they take that up later. They do confirm that both versions have Goldilocks jumping out of a window, and Mrs. Poremba teaches about both story structure and book handling skills in terms of beginnings, middles, and ends.

Mrs. Poremba says, "Let's see if I can find–where would I find that part of the book? Would I find it—"

"In the back," answers a kindergartner.

"—in the very beginning?"

"No."

"No? It didn't happen in the very beginning?"

Several kindergartners express the same idea: "No." "Back." "At the end."

"Toward the back of the book, at the end of the story?" asks Mrs. Poremba. "At the very back?"

"No."

"Am I close to it? Am I close if I turn it?" Thus she locates Paul Galdone's having Goldilocks jumping out of a window.

Mrs. Poremba pursues this comparison of the two books and makes even more explicit the role of the print in a book. She returns the class to an issue that had risen during Mrs. L.'s reading of Jan Brett's version, how she referred to the papa bear as "the great huge bear." "Do you remember what Paul Galdone called—"

" 'The great big bear,' " interjects Ian.

"He did? Is there a way we can find out what he called the big bear?"

"Read it," suggests a kindergartner.

"Read it? Where?" asks Mrs. Poremba. Then she displays pages, and asks, "Would I find those words here? Does it say anything about the great big bear here?"

"No."

"OK. Let me keep looking." When showing the first page of the story elicits an affirmative guess from some kindergartners, Mrs. Poremba responds, "Well, let me look at those words on this page to see if we can find what Paul Galdone calls the largest bear." She reads the page, and nowhere are the words "the great big bear."

When she shows the page whose illustration is of the biggest bear, more children think that page may yield better results. "Yeah!"

"Where?"

"Right there," say several kindergartners.

Mrs. Poremba seeks clarification: "The words by the large bear might tell what Paul Galdone called him?"

"Yeah."

"Well, let me check those words out to see if that gives us the information we need." Mrs. Poremba reads, " 'And the other was a great big bear.' Does that tell us?"

"Yeah!" shout several kindergartners together.

"They did! We found them!" says Mrs. Poremba.

The kindergartners now initiate many other comparisons, including whether or not the bears are clothed, which Goldilocks is prettier, whether or not their bowls are decorated, and—reviving an earlier issue—where Goldilocks landed when she jumped out of the window. Eric D. says about Paul Galdone's version, "And there's no roof she jumped on in this story."

"Ah! In Paul Galdone's story she didn't jump on the roof," Mrs. Poremba confirms, and then she recalls the earlier noticing of that. "We looked at that—"

"She jumped right on the ground," says Eric.

"She jumped right on the ground."

Freddy quibbles, "And the other one too, she jumped on the ground."

Eric will not be deflected that easily. "No," he says. "She jumped on the roof first, and then she jumped on the ground."

Mrs. Poremba raises the question of what the bears had in their bowls. As with the "great big bear" search, this requires locating in Paul Galdone's book a likely page based on the illustration ("the porridge page," as Ian calls it) *and* reading the text. Mrs. Poremba says, "Here it says—" And she reads, " 'They each had a bowl for their—' "

" '—porridge,' " the kindergartners finish together.

" '—porridge,' " Mrs. Poremba repeats. "Yes, this is the page I can find out what was in the bowl. It's porridge."

Eric D. confirms the similarity of the two versions: "In the other book, there's porridge too."

A Third Version of *The Three Bears*

On the next day, the 4th day of the bear unit, Mrs. Poremba reads still another version of the Three Bears story. This one allows even more comparisons, for it is Marilyn Tolhurst's *Somebody and the Three Blairs* (1991), an amusing story of the Blair family—father, mother, and baby humans—who go out for a walk while their breakfast cools and are visited by Somebody. Somebody is a small bear who wreaks havoc in their house before falling asleep and being discovered by the Blairs when they return home. The kindergartners appreciate what these books have in common, and they show they know what to expect from Mrs. Poremba's book reading routine.

After Mrs. Poremba points to and reads the title on the book cover, she also reads about the author and illustrator: "The person who wrote this book is 'Marilyn Tolhurst,' and the illustrations are by 'Simone Able.' "

Kindergartners immediately shout two familiar next steps in this routine: "Two people!" and "Title page!"

"Two people worked together," confirms Mrs. Poremba. "That's right, two people." They talk about the illustrations on the book's cover. Then Mrs. Poremba says, "Jason is very interested in seeing the title page, and I wanted to show it to him. Jason, on the title page, it always tells us the name of the story again." She points to and reads the title and author's name again.

After reading this third version of the Three Bears story, Mrs. Poremba sets all three out on the carpet and has the children indicate their favorites by sitting in rows before their choices. They make a human bar graph ("It's a graph made with real things, because you're going to be the graph!"). Mrs. Poremba summons the children one at a time by holding up cards bearing their names. Each kindergartner's face lights up with recognition of his or her name, and the class giggles with delight as they watch the lines form. When the graph is complete, the children already know which book is the favorite of the greatest number of their classmates; the row for *Somebody and the Three Blairs* is noticeably longer than the others. Still, they confirm that finding by counting the number of children in each row and comparing numbers.

Fact versus Fiction

On the next day, the 5th day of the bear unit, Mrs. Poremba's kindergartners are ready for a new kind of comparison, one between fictional and nonfictional books about bears. She begins by displaying Paul Galdone's *The Three Bears* and directing, "I want you to think about the things that the bears in this story do." The kindergartners recall—and Mrs. Poremba confirms by showing pictures—that the three bears read books, sleep in beds, eat porridge from bowls, sit in chairs, live in a house. Then Mrs. Poremba suggests, "I want you to think about pretend bears and what real bears would do."

"Sleep in caves," says a kindergartner.

"Real bears would sleep in caves, not in houses," Mrs. Poremba confirms.

"And real bears would eat fish," says Eric D.

"Real bears might eat fish instead of porridge."

"And real bears won't eat, real bears, um, don't use bowls," continues Eric.

"Real bears don't use bowls," Mrs. Poremba repeats.

"And they don't use beds and books," another kindergartner offers.

Erin adds, "Pretend bears are not like real bears."

Freddy's contribution is "Real bears scratch people," to which a classmate adds, "They can eat you."

Eric C. elaborates, "If you stay still and close your eyes and pretend you're dead, they won't get you."

This reminds Jason of something he has learned from the movies: "Teacher! Teacher! Teacher!" he calls out. "You know what? Tyrannosaurus Rex, if they try to get you, if you stay still, they can't see you."

Additional talk includes the observation that bears in cartoons are pretend bears, like those in the fictional books the class has been reading. Then Mrs. Poremba says, "I think you are beginning to understand very well the difference between storybook pretend bears and real bears. Are there books that can be written about real bears—"

"Yeah," answer several kindergartners together.

"—showing you what real bears do?"

"Yeah."

Mrs. Poremba describes going to the school library where the librarian looked in the card catalog for books about bears. "She pulled out one of the drawers, and she started filing through the cards, and she came to a part of the drawer that had a big letter *B* on it—"

"Bear!" shouts Kaitlynn, and others echo this.

"Exactly. She was looking for things about bears. . . . And she and I went looking and hunting on the shelves, and we found all of these books"—Mrs. Poremba explains that actually some of the books she is displaying are her own, from her house—"about real bears. The bears in this page don't sit in chairs; they don't eat porridge from a bowl; they don't sleep in beds; they don't live in houses; they don't wear clothes. These are the real kind that are really out in the forest." The kindergartners have scooted closer and closer to Mrs. Poremba's chair. She pauses to get a stack of name cards, one for each kindergartner, from the attendance board. "Let me tell you what we're going to do. Today we're going to be researchers."

Kindergarten Research

"What is that?" asks Tara G.

"Researchers are very important people who are trying to learn important things. You are going to be a researcher today. *You're* going to be a very important person who is trying to learn important things. Today we're going to try to find out and learn as much as we can about real bears, not the kind in the Three Bears storybooks, but real bears in books that show us what real bears look like and what real bears do. Here's what we're going to do. You're going to work with another kindergarten research partner."

Mrs. Poremba explains that partners can choose a book and go together to any part of the room to study it. "As you're looking, you can be talking to each other. You can say, 'Hey look at what this real bear is doing! Look at what this real bear looks like. Huh! Look at the color of his fur!" Thus Mrs. Poremba describes the reference function of nonfictional books.

Next she talks about the reporting and recording functions of written language. She explains that when partners "find something that's very important about real bears, something so important that you want it written down so we can remember it" they can bring their book to one of today's adult helpers who "will write your idea down just the way you tell her on a card."

When cards are filled out, kindergartners are to bring them to Mrs. Poremba, who will put them on a "Bear Facts" chart displayed on the easel. "The things that you're telling us about are called facts. We're going to write bear facts today. Facts are real things about real bears, things that are true. So when you see the words "Bear Facts," you know that the things that are going to come up here on your cards are real, true things about bears. That's what a fact is; it's a truth."

Mrs. Poremba calls on me so that I can emphasize the distinction between "two different kinds of books": storybooks like *The Three Bears* ("What kind of bears were in those storybooks?" I ask, and the kindergartners answer, "fake" and "pretend") and "fact books," those that are set out now near where I am sitting for the kindergartners' research. Mrs. Poremba encourages kindergartners to listen to their classmates' ideas, and "if you hear a lot of people saying the same thing, . . . you might say, 'Hmm, we already have that fact . . . let's find something new to write on a card.' " Mrs. Poremba shuffles the name cards and draws two at a time to assign partners and demonstrates studying a book—not just fanning the pages, but looking at the cover and each page deliberately. She models a researcher's talk: " 'Ah, look what's on that cover. Look at all those polar bears. My goodness, there must be someone back there [inside the book] who knows a lot about polar bears. Hmmm, I think I'll go through each of the pages— Oh, and look what's on the inside cover. Wow!' . . . And you would carefully turn the pages and stop when you see something really interesting that you can tell about a polar bear and stop and talk about it with your partner. And if it's an important fact that you want written down, find a grown-up and we will help you with that."

As pairs bring their cards with dictated facts to Mrs. Poremba, she has them sort the cards for display in two columns on the Bear Facts chart, one headed "What bears look like" and one, "What bears do" (portions of these charts appear in Figure 10.1). In the end, the "What bears do" column has so many fact cards that, taped together, they hang below the bottom of the chart, over the easel's ledge, almost to the floor. Many kindergarten-researcher pairs have dictated more than one bear fact.

Sharing Research Findings

Later in the day, the kindergartners meet Mrs. Poremba by the easel. She begins, "Something researchers do after they've finished writing their important facts down is they go back and they reread them and they think about what the important facts are. And that's what we're going to do now."

Mrs. Poremba begins, "So people got these ideas from doing their reading." Thus she validates looking at pictures as a kind of reading for kindergartners. "Let's find out what the ideas are. Under here about "What bears look like," Jason and Nathan say, 'Bears have big teeth, and they have a lot of meat.' That's important." She makes an explicit statement like this about the value of the kindergartners' work after reading every card. After Erin and Freddy "Panda bears look like polar bears and black panther

What bears look like:

Jason and Nathan: Bears have big teeth, and they have a lot of meat.

Ian and Elise: Some bears are brown, and they have white claws.

Erin and Freddy: Panda bears look like polar bears and black panther bears put together.

Eric C. and Zack: Black bears have long claws. They are all black, but with white fur by their black noses.

Sarah and Tara G.: Bears are really furry.

Eric D. and Meagan: Bears have a skeleton and muscles.

Freddy and Erin: Some bears have striped arms and white faces. Bear claws are very sharp and they can cut you.

What bears do:

Eric C. and Zack: Bears fight with their claws and they growl. Stand up and fight.

Kaitlynn and Alyssa: Polar bears jump in snow and water.

Sarah and Tara G.: Panda bears hold their baby and hide inside a tree hole.

Freddy and Erin: A bear is eating a fish, and another bear is catching a fish.

Ian and Elise: Polar bears hold things for each other with their front feet.

What bears do: (cont.)

Eric C. and Zack: A polar bear swims with his legs and does the bear paddle.

Eric D. and Meagan: Panda bears eat bamboo.

Jeff and Tara J. Bears like honey but should stay away from bees. Bears eat deer.

Tara G. and Sarah: Panda bears eat tree branches.

Erin and Freddy: Bears eat berries. Polar bears live under ice and snow to stay safe.

Alyssa and Kaitlynn: Polar bears live in the same place as reindeer.

Elizabeth and Steven: Bears sleep in winter.

Eric C. and Zack: Panda bears eat plants.

Sarah and Tara G.: Panda bears protect their babies from wolves with their teeth and claws.

Elizabeth and Steven: Mother bears snuggle with their babies.

Nathan and Jason: Polar bears can swim in cold, icy water.

Jeff and Tara J.: Sticks stab polar bears and it would hurt them. Fire would also hurt polar bears.

Elizabeth and Steven: Bears play together.

Kaitlynn and Alyssa: Polar bears and arctic foxes live in the same place because they are friends.

FIGURE 10.1. Fact sheet.

bears put together," she says, "What a neat way to describe a panda bear!" After Freddy and Erin's "Some bears have striped arms and white faces. Bear claws are very sharp and they can cut you," she says, "Wow!"

Eric C. immediately adds, "That is really important."

Mrs. Poremba responds, "That's very important. I agree, Eric."

Other kindergartners chime in: "I agree too." "Me too." "Me too."

Under "what bears do," Eric D. and Meagan's "Panda bears eat bamboo" prompts conversation. Tara G. asks, "What's bamboo?"

Jason volunteers, "That's what they eat—tree bamboo, like coconut tree."

Eric D. elaborates, "There's, there's no, there's no bamboo or no panda bears out here." Meagan sidles up to her research partner to share the credit for this additional fact. Eric continues, "They're, they're out in China."

After reading Tara G. and Sarah's "Panda bears eat tree branches," Mrs. Poremba facilitates a connection: "I wonder if the tree branches you saw them eating might have been bamboo. I wonder."

Zack nods, "Yeah!"

Tara G. agrees, "Yes!"

Before reading Elizabeth and Steven's third bear fact, Mrs. Poremba celebrates their collaboration and their productivity: "Boy, Elizabeth and Steven did a lot of work together." This fact, "Bears sleep in winter," prompts talk about vocabulary.

Several kindergartners comment: "I know that already." "I know that." "I know that."

Mrs. Poremba asks, "I wonder what word tells about—"

"Hibernating," Tara G. answers before Mrs. Poremba finishes her question, and several kindergartners echo her.

Other Uses for the Bears Facts Chart

The Bear Facts chart remains in Mrs. Poremba's room for some weeks after the bear unit is finished. Several kindergartners refer to it during their routine, beginning-of-the-day sign-in writing. During the next 2 weeks, Tara G., Jason, and Ian include the word *bear* in their sign-in writing and are able to identify their copying source as the Bear Facts chart. Over a month later, Tara J. copies all of Ian and Elise's "Some bears are brown, and they have white claws" (see Figure 10.2).

FIGURE 10.2. Tara J.'s sign-in sheet with bear facts.

Sharing Dictated Bear Stories: Fact versus Fiction

Mrs. Poremba's kindergartners had other experiences of writing by dictating during the bear unit. Mrs. Poremba sends "Home Link" notes to parents to involve them with their children's learning. During the first week of the bear unit, a Home Link note asked parents to help their children make cut-and-paste bears from a simple paper form attached to the note and then to talk with their children about their bears. A parent might ask the bear's name and what the bear likes to do. Then the child was to "make up a story about [the] bear" and the parent was to write the story "word for word" on a lined sheet headed "My Bear Story."

Today Mrs. Poremba shows Tara J.'s bear and reads her story: "There was a bear named Jenny. Her Papa Bear said, 'Do you want to go on a ride around the block on a bear bike?' " And then they ate dinner. And then after dinner, I asked if I could play with my bear friend. Her name was Courtney. And then after I played with my bear friend, I played with another friend. And her name was Ann. And we played on the swing set. The end." Mrs. Poremba then shows Eric D.'s bear and reads his story: "Once upon a time, George the Bear played outside in the woods. George likes to throw rocks in the river. He likes to catch fish for his family to eat for breakfast, lunch, and dinner. He likes to pick berries off the mulberry bush. He also likes to climb apple and orange trees. George jumps over the river, and he likes to climb down the mountains. George goes inside his cave and goes to bed. He is tired. Now it's morning, and George is getting up from his good night's sleep. George wants to catch some fish for breakfast, and he's ready to pick berries again for dessert."

Both of these stories are strings of events, related and ordered by what their authors experience in their own daily lives. But there is one striking difference between them. After reading Tara's story, Mrs. Poremba asks, "Would that be a story about a real bear or a pretend bear?"

"Pretend," answer several kindergartners together.

Eric decorated his George the Bear figure with a bow tie and surrounded him with some human trappings, such as three meals a day, but after hearing Eric's story, Freddy immediately shouted, "That's a real bear story."

Mrs. Poremba has to agree. "Yes, Freddy! Real bears do the things that George did. Real bears would catch fish and eat berries."

Ian argues, "Yeah, but they can't jump across the river."

Mrs. Poremba interprets George's jumping more liberally: "Did anybody see bears in the water crossing rivers in their book?"

Freddy says, "Me!" Other kindergartners echo his claim.

Jason clarifies, "Yeah, because they can walk in the water."

Sharing Dictated Bear Stories: Meaning–Form Links

Both Tara's and Eric's stories are long. They fill up the lined page Mrs. Poremba sent home with the Home Link note. But not all the children's stories are so long. On Monday of the second week of the bear unit, more children bring their cut-and-paste bears and dictated stories. Mrs. Poremba reads Sarah's: "Once upon a time, there was a bear named Natalie Church. And she went to jump in the hay. Then she came back. She found another friend to play on a swing set. Then they jumped off of the swing. The end."

"That's short," notes Zack

"Some stories can be short," confirms Mrs. Poremba, and she shows why this reading was short. "Let me show Sarah's words of her story."

"It got wroten with pen," Sarah tells.

When it is Eric C.'s turn, Mrs. Poremba takes advantage of the opportunity to demonstrate again the link between the amount of writing and the length of a reading. This is a simple idea that we take for granted, but it is more basic and just as important as the link between sounds and letters that so often preoccupies parents and teachers of beginning readers. "Eric's is a very long story," Mrs. Poremba says, "I just wanted to show you Eric C.'s story before I begin reading."

"Long!" exclaim several kindergartners.

"Now there's even more on the back," notes Mrs. Poremba.

"Whoah!"

The reaction to Alyssa's story demonstrates the difficulties for kindergartners of distinguishing between real and pretend. Alyssa writes in the first person and includes eating porridge and swinging on a swing set and riding bikes with her friend Jeannette. Immediately after the reading, Tara J. remarks, "That's a real story because she does really have a friend named Jeannette." Mrs. Poremba binds the kindergartners' bear stories into book, which becomes a popular Reading center choice during free-choice time.

PUTTING IT ALL TOGETHER:
AN ART PROJECT, WRITING BY DICTATION,
AND USING KINDERGARTEN RESEARCH FINDINGS

A second art project and writing-by-dictation activity occurs on Tuesday of the second week of the bear unit. This is completed in school, and Mrs. Poremba again demonstrates the reference function of nonfictional books.

Each kindergartner, on a large, dark-blue, construction paper background, glues a bear that he or she makes from freely cut pieces of brown, black, or white construction paper. Then he or she paints a forest or mountain or snowscape setting for the bear. Mrs. Poremba introduces the project: "Kindergartners, we have been talking and learning lots and lots about bears. Do you remember the day that we read and did all that bear research? You learned facts about bears. . . . Today, I'm going to give you an opportunity to use your own ideas to show things you've learned about bears." She shows the different colors of construction paper and asks about the colors bears can be. She says, "We have our books right here that show real bears doing real bear things. Here's our polar bear that we talked about. And some more polar bears."

"I had that book," Kaitlynn recalls.

"There are our brown bears," continues Mrs. Poremba. "And here's a panda."

"Oh, we had that book," Tara G. says.

Mrs. Poremba shows pictures from the book as she asks what colors of paper kindergartners will use to make a panda bear. "This book would be a great book to show you the colors to use for a panda bear." She models making a polar bear. "Oh, I can't remember how many legs a polar bear has."

"Four," several kindergartners suggest.

"Are you sure?"

"Yeah."

"Where could I look to be absolutely sure?"

"They have two on both sides," Jason explains.

"In a book," say a few kindergartners.

"I wonder if I could find out in this book how many legs a polar bear—Wow! It shows it right here. 1-2-3-4. . . . Okay, so I need four legs." Later, she asks, "Do polar bears have tails?"

"Yeah," answer some kindergartners.

"No," answer others.

"Some do," says one kindergartner.

"Um, can you check in that book, Steven, just check to see if polar bears have tails, for me, please?"

There is silence while Steven does his research.

"Yes, it does," he reports and he shows the evidence.

"Oh, there is a little thing there. OK. Well, that helps me. I didn't realize that. . . . Some bears might not have tails. You'll have to check the books to see about that."

When Mrs. Poremba makes her polar bear's ears, a quick question to Steven, who still has the book, settles the question of whether they should be black or white. "White," he reports. Again, when she models painting a setting for her polar bear, Mrs. Poremba refers to the books to determine that there are no trees because "I want to make this polar bear look like he's in a place where a polar bear really would live."

Mrs. Poremba had planned that on the next day the kindergartners would dictate captions for their pictures for her, her aide Mrs. Roloff, and me to write, but Jason finishes his picture so early and has so much to say about it that she begins the caption writing after the art activity.

More Fictional Books about Bears

This emphasis on factual books about bears does not mean the end of reading fictional bear books. Among those Mrs. Poremba reads to the class during the last 2 weeks of the bear unit are *Bears, Bears, Everywhere* (Connelly, 1988), *Brown Bear, Brown Bear, What Do You See?* (Martin, 1967), and *The Teddy Bears' Picnic* (Kennedy, 1991). The kindergartners often choose these books during partner reading time or when they visit the Reading center during free-choice time. When the kindergartners' third grade buddies visit for the first time at the end of September, Erin reads *Brown Bear, Brown Bear, What Do You See?* (Martin, 1967) and Paul Galdone's *The Three Bears* (1972) to her buddy.

The first reading of *Bears, Bears, Everywhere*, on Tuesday of the 2nd week of the bear unit, is from a big book version displayed on the easel. This book is an easy contrast with factual books, for it is very fanciful; its cover shows bears riding bicycles and doing other human activities. Mrs. Poremba asks the kindergartners to think about whether this book is about real or pretend bears and then to turn and tell a friend.

"Pretend," whisper several pairs of kindergartners to one another.

Ian is a dissenter. "Real bears wouldn't—" begins his partner.

"Yeah, they would—if they were in the circus," Ian asserts.

"Oh well, there's an idea. I hadn't thought of that," responds Mrs. Poremba. Ian's answer and Mrs. Poremba's response are part of a conversation about this book; they demonstrate that already in mid-September Mrs. Poremba's students know that a wide range of ideas is welcome, that she is not quizzing them for one expected correct answer.

Mrs. Poremba suggests, "Why don't we read, and then we'll get more ideas about whether this is about real bears or pretend bears, bear facts or pretend things about bears." Each page's text is a predictable rhyme that uses a pattern beginning always with *Bears, bears, everywhere* and ending always with *Bears* _____, the blank filled with a statement of a most un-bear-like activity, such as drawing squares, climbing stairs, chasing hares, riding mares, taking dares, eating pears, paying fares, selling wares. One page has bears in pairs, another has bears in lairs. These unusual words require much discussion. For example, bears in pairs causes some confusion. "I wonder what it means—'bears in pairs?' " Mrs. Poremba asks.

Jason knows. "Two together make a pair."

Mrs. Poremba responds, "Oh, there are two together. So this isn't the kind of pear that you buy at the store and eat, like a fruit. This is a different way to use the word *pair*. Jason said that a pair is when two things are together. Look at your shoes. Like a pair of socks."

The children try out this idea. They shout their examples, and Mrs. Poremba repeats many of them: "Pair of shoes!" "Pair of earrings!" "Pair of shoelaces!" "Pair of eyes!" "Ears!" "Pair of arms!" "A pair of legs!"

"Ooo, great job!" says Mrs. Poremba.

But the children are not finished. "A pair of toes!" suggests one kindergartner.

"A pair of toes!" laughs Mrs. Poremba.

Two more kindergartners have suggestions: "No—a pair of elbows." "A pair of fingers."

"So things that come in twos—" says Mrs. Poremba.

"A pair of earrings!" repeat several kindergartners.

"A pair of earrings. Thank you," replies Mrs. Poremba.

"A pair of bumps on your leg," suggests another kindergartner.

"Things that come in twos are pairs," concludes Mrs. Poremba. "Ready? OK," she adds, for *she* is ready to continue reading.

But a kindergartner suggests still one more example: "Two lips!"

"A pair of lips," confirms Mrs. Poremba. "Let's read the words right—"

"Two noses!"

Several pages later there are bears eating pears. "Look at what they're eating here," directs Mrs. Poremba.

Several kindergartners answer, "Pears!"

"Now that's a new way to use the word *pear*," observes Mrs. Poremba. "Here's the pear that's a fruit, and back here—" Mrs. Poremba stops to find the "Bears in pairs" page.

"—is a pair of people," finishes Jason.

"—a pair that means two together," finishes Mrs. Poremba.

Mrs. Poremba directs the reading of this page, " 'Bears—' "

Again, several kindergartners join this familiar part, " '—bears, everywhere. Bears—' "

"What are they doing?" asks Mrs. Poremba.

"Eating," answer some kindergartners.

" '—eat pears,' " finish Mrs. Poremba and some of the kindergartners.

"He's a friend," explains a kindergartner.

"And there they are munching on their pears," notes Mrs. Poremba.

Little Book Reading of a Familiar Story

Two days later, the kindergartners receive personal little book versions of *Bears, Bears, Everywhere*, and they read them to the teddy bears that they have brought to school, to partners, or in small groups. Jason, Meagan, and Erin are reading together. Their recall of whole-class readings of the big book version of this story, the book's picture clues, and the repetition and rhyming pattern help them to read fairly accurately. But the "Bears in lairs" page causes confusion. The picture shows bears among a group of lions in their lair. Erin thinks the lower-case *l* at the beginning of *lairs* is an upper-case *I*. Jason disagrees. He crosses the room to appeal to Mrs. Poremba, who is walking among the small groups of readers. "Teacher, what's this called?" he asks.

Mrs. Poremba gives him a meaning clue and a sound clue: "Oh, what is it called when a lion family is together? They're in a *llllll*—"

"Lair," answers Jason.

"Lair," repeats Jason. Then he names the letter, "*l*." He goes back to report to his group.

The kindergartners take home their little book versions of *Bears, Bears, Everywhere*. Weeks later, when they are given personal copies of another book, Freddy says that he still reads from *Bears, Bears, Everywhere*. "You know what?" he says. "I'm still working on my bear book."

Conversation That Includes Instruction

When teachers read books interactively, when they read *with* their students instead of *to* their students, when they build conversation into their book reading, then talk about sounds and letters is easily included. This is the case with Mrs. Poremba and her kindergartners. For example, during their first reading of their big book edition of *Bears, Bears, Everywhere*, Mrs. Poremba's first question was "Where could I look to find the name of the story?"

One kindergartner answers, "the title page," another, "the cover." But another indicates where to look on the cover by saying, "*B*!" and many others repeat this suggestion.

Mrs. Poremba asks, "What do you mean, *B*? . . . OK. I would look right up here—

and I noticed that some of you said the letter *B*, because that's the very first letter in the word *Bears*. Here's another one," says Mrs. Poremba, pointing to the *B* at the beginning of the second word of the title. "This story is called *Bears, Bears, Everywhere*."

On the second page of the book, Mrs. Poremba uses the repeated *B* words to teach about an aspect of form. She directs the kindergartners' attention to the first words on the page, the same words as in the book's title. "I wanted to show you something here. Do you see that *B* in the beginning of *Bears*? Well, look at this one." Mrs. Poremba points to the lower-case *b* at the beginning of the second word, *bears*.

" 'Bears, bears everywhere,' " reads Deborah.

"But look at this *bear*. Look at this *B*."

"Lower-case," notes Eric D. This is true, and, of course, it is unlike the upper-case beginning of the second word in the title on the book's cover.

"It's a lower-case *B*. So *B*'s can come in capitals like that—"

Eric D. explains, "Um, if they—if there was a top, there would be a *B* just like that."

"Mmm hmm," confirms Mrs. Poremba.

"I like capitals," notes one kindergartner.

Mrs. Poremba turns the page. "Look at the bears—"

" 'Bears, bears—' " begins one kindergartner, and several others join in, " '—everywhere.' "

Another lesson about form presents itself on the very next page, this time about the importance of letter order in writing. The bears on this page are on chairs.

"—sitting in chairs," suggests one kindergartner.

"*No!*" suggests another kindergartner.

"What's this word?" asks Mrs. Poremba, pointing to *on*.

Two more kindergartners voice their suggestions: "*And*." "*No*."

"Look at this word," repeats Mrs. Poremba.

"*No*," repeats another child.

"*Zero!*" shouts Zack.

"Does anybody know what *O-N* spells?

"*No*," answer several children.

"*On!*" shouts one child.

"*On*," echoes another kindergartner.

"Let me show you," says Mrs. Poremba, and she picks up a small erasable board and a marker.

One kindergartner continues reading from the big book: " 'On chairs.' "

Mrs. Poremba directs the children's attention to her erasable board writing: "Here is how you spell *no*."

"N-O," notes Tahra.

"How do you spell it?" continues Mrs. Poremba. "With *n* first and then—"

Eric D. exclaims, "Oh I get it! I get it. The *O* has to be on that side and the *N*'s on that side."

"Yes," explains Mrs. Poremba, "when the *O* is on this side and the *N* is second, that's the word *on*."

"Oh!" says one kindergartner.

"It's like a pattern!" says Tahra. The children are used to finding patterns in the shapes on which the numbers of the calendar are written.

"It *is* kind of," agrees Mrs. Poremba.

Several kindergartners exclaim: "*On!*" "*On.*" "*On.*" " 'On chairs!' " "It's '*On chairs*' !" " 'On chairs' !"

"So it's, 'Bears—" says Mrs. Poremba.

" '—on chairs,' " read Mrs. Poremba and several students together.

Mrs. Poremba makes explicit a connection between this reading and her students' writing: "Some of you have been writing *on* in your sign-in sheets." (See Figure 10.3 for a sign-in sheet using the word *on*.)

"I have," say several kindergartners.

Brown Bear Bread: Kindergartners Talk among Themselves

The next day, a recipe for Brown Bear Bread, written on chart paper, is displayed on the easel. During free-choice time, Ian points out another *b* word repetition. He tells Mrs. Poremba that *Bear* and *Bread* start the same, with a *b*. This observation is no accident. Mrs. Poremba had prepared the kindergartners to notice such things by her own observation the day before in *Bears, Bears, Everywhere*, and she had directed them in the morning—long before they would sit down to read it together—to study the posted recipe. Such study in advance of reading together is part of the What Can You Show Us? routine. She had said, "After I excuse you today and tell you may go over to the carpet, there's a special job that I would like you to do. I want you to make sure that you visit

FIGURE 10.3. A September 17 sign-in sheet with *on*.

the easel today, because there's something up here that I want you to look at carefully. I want to see kindergartners talking about what they see and sharing their ideas with each other about what is right here on the easel. So make sure that you visit the easel before you come to sit down on the carpet. And when you visit the easel, don't just take a quick look and leave. Really look at it carefully and get that brain thinking about what this is about here."

Ian's comment is not the only one to reveal such thinking. During their visits to the easel, a conversation among several kindergartners reveals their thinking about other forms, especially numerals. But even more striking is the kindergartners' knowledge that this piece of writing must make sense; its meanings must be consistent and serve a unified purpose.

The Brown Bear Bread recipe, of course, includes numbers telling what quantities of ingredients to use; these are all 1's and 2's (e.g., 1 egg, 2 cups flour) (see Figure 10.4). There are small pictures of cups, measuring spoons, eggs, and sticks of butter to give clues for the reading of the recipe. There are numbers to tell how long and at what temperature to bake (375° for 12 minutes), and the steps of the recipe are numbered 1 to 7.

Mrs. Roloff joins the group of kindergartners at the easel. "That's a lot of words on there," she says.

Erin, pointing to the picture clues, says, "Yeah, we looked at these—"

Mrs. Roloff points to numbers. "And look at these, too—"

"—these are cups," says Erin, still attending to the pictures.

"—all these numbers," finishes Mrs. Roloff.

"These are cups. Cups!" repeats Erin.

"That means cups?" asks Mrs. Roloff.

"Mmm hmm," answers Erin.

Mrs. Roloff points to a *1* followed by a picture of an egg. "What do you think this is?"

"*10!*" answers Erin.

Mrs. Roloff accepts this. It does look like a *10*. One kindergartner begins counting backwards from *10*: "*10-9-8-*"

Erin reads all the *1*'s and *2*'s.

"Lots of spoons," observes Zack.

Step 5 is a direction to arrange and pat balls of dough into a bear shape. It says, "Make balls" (there is a picture of dough balls) and "Put on pan" (there is a picture of a bear made up of circles). "Five bears!" reads Erin. "Four bowls," she continues, reading Step 4 which says, "Mix together" with a picture of two bowls with an ampersand between them.

They count the 1s and 2s.

"Wow, this is a big number," says Mrs. Roloff about 375.

"Three!" says Erin.

"Look at all those numbers together—"

Erin starts to revise her reading of this big number: "*30—*"

"—3, 7, 5. Wow!" says Mrs. Roloff, pointing to each digit as she reads.

"Thir—" repeats Erin. Then she revises again, "A hundred and, um—"

Brown Bear Bread

1. Grease pan.

2. Mix with a spoon in a bowl:

   1   BUTTER   butter and 1   butter

   1   molasses

   1   brown sugar

   1   egg

3. Mix in another bowl with a spoon:

   2   flour

   1   flour
   2   soda
   1   ginger
   1   cinnamon

4. Mix together   and

5. Make balls.   Put on pan.

6. Decorate.

7. Bake at 375 degrees for 12 minutes.

FIGURE 10.4. The Brown Bear Bread recipe.

"You think that's a hundreds number?" asks Mrs. Roloff.

"A hundred and fifty?" wonders Erin.

"Ooo. I think you're getting very close. It is a hundreds number. It is a very high number."

Jeff joins the group and reads the numerals that number the steps of the recipe. Then others read all the 1's and 2's, and a kindergartner reads, "2 cups."

No one has identified this as a recipe. There is a picture of a bear at the top, next to the words *Brown Bear Bread*. Some kindergartners think it is a text about the story of Goldilocks and the Three Bears.

A new group forms at the easel: Ian, Freddy, and Jason.

"What the heck?!" one of them asks.

"I don't know," answers another.

They identify numbers and read the pictures of cups and spoons and bowls.

Jason attempts a reading: "No, it says, 'The bear—the bear'—I don't know what it says!"

One of these boys asks Mrs. Poremba, "What does it say?"

"Talk it over with Jason," she replies. "He's got some good ideas going there."

"Hey, you know what? I think it talks about what the three bears did," speculates Ian.

"1, 2, 3 bowls," reads Jason. "Number 10," he continues, reading the 1 and the picture of an egg just as Erin had.

"Bear," reads Freddy.

The boys continue to read some numbers and to be stumped by other parts of the recipe: "I don't know what that says." "I don't know."

Ian asks, "What have you figured out, Jason? What have you figured out?"

Jason answers by identifying parts of text: "Well, I figured out '1'—"

Ian interrupts, "You know what I figured out?"

"What?"

Ian persists with his theory of the overall meaning of the text, "This whole thing is about what the three bears did."

"That's what I said," agrees Freddy.

"Well, what is this gonna be?" asks Jason, still wanting to identify discrete parts of the text.

The boys continue to speculate about individual words and pictures, but now within the Three Bears framework. One of them says, "This is how you make porridge."

Jason wants certainty. "Teacher, what does this say?" he asks Mrs. Poremba, who has already begun opening-of-the-day activities with the rest of the class.

Mrs. Poremba replies from across the room: "Hmmm. Any ideas there, guys?"

"We know it's from *The Three Bears*," answers Jason in a tentative voice.

"You know it's from *The Three Bears*?"

"You can tell by the bear," explains Jason.

"There's a bear up there," Mrs. Poremba confirms, but she does not give a definitive answer. She knows that would terminate the boys' conversation. "I just wanted you to look at it. We're going to talk more about it later. You seem to be busy thinking."

Freddy begins to identify the picture clues: "There's the big bear. There's the middle-sized bear." He points to the big bear picture at the top of the poster and the smaller picture of a bear that is part of Step 5 of the recipe.

Jason follows this lead: "There's the little glass. There's the big glass." He points to the different-sized measuring cups pictured in the recipe.

"THE GREAT BIG DADDY GLASS," says one of the boys in a great big voice.

Jason's name is drawn as one of today's helpers. "Jason! Jason!" calls Jeff. "Jason, you're the helper today!"

"Oh!" replies Jason, ready to abandon his easel work.

But Mrs. Poremba tells him, "Jason, if you and Freddy want to continue talking about the easel, you have a few more minutes."

"Baby Bear's spoon, Mommy Bear's spoon, Daddy Bear's spoon," says Freddy about picture clue spoons.

Ian has an idea about one of the cup pictures. "You know what that is?! That's the, that's the cradle!"

Brown Bear Bread: Whole-Class Conversation

Later in the morning, Mrs. Poremba reads *Brown Bear, Brown Bear, What Do You See?* (Martin, 1967) with the class and then she says, "I'd like you to look up at the easel, and I need some ideas for what is going on here."

Ian responds, "About *The Three Bears*."

Several children repeat this suggestion. Mrs. Poremba calls on Jason to explain. "Because of the bowls and spoons," Jason says, repeating his and Ian's and Freddy's earlier speculation.

As Mrs. Poremba calls on Ian for another idea, Jason adds, "And the bear at the top."

And so Ian says, "Actually, Jason already said it."

"You noticed the bear at the top," Mrs. Poremba acknowledges. "So something about bears. Kaitlynn."

"There's a 3 on there, and that means the Three Bears," explains Kaitlynn.

"Ahh. Jeff?"

"There's the table," says Jeff about a picture of a pan.

"You noticed a table. *Maybe* that's a table, and maybe it's something else."

At his turn, Zack says, "Um. There's a spoon. And there's a bear up there."

Mrs. Poremba gives a hint: "I wonder what we would use things like bowls and spoons—"

"Porridge!" shouts Freddy, repeating another notion from his and Ian's and Jason's earlier talking together at the easel.

Other kindergartners repeat this hypothesis, and other Three Bear notions are offered.

"There's three spoons," observes Eric D.

"Three spoons and three bowls," adds another kindergartner.

"So we think it's something about eating," concludes Mrs. Poremba.

Freddy repeats his porridge suggestion.

"Possibly porridge," says Mrs. Poremba. "Maybe it would help you if I read something to you."

"Yeah!" respond the kindergartners together.

"Where should I, what should I read?"

Two kindergartners show they know that letters have something to do with what Mrs. Poremba will read. "P-g!" suggests one, perhaps thinking that Mrs. Poremba will read the word *porridge*.

"B-B-B-B-B-" says Kaitlynn, looking at all the B words in *Brown Bear Bread*.

"If we wanted to find out what this was about, where would we have to look?" repeats Mrs. Poremba. "What part of this? At the bottom, or—"

"Top!" say several kindergartners.

"At the top? Let's try the top," responds Mrs. Poremba. "Up here it says, 'Brown Bear Bread.' "

"Brown Bear Bread?" repeats Tara G., not sure what that means.

"We're making bread!" declares Eric D.

"A song!" suggests another kindergartner.

"It could be a song," responds Mrs. Poremba. "Eric had a different idea. What did you think, Eric?"

"We can make bread."

"Maybe this would tell us how to make bread. What would we call it if you're going to make something at home, and you look at something that's written down that tells you how to make something, what is it called?"

"A recipe!" answers one kindergartner.

"It's called a recipe. Actually that is exactly what this is! . . . This is a recipe, and today we're going to make some—" Mrs. Poremba points again to the title at the top of the poster paper—" 'Brown Bear Bread.' "

Mrs. Poremba directs the children to stand and stretch and then wash their hands.

The children stand and move about, one of them reading, "It says, 'Brown Bear Bread!' "

Making Brown Bear Bread

Making Brown Bear Bread is also an opportunity to use numbers and letters and words in an authentic, functional way. The kindergartners use their number knowledge and their meaning-making strategies to combine the right portions of ingredients to make a gingerbread-like snack for their own consumption at snack time later.

As they begin to follow the recipe's directions for making Brown Bear Bread, Jason asks, "Teacher, what are we going to do with it?"

And Jeff asks, "Are we going to snack with this?"

Mrs. Poremba answers, "Yup. This will be our snack today. Good idea, Jeff."

Step 3 includes adding two teaspoons of soda. "Where are we?" asks Mrs. Poremba.

"We're on the next thing. Right up here, kindergartners," says Mrs. Roloff, standing by the easel and pointing to a 2, a picture of a measuring spoon, and the word *soda*.

"Spoons!" several kindergartners read.

"How many?" asks Mrs. Roloff.

"Two."

" 'Two spoons soda,' " reads Mrs. Roloff.

"OK," says Mrs. Poremba.

When it is time to make the eyes on the gingerbread bear, a kindergartner says, "Now comes the eyes."

Mrs. Poremba holds up a box of raisins. "I brought some—"

"Raisins!" say the kindergartners.

"I tell you what," says Mrs. Poremba, "if you don't like raisins, you don't have to be concerned, because—"

Several kindergartners voice their tastes: "I do!" "I don't!"

"I have to stop talking," says Mrs. Poremba, "because I got interrupted. I'm trying to say something—"

"Interrupting is not nice," says Tara G., interrupting.

"Yeah, I keep getting interrupted," says Mrs. Poremba. "Are you ready to listen now?"

"Yes," answer several kindergartners together.

"If you don't care for raisins, you don't have to be concerned because you can have a piece of the bear that doesn't have a raisin on it."

When it is time to combine the dry and wet ingredients, Mrs. Poremba observes, "We are running really late, guys." She organizes a line of kindergartners who will take turns stirring.

Mrs. Poremba again directs the kindergartners' attention to the print on the recipe. "What I want you to do now is put your eyes up on the recipe, and we'll see what we're going to do with these two things that you mixed together."

Next on the recipe is step 5 ("Make balls") with a picture of five little dough balls (though this is not intended to represent the exact number of balls required), and "Put on pan" with a picture of a dough bear on a pan.

"Five bears," one kindergartner incorrectly reads.

"Five bears, for eight—nineteen kids?" questions Ian.

They work out a correct reading of Step 5, and the kindergartners make balls and shape them on the pan for their gingerbread bear's stomach, legs, head, and ears. After the gingerbread bear is complete, Mrs. Poremba announces free-choice time.

The Unit's End and Beyond

On next-to-last day of the 2-week bear unit, Mrs. Poremba sends a Home Link note home with the kindergartners requesting that they bring small, nutritious snacks to school the next day. On the last day of the unit, she reads *The Teddy Bears' Picnic* (1991), and she and the kindergartners and their teddy bears have a picnic on the playing field next to the playground.

The ripple effects of the bear unit continue even after it is finished and the class moves on to another unit. The next week, at the Writing center, Tara J. draws a bear

and names it Trina after her aunt. Three weeks later, Freddy's sign-in writing includes
What bears look: and What bears do:, copied from the Bear Facts chart still on display. A week later, Eric C. brings a salamander to school. During sign-in writing, Ian
asks me how to spell *salamander*. He has already drawn a salamander and written
FactS. Now he writes the word above the picture as I spell it. Not until the next
school day's free-choice time do we have time to work together writing salamander
facts from a book in the Reading center's science book shelf, *World Book's Young Scientist: Volume 6. Animals* (1991). I show Ian the index and ask him what letter to look
under for *salamander*. He says, "*S*," and he is able to tell me when to stop paging
because we are at the *S* words in the index.

"Guess what?" I ask. "Look at what that first word is."

" 'Salamander!' " Ian reads.

I direct Ian to write down the page numbers for *salamander*, which he does on the
back of his sign-in sheet.

When we find those pages and talk a bit about what we see and what I read there,
Ian says, "But I don't want to write that. I want you to." So I agree to write what Ian dictates, as the class had done for the Bear Facts chart and the bear art project captions.
Ian's dictations are based on what we read. When I read that adult newts and salamanders spend much more time in water, Ian asks, "Can you just write 'Adult salamanders
spend much more time in the water'?" Our finished text has five sentences about salamanders (see Figure 10.5). I read it to Ian and he takes it home.

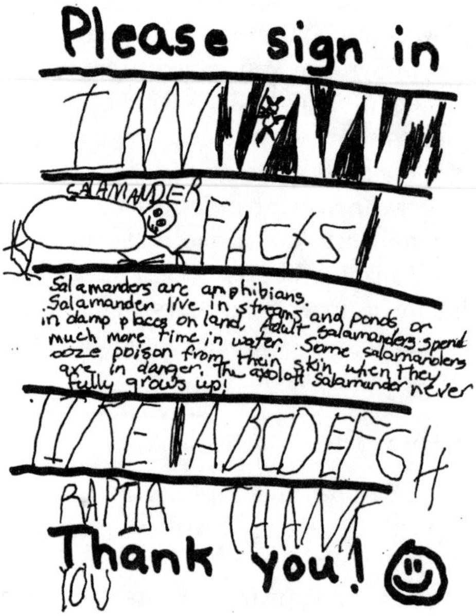

FIGURE 10.5. Ian's sign-in sheet with salamander facts.

LITERACY TEACHING AND LEARNING OUTSIDE OF THE THEMATIC UNIT

Not all reading and writing during the bear unit was about bears. At the beginning of this chapter we briefly described the Words for Today routine. Mrs. Poremba introduced it during the 1st week of the bear unit. The words she elicited and wrote as a shared writing activity were mostly weather words (appropriately so, for, as we have seen, the routine started as More Weather Words). This was an excellent opportunity for talk about sounds and about meaning–form links, such as length of word and sound–letter correspondences. For example, on the very day that Mrs. Poremba introduced More Weather Words, Tara J. suggested *wet*, and that became a favorite word for weeks. Thus, Mrs. Poremba had frequent opportunities to comment that it was a short word and to demonstrate the correspondence between its sounds and its spelling. When Eric D. suggests *wet* on the 4th day of doing More Weather Words, Mrs. Poremba says, "Www-et. We've been using that word a lot lately too. Www-et. Watch me carefully as I write that word. This is a word we've been using a lot. Wwww—ehhh-t" (Richgels, 2003). On the next school day, when Steven suggests *wet*, Mrs. Poremba says, "Wet. We have that word up here a lot on our graph, don't we? Wwwet. Starts with a W. It's a small word. Watch me write that. W-e-t. Look at how small, only three letters in *wet*. It's a small word" (Richgels, 2003). On October 12, when *wet*, still a favorite, is again a More Weather Words item, Katilynn copies it on her sign-in sheet.

Mrs. Poremba's and her students' talk about *wet* was not only about sounds and letters and the length of the word. They also talked about meanings. Of course, *wet* was meaningful as a weather word during a rainy time of the fall, but the meaning talk went beyond that. On the same day that Tara first suggested *wet*, Eric D. suggested a synonym, *damp*.

"But what does *damp* mean?" asks Mrs. Poremba.

"*Damp* means wet," answers a kindergartner. (Richgels, 2003)

And that became another favorite word. When Steven suggests it 3 days later, Mrs. Poremba again asks, "*Damp*. What does *damp* mean?"

"Not real wet," answers Steven.

"That's a very good way of telling us what damp means. I like that idea." Mrs. Poremba says the first sound and then the whole word: "D-*damp*."

"D," say several kindergartners.

Mrs. Poremba writes *damp*. (Richgels, 2003)

CHAPTER SUMMARY

This chapter's description of a 2-week bear unit in Mrs. Poremba's kindergarten includes many examples of teaching and learning strategies that we recommended in earlier chapters. Mrs. Poremba involved her students in several kinds of writing, including individual, self-directed sign-in writing and writing by dictation. As the year progressed and the kindergartners' abilities increased, they continued to write about unit topics in self-directed writing on sign-in sheets and at the Writing center. The amount and sophistication of their writing increased as shown in their writing in journals, on laminated story-starter folders (with a picture and "Once upon a time" at the top), during play, and in the Words for Today routine (see the beginning of this chapter). We have seen here that Mrs. Poremba's students participated in the What Can You Show Us? routine with a variety of texts, in interactive readings of fictional and nonfictional picture books, and in individual and partner reading of books that Mrs. Poremba had already read to the class, including personal, little book copies of big books. These activities continued throughout the year. For each new unit, Mrs. Poremba stocked the Reading center with a text set of fictional and factual books on the unit topic. The kindergartners honed their ability to distinguish between fiction and nonfiction (Richgels, 2002); they continued to use nonfictional books for "kindergarten research"; and increasingly they used books of all kinds as sources for their individual writing on sign-in sheets, at the Writing center, and on story-starter folders. Mrs. Poremba embedded instructional talk about phonemic awareness and sound–letter correspondences in all of these activities, especially during interactive reading and shared writing and both in her individual response to and in her celebration before the whole class of kindergartners' sign-in writing. This instructional talk was often student-initiated and student-centered because it frequently occurred in the context of What Can You Show Us? and Words for Today. For additional descriptions of all of these activities throughout the year, see Richgels (2003).

A Primer on Phonics for Teachers

SOME BACKGROUND

Phonics, in general, is instruction that helps children to learn the relationships between letters and sounds and to use that knowledge when sounding out or decoding words and in spelling words. First, children are taught to connect phonemes to consonants, then short vowels, digraphs and blends, and finally long vowels. Different phonics programs may teach the letter-sound correspondences in different orders. For example, some programs teach a few consonants and then introduce one or two short vowels so that children can begin blending and spelling words. Regardless of the order in which the letters are introduced, children are usually taught (at least in the beginning of phonics instruction) only one phoneme associated with one letter. This explains why consonants and short vowels are taught first—most consonants and short vowels are highly regular, with each letter generally representing one phoneme. Later, children are taught that some letters (a few consonants and many double-vowel spellings) are related to several different phonemes), and that one phoneme (such as the long *a*) can be related to several spellings (such as in the words *wait, pay, weigh, cake,* and *break*).

Effective teachers of phonics know what a phoneme is. Ehen asked what a phoneme is, teachers most often answer that a phoneme is a sound represented by a letter. However, phonemes have nothing to do with letters. Phonemes are actually the smallest units of sound that matter in a language. In other words, it is the combining and contrasting of phonemes that makes words possible. Consider, for example, the *p*-phoneme, the short-*i* phoneme, and the *g* phoneme. (We write about them this way to make clear we are discussing sounds and not letters). These three phonemes are combined to make the word *pig*, and the *p*-phoneme and the *b*-phoneme are contrasted when distinguishing the words *pig* and *big*. The difference in the pronunciations of the *p* sound and the *b* sound is slight. It is only that for the *p* sound we do not use our voice and for *b* sound we do; everything else—how we use our tongue and throat, how we shape our lips, how we part our teeth—is identical. Yet speakers and listeners rely on that very small difference, that contrast; it is all that signals two very different English meanings, an animal that says "oink" versus a dimension of size, the opposite of small.

Another linguistic fact about phonemes that teachers must know is that phonemes are not discrete entities, but rather are categories within which there is much variation. For example, even while it is important in spoken language to be able to perceive the slight difference between the *p* sound and the *b* sound in *pig* and *big*, it is equally important to ignore differences in pronunciations of the *p* sound, for example, in *wrapped* and *rapid*. We do ignore this difference when we teach children about the *p* phoneme as if there is only one, when in fact there is a whole category of them (notice also the real, but ignored difference between the *p* sounds in *spot* and *pot*; to notice this difference, we dangle a piece of paper before our mouths when we say the two words). The following presents information about the usual categories of information taught in phonics programs. This information represents what children learn up to and including in second grade. Therefore, much of this information is beyond what preschool and kindergarten teachers actually need. However, in order to keep in mind the larger picture of where children will go in conventional reading and spelling instruction, we present it here.

LETTER–SOUND RELATIONSHIPS

Initial Consonant Letter-Sounds (one letter spells one phoneme)		Final Consonant Letter-Sounds (one letter usually spells one phoneme although in some instances two letters spell one phoneme*)	
b	boy	b	tub
d	dog	d	mud
f	foot	f	if, stiff*
h	hand	g	pig
j	jelly	k (ck)	stick*
k	king	l	mill*
l	leg	m	swim
m	man	n	van
n	nose	p	map
p	pot	t	hat
r	rope		
t	toe		
v	van		
w	wig		
y	yawn		
z	zebra		

Initial Consonant Blends (two or three letters spell two or three phonemes)		Final Consonant Blends (two phonemes spell two phonemes)	
br	bride	st	most
cr	crow	sk	mask
dr	drum	ld	sold
fr	frog	mp	jump
gr	green	nd	band

Initial Consonant Blends
(cont.)

pr	prince
tr	tree
scr	scream
spr	spray
str	strong
bl	blue
cl	clock
fl	fly
gl	glass
pl	plate
sl	slow
spl	splatter
sc	score
sm	smart
sp	sport
sw	swim
sk	skirt
sn	snail
st	start
qu	quiet

Final Consonant Blends
(cont.)

lf	shelf
lt	melt
nt	sent

Initial Consonant Digraphs
(two letters spell one phoneme)

sh	shoe
ch	chair
wh	white
th	thumb

Final Consonant Digraphs
(two letters spell one phoneme)

sh	dish
ch	peach
th	math
nk	thank
ng	ring

Variant Consonants
(consonants that have more than
one phoneme associated with them)

c	cake, ice
g	goat, giant
s	sun, his, sure
x	box, xylophone

Silent Consonants
(consonants that are not sounded)

d	judge
gh	fight
w	wrong
t	watch
b	climb

Short Vowel
(usually spelled with one letter;
each sound associated with one spelling)

a	hat
e	net
i	pig
o	dog
u	duck
o͝o	foot

Long Vowel
(usually spelled with two letters; each
sound associated with several spellings)

a	rain, pay, cake, weigh, prey
e	feet, mean, she, chief, happy
i	pipe, might, cry, mild
o	home, boat, slow, sold
u	cube
o͞o	tube, boot, blue, blew,

R-Controlled Vowels
(vowel altered by r-phoneme and
associated with one or more spellings)

ar	car, carve
air	chair, care,
er	her, bird, nurse
eer	steer, fear
ire	fire
ore	more, for, roar, war, four
our	hour
oor	tour

Other Vowels
(not long or short; or associated
with more than one phoneme)

ea	beat, bread
ow	clown, blow
ou	out, would, rough, though
au	August
aw	awful
oi	boil
oy	boy

Literacy Assessments

This appendix presents sheets that may be reproduced and used as literacy assessments. Each assessment includes an administration/scoring sheet that the teacher uses to tell children how to do the assessment and as a scoring sheet. Each assessment also includes a child sheet that the child may use to complete the assessment. Directions for how to administer and score the assessments are found in Chapter 3.

Upper-Case Alphabet Recognition Administration, Scoring, and Child Sheet

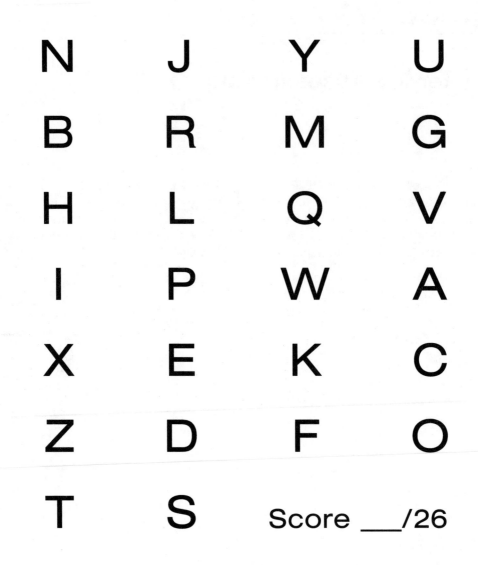

N	J	Y	U
B	R	M	G
H	L	Q	V
I	P	W	A
X	E	K	C
Z	D	F	O
T	S		

Score ___/26

Lower-Case Alphabet Recognition Assessment
Administration, Scoring, and Child Sheet

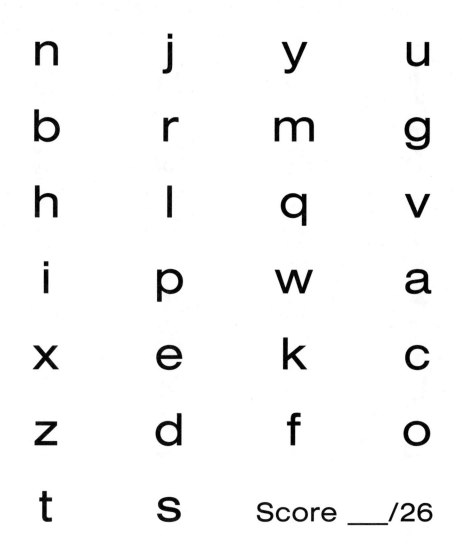

n	j	y	u
b	r	m	g
h	l	q	v
i	p	w	a
x	e	k	c
z	d	f	o
t	s	Score ___/26

Alphabet Production Assessment Administration and Scoring Sheet (letters are scored as correct in either upper- or lower-case form)

j	y	n	u
r	m	b	g
l	q	h	v
p	w	i	a
e	k	x	c
d	f	z	o
s	t	Score ___/26	

Alphabet Production Assessment Child Sheet

_____   _____   _____   _____

_____   _____   _____   _____

_____   _____   _____   _____

_____   _____   _____   _____

_____   _____   _____   _____

_____   _____   _____   _____

_____   _____

Rhyming Assessment Administration and Scoring

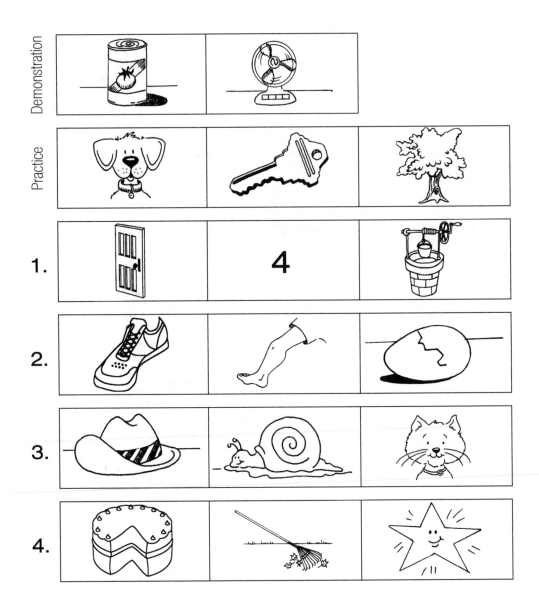

(cont.)

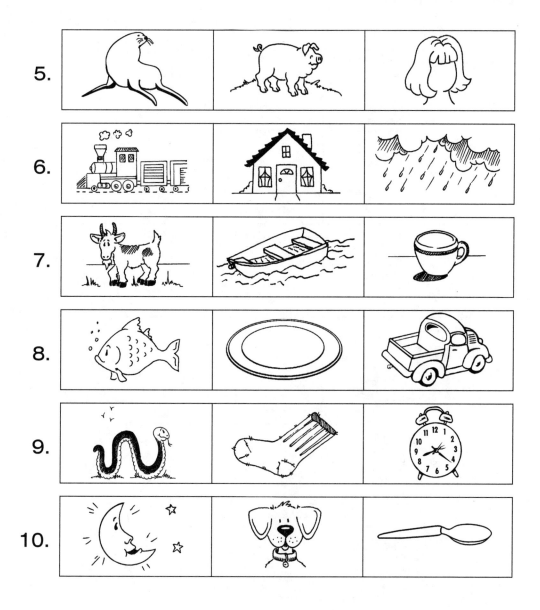

5.

6.

7.

8.

9.

10.

Score_____/10

Alliteration (Beginning Phoneme) Assessment Administration and Scoring

(cont.)

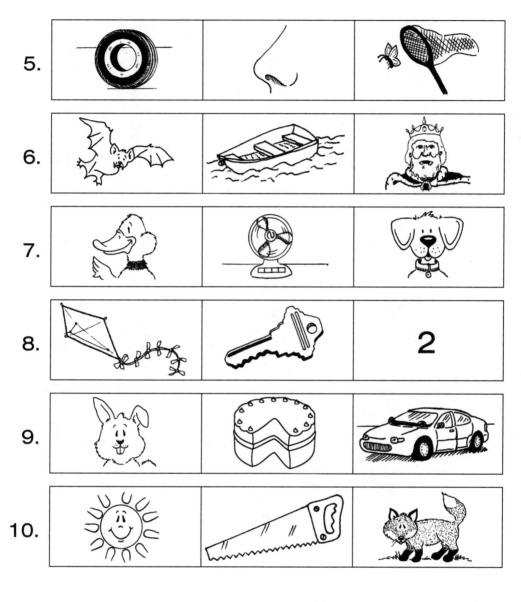

5.

6.

7.

8.

2

9.

10.

Score_____/10

Letter–Sound Assessment Administration and Scoring Sheet

Demonstration		D	

Practice		R	S	B

1.		✗	H	L

2.		P	M	S

3.		K	S	T

4.		B	F	H

(cont.)

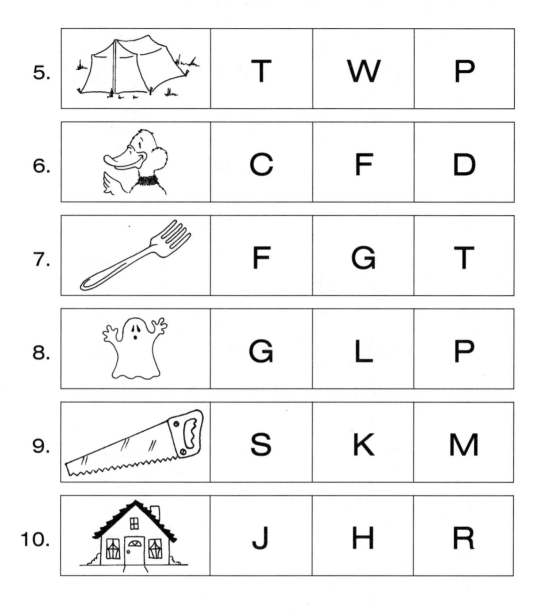

5.		T	W	P
6.		C	F	D
7.		F	G	T
8.		G	L	P
9.		S	K	M
10.		J	H	R

Score_____/10

Blending Onset and Rime Assessment
Administration and Scoring Sheet

Demonstration	/f/	/ish/	fish
Practice	/th/	/umb/	thumb
Practice	/b/	/oot/	boot
1.	/b/	/ed/	bed
2.	/s/	/ocks/	socks
3.	/t/	/ire/	tire
4.	/p/	/ot/	pot

(cont.)

5.	/g/	/irl/	girl
6.	/w/	/eb/	web
7.	/sh/	/ark/	shark
8.	/l/	/eaf/	leaf
9.	/s/	/un/	sun
10.	/f/	/an/	fan

Score_____/10

Segmenting Onset and Rime Assessment
Administration and Scoring Sheet

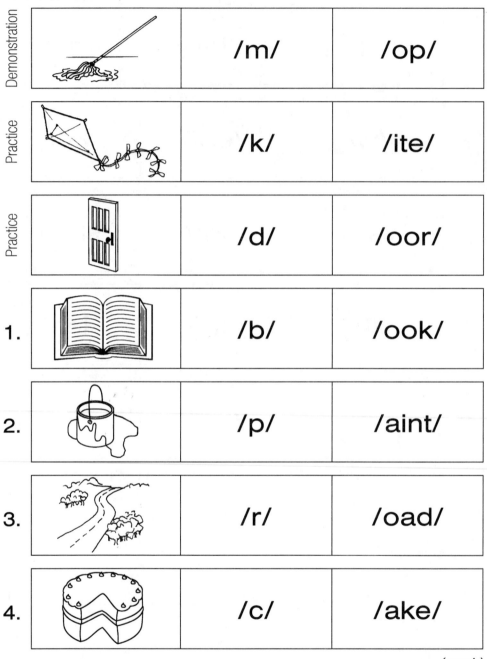

Demonstration		/m/	/op/
Practice		/k/	/ite/
Practice		/d/	/oor/
1.		/b/	/ook/
2.		/p/	/aint/
3.		/r/	/oad/
4.		/c/	/ake/

(cont.)

5.		/d/	/uck/
6.		/t/	/ub/
7.		/f/	/ox/
8.		/j/	/ump/
9.		/ch/	/air/
10.		/m/	/oon/

Score_____/20

Segmenting Onset and Rime Assessment
Child Sheet

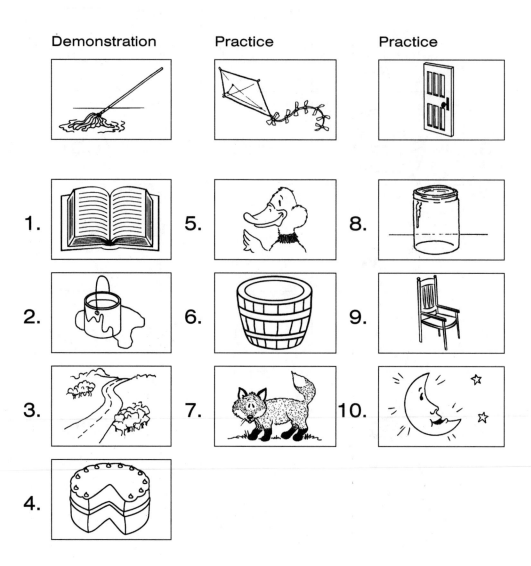

Demonstration   Practice   Practice

1.   5.   8.

2.   6.   9.

3.   7.   10.

4.

Segmenting Phonemes Assessment Administration and Scoring Sheet

Demonstration		/t/	/ie/
Practice		/a/	/pe/
1.		/k/	/ey/
2.		/sh/	/oe/
3.		/i/	/ce/

(cont.)

Demonstration		/c/	/u/	/p/
Practice:		/ch/	/i/	/ck/
4.		/l/	/i/	/p/
5.		/d/	/o/	/g/
6.		/r/	/ai/	/n/
7.		/f/	/ee/	/t/
8.		/n/	/o/	/se/
9.		/sh/	/ee/	/p/
10.		/c/	/a/	/t/

Segmenting Phonemes Assessment Child Sheet

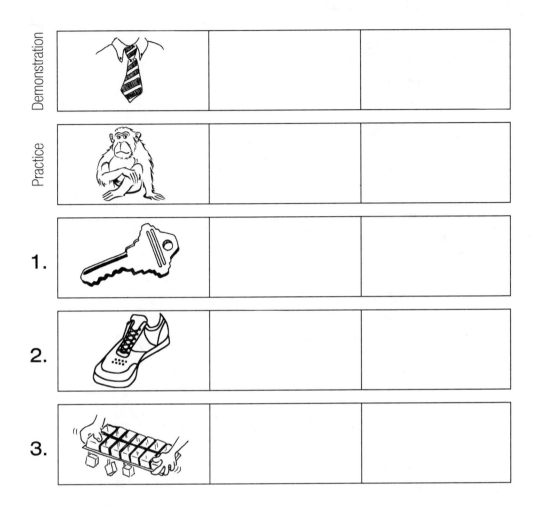

(cont.)

Segmenting Phonemes Assessment
Child Sheet (p. 2 of 2)

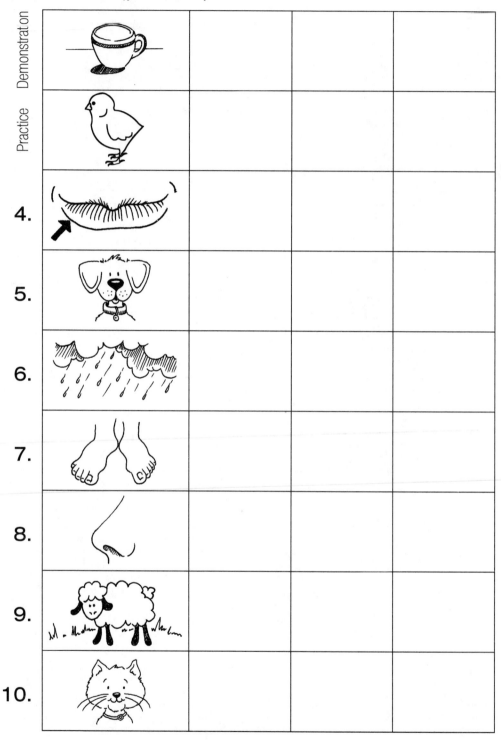

Demonstration

Practice

4.

5.

6.

7.

8.

9.

10.

References

Adams, M. (1990). *Beginning to read*. Cambridge, MA: MIT Press.

Adams, M. (2001). Alphabetic anxiety and explicit, systematic phonics instruction: A cognitive-science perspective. In S. Neuman & D. Dickinson (Eds.), *Handbook of early literacy research* (pp. 66–80). New York: Guilford Press.

Adams, M., Foorman, B., Lundberg, I., & Beeler, T. (1998). *Phonemic awareness in young children: A classroom curriculum*. Baltimore, MD: Paul H. Brookes.

Alborough, J. (2001). *Duck in a truck*. New York: HarperCollins.

Allington, R. (1995). Literacy lessons in the elementary schools: Yesterday, today, and tomorrow. In R. Allington & S. Walmsley (Eds.), *No quick fix: Rethinking literacy programs in America's elementary schools* (pp. 1–15). New York: Teachers College Press.

Au, K. H. (1980). Participation structures in a reading lesson with Hawaiian children: Analysis of a culturally appropriate and instructional event. *Anthropology and Education Quarterly, 11,* 91–115.

August, D., & Hakuta, K. (Eds.). (1997). *Improving schooling for language-minority children: A research agenda*. National Research Council and Institute of Medicine. Washington, DC: National Academy Press.

Baghban, M. (1984). *Our daughter learns to read and write: A case study from birth to three*. Newark, DE: International Reading Association.

Ballenger, C. (1999). *Teaching other people's children: Literacy and learning in a bilingual classroom*. New York: Teachers College Press.

Barone, D. (1999). *Resilient children: Stories of poverty, drug exposure, and literacy development*. Newark, DE: International Reading Association.

Barrera, R., Ligouri, O., & Salas, L. (1992). Ideas literature can grow on: Key insights for enriching and expanding children's literature about the Mexican-American experience. In B. Harris (Ed.), *Teaching multicultural literature in grades K–8* (pp. 203–241). Norwood, MA: Christopher-Gordon.

Barton, B. (1981). *Building a house*. New York: Puffin.

Beall, J. (2001). *Wee sing in the car*. New York: Price Stern Sloan.

Bear, D. R., Invernizzi, M., Templeton, S., & Johnston, F. (2000). *Words their way: Word study for phonics, vocabulary, and spelling instruction*. Columbus, OH: Merrill.

Beaver, J. (1997). *Developmental reading assessment*. Parsippany, NJ: Celebration Press.

Bishop, R. S. (1992). Multicultural literature for children: Making informed choices. In V. J. Harris

(Ed.), *Teaching multicultural literature in grades K–8* (pp. 37–53). Norwood, MA: Christopher-Gordon.

Bissex, G. (1980). *GYNS AT WRK: A child learns to write and read.* Cambridge, MA: Harvard University Press.

Bloodgood, J. W. (1999). What's in a name? Children's name writing and literacy acquisition. *Reading Research Quarterly, 34,* 342–367.

Brady, S., Fowler, A., Stone, B., & Winbury, N. (1994). Training phonological awareness: A study with inner-city kindergarten children. *Annals of Dyslexia, 44,* 26–59.

Branscombe, A. (1991). "But it ain't real!": Pretense in children's play and literacy development. In J. F. Christie (Ed.), *Play and early literacy development* (pp. 91–115). Albany: State University of New York Press.

Brett, J. (1987). *The three bears.* New York: Putnam.

Brewer, J. A. (1998). Literacy development of young children in a multilingual setting. In R. Campbell (Ed.), *Facilitating preschool literacy* (pp. 119–130). Newark, DE: International Reading Association.

Briggs, R. (1970). *Jim and the beanstalk.* New York: Coward-McCann.

Brown, M. (1942). *The runaway bunny.* New York: Harper & Row.

Brown, M. (1947). *Goodnight, moon.* New York: Harper & Row.

Burningham, J. (1993). *Mr. Gumpy's motor car.* New York: Crowell.

Byrne, B., & Fielding-Barnsley, R. (1991). Evaluation of a program to teach phonemic awareness to young children. *Journal of Educational Psychology, 83,* 451–455.

Canizares, S., & Chessen, B. (1998). *From egg to robin.* New York: Scholastic.

Carger, C. (1993). Louie comes to life: Pretend reading with second language emergent readers. *Language Arts, 70,* 542–547.

Carle, E. (1986). *The grouchy ladybug.* New York: Harper & Row.

Casbergue, R. M., & Plauché, M. B. (2003). Immersing children in nonfiction: Fostering emergent research and writing. In D. M. Barone & L. M. Morrow (Eds.), *Literacy and young children: Research-based practices* (pp. 243–260). New York: Guilford Press.

Catts, H. W., Fey, M. E., Zhang, X., & Tomblin, J. B. (2001). Estimating the risk of future reading difficulties in kindergarten children: A research-based model and its clinical implementation. *Language, Speech, and Hearing Services in Schools, 32,* 38–50.

Chandler, K. (2000, November). Functional illiteracy. *The Advisor, 26,* 3.

Chaney, C. (1992). Language development, metalinguistic skills, and print awareness in 3-year-old children. *Applied Psycholinguistics, 13,* 485–514.

Christie, J. F. (1991). Psychological research on play: Connections with early literacy development. In J. F. Christie (Ed.), *Play and early literacy development* (pp. 27–43). Albany: State University of New York Press.

Christie, J., & Enz, B. (2002, April). *Using environmental print to help children learn the code.* Paper presented at the annual meeting of the International Reading Association, San Francisco.

Clarke-Stewart, K. A., & Beck, R J. (1999). Maternal scaffolding and children's narrative retelling of a movie story. *Early Childhood Research Quarterly, 14,* 409–434.

Clay, M. M. (1985). *Early detection of reading difficulties* (3rd ed.). Auckland, New Zealand: Heinemann.

Clay, M. M. (1993). *An observation survey of early literacy achievement.* Auckland, New Zealand: Heinemann.

Clay, M. M. (1998). *By different paths to common outcomes.* York, ME: Stenhouse.

Cochran-Smith, M. (1984). *The making of a reader.* Norwood, NJ: Ablex.

Collins, A., Brown, J. S., & Newman, S. (1989). Cognitive apprenticeships: Teaching the crafts of reading, writing and mathematics. In L.R. Resnick (Ed.), *Knowing, learning and instruction* (pp. 453–491). Hillsdale, NJ: Erlbaum.

Comber, B. (2000). What *really* counts in early literacy lessons. *Language Arts, 78,* 39–49.

Connelly, L. (1988). *Bears, bears, everywhere* (N. C. Koeller, Ill.). Cypress, CA: Creative Teaching Press.

Cornell, E. H., Senechal, M., & Brodo, L. S. (1988). Recall of picture books by 3–year-old children: Testing and repetition effects in joint reading activities. *Journal of Educational Psychology, 80,* 537–542.

Cowley, J. (1989). *Yuck soup.* Bothell, WA: Wright Group.

Cunningham, P. (2000). *Phonics they use: Words for reading and writing.* New York: Longman.

Delgado-Gaitan, C., & Trueba, H. (1991). *Crossing cultural borders: Education for immigrant families in American.* Philadelphia: Falmer Press.

dePaola, T. (1988). *The legend of the Indian paintbrush.* New York: Alladin.

Diamond, B. J., & Moore, M. A. (1995). *Multicultural literacy: Mirroring the reality of the classroom.* White Plains, NY: Longman.

Dickinson, D. K., & Smith, M. W. (1994). Long-term effects of preschool teachers' book readings on low-income children's vocabulary and story comprehension. *Reading Research Quarterly, 29,*104–122.

Dickinson, D. K., & Sprague, K. E. (2001). The nature and impact of early childhood care environments on the language and early literacy development of children from low-income families. In S. B. Neuman & D. K. Dickinson (Eds.), *Handbook of early literacy research* (pp. 263–280). New York: Guilford Press.

Dickinson, D. K., & Tabors, P. O. (2001). *Beginning literacy with language.* Baltimore, MD: Brookes.

Duke, N. (2000). Print environments and experiences offered to first-grade students in very low- and very high-SES school districts. *Reading Research Quarterly, 35,* 456–457.

Duke, N. K., & Kays, J. (1998). "Can I say 'once upon a time'?": Kindergarten children developing knowledge of information book language. *Early Childhood Research Quarterly, 13,* 295–318.

Dunn, J. (1976). *The little duck.* New York: Random House.

Dunn, L., & Dunn, L. (1981). *Peabody Picture Vocabulary Test—Revised* Circle Pines, NM: American Guidance Service.

Edwards, P. A., & Danridge, J. C. (2001). Developing collaboration with culturally diverse parents. In V. J. Risko & K. Bromley (Eds.), *Collaboration for diverse learners: Viewpoints and practices* (pp. 251–272). Newark, DE: International Reading Association.

Ehlert, L. (1995). *Snowballs.* Orlando, FL: Harcourt Brace.

Ernst-Slavit, G., Han, J. W., & Wenger, K. J. (2001). Reading at home, reading at school: Conflict, communication, and collaboration when school and home cultures are different. In V. J. Risko & K. Bromley (Eds.), *Collaboration for diverse learners: Viewpoints and practices* (pp. 289–309). Newark, DE: International Reading Association.

Feldgus, E., & Cardonick, I. (1999). *Kid writing: A systematic approach to phonics, journals, and writing workshop.* Bothell, WA: Wright Group.

Ferreiro, E. (1986). The interplay between information and assimilation in beginning literacy. In W. H. Teale & S. Sulzby (Eds.), *Emergent literacy : Writing and reading* (pp. 15–49). Norwood, NJ: Ablex.

Fillmore, L. (1991). When learning a second language means losing the first. *Early Childhood Research Quarterly, 6,* 323–346.

Fitzgerald, J. (1989). Research on stories: Implications for teachers. In K. D. Muth (Ed.), *Children's comprehension of text: Research into practice* (pp. 2–36). Newark, DE: International Reading Association.

Fleming, D. (1991). *In the tall, tall grass.* New York: Henry Holt.

Fletcher, N. (1993). *See how they grow: Penguins.* New York: Dorling Kindersley.

Fontanel, B. (1989). *The penguin: A funny bird.* Watertown, MA: Charlesbridge.

Fountas, I., & Pinnell, G. (1996). *Guided reading: Good first teaching for all children*. Portsmouth, NH: Heinemann.

Fractor, J., Woodruff, M., Martinez, M., & Teale, W. (1993). Let's not miss opportunities to promote voluntary reading: Classroom libraries in elementary school. *Reading Teacher, 46*, 476–484.

Galdone, P. (1972). *The three bears*. New York: Scholastic.

Gardner, M. (1990). *Expressive One-Word Picture Vocabulary Test—Revised*. Novato, CA: Academic Therapy.

Gibbons, F. (1999). *Mama and me and the Model T*. New York: Morrow.

Gibson, J. T. (1999). *Developing strategies and practices for culturally diverse classrooms*. Norwood, MA: Christopher-Gordon.

Gleason, J. B. (Ed.). (2001). *The development of language* (5th ed.). Boston: Allyn & Bacon.

Goldenberg, C., & Gallimore, R. (1991). Local knowledge, research knowledge, and educational change: A case study of early Spanish reading improvement. *Educational Researcher, 20*, 2–14.

Goldenberg, C., & Gallimore, R. (1995). Immigrant Latino parents' values and beliefs about their children's education: Continuities and discontinuities across cultures and generations. In P. Pintrich & M. Maehr (Eds.), *Advances in motivation and achievement: Culture, ethnicity, and motivation* (Vol. 9, pp. 183–228). Greenwich, CT: JAI Press.

Halliday, M. A. K. (1975). *Learning how to mean: Explorations in the development of language*. London: Edward Arnold.

Halliday, M. A. K. (2002). Relevant models of language. In B. M. Power & R. S. Hubbard (Eds.), *Language development: A reader for teachers* (2nd ed., pp. 49–53). Upper Saddle River, NJ: Merrill.

Hargrave, A. C., & Senechal, M. (2000). A book reading intervention with preschool children who have limited vocabularies: The benefits of regular reading and dialogic reading. *Early Childhood Research Quarterly, 15*, 75–90.

Harlan, J., & Rivkin, M. (2000). *Science experiences for the early childhood years: An integrated approach* (7th ed.). Columbus, OH: Merrill.

Harste, J., Burke, C., & Woodward, V. (1983). *The young child as a writer-reader and informant*. Bloomington: Indiana University Press.

Hart, B., & Risely, T. (1995). *Meaningful differences in the everyday experiences of young American children*. Baltimore, MD: Brookes.

Helburn, S. (1995). *Cost, quality and child outcomes in child care centers*. Denver, CO: Department of Economics, Center for Research in Economics and Social Policy, University of Colorado at Denver.

Helm, J., & Katz, L. (2001). *Young investigators: The project approach in the early years*. New York: Teachers College Press.

Helm, J., Beneke, S., & Steinheimer, K. (1998). *Windows on learning: Documenting young children's work*. New York: Teachers College Press.

Hiebert, E., & Taylor, B. (2000). Beginning reading instruction: Research on early interventions. In M. Kamil, P. Mosenthal, P. Pearson, & Barr, R. *Handbook of reading research* (Vol. III, pp 455–482). Mahwah, NJ: Erlbaum.

Hildreth, G. (1936). Developmental sequences in name writing. *Child Development, 7*, 291–303.

Hoff, S. (1958). *Danny and the dinosaur*. New York: Harper & Row.

Hunt, K. (1965). *Grammatical structures written at three grade levels*. [National Council of Teachers of English Research Reports, No.3]. Champaign, IL: National Council of Teachers of English.

Hutchins, P. (1968). *Rosie's walk*. New York: Macmillan.

International Reading Association and National Association for the Education of Young Children.

(IRA/NAEYC). (1998). Learning to read and write: Developmentally appropriate practices for young children. *Reading Teacher, 52,* 193–216.

Intrater, R. (1995). *Two eyes, a nose, and a mouth.* New York: Scholastic.

Isbell, R. (1995). *The complete learning center book.* Beltsville, MD: Gryphon House.

Isbell, R. T., & Exelby, B. (2001). *Early learning environments that work.* Beltsville, MD: Gryphon House.

Johnston, F., Invernizzi, M., & Juel, C. (1998). *Book buddies: Guidelines for volunteer tutors of emergent and early readers.* New York: Guilford Press.

Johnston, R. S., Anderson, M., & Holligan, C. (1996). Knowledge of the alphabet and explicit awareness of phonemes in pre-readers: The nature of the relationship. *Reading and Writing: An Interdisciplinary Journal, 8,* 217–234.

Kennedy, J. (1991). *The teddy bear's picnic* (A. Day, Ill.). New York: Simon & Schuster.

Klenk, L., & Kibby, M. (2000). Re-mediating reading difficulties: Appraising the past, reconciling the present, constructing the future. In M. Kamil, P. Mosenthal, P. Pearson, & R. Barr (Eds.), *Handbook of reading research* (Vol. III, pp. 667–690). Mahwah, NJ: Erlbaum.

Kovalski, M. (1987). *The wheels on the bus: An adaptation of the traditional song.* New York: Little, Brown.

Krashen, S. (1982). *Principles and practices in second language acquisition.* Oxford, England: Pergamon.

Ladson-Billings, G. (1994). *The dreamkeepers: Successful teachers of African American children.* San Francisco: Jossey-Bass.

Lesman, P., & deJong, P. (1998). Home literacy: Opportunity, instruction, cooperation and social-emotional quality predicting early reading achievement. *Reading Research Quarterly, 33,* 294–318.

Lester, H. (1998). *Tacky in trouble.* New York: Scholastic.

Leung, C. B. (1992). Effects of word-related variables on vocabulary growth through repeated read-aloud events. In C. Kinzer & D. Leu (Eds.), *Literacy research, theory, and practice: Views from many perspectives* (pp. 491–498). Chicago: National Reading Conference.

Levy, A. K., Wolfgang, C. H., & Koorland, M. A. (1992). Sociodramatic play as a method for enhancing the language performance of kindergarten age students. *Early Childhood Research Quarterly, 7,* 245–262.

Lindamood, C., & Lindamood, P. (1975). *Auditory discrimination in depth.* Columbus, OH: Science Research Associates/McGraw-Hill.

Lonigan, C. J., Burgess, S. R., Anthony, J. L., & Baker, T. (1998). Development of phonological sensitivity in 2– to 5–year-old children. *Journal of Educational Psychology, 90,* 294–311.

Maclean, M., Bryant, P., & Bradley, L. (1987). Rhymes, nursery rhymes, and reading in early childhood. *Merrill–Palmer Quarterly, 33,* 255–281.

Manning-Kratcoski, A., & Bobkoff-Katz, K. (1998). Conversing with young language learners in the classroom. *Young Children, 53,* 30–33.

Martin, B., Jr. (1967). *Brown bear, brown bear, what do you see?* (E. Carle, Ill.). New York: Holt, Rinehart & Winston.

McFadden, T. U. (1998). Sounds and stories: Teaching phonemic awareness in interactions around text. *American Journal of Speech–Language Pathology, 7,* 5–13.

McGee, L. M. (1998). How do we teach literature to young children? In S. Neuman & K. Roskos (Eds.), *Children achieving: Best practices in early literacy* (pp.162–179). Newark, DE: International Reading Association.

McGee, L. M. (2003). Book acting: Story telling and drama in the early childhood classroom. In D. M. Barone & L. M. Morrow (Eds.), *Literacy and young children: Research-based practices* (pp. 157–172). New York: Guilford Press.

McGee, L. M., & Richgels, D. J. (1989). "K is Kristen's": Learning the alphabet from a child's per-spective. *Reading Teacher, 43,* 216–225.

McGee, L. M., & Richgels, D. J. (2000). *Literacy's beginnings: Supporting young readers and writers* (3rd ed.). Boston: Allyn & Bacon.

McGee, L. M., & Tompkins, G., (1981). The videotape answer to independent reading compre-hension activities. *Reading Teacher, 34,* 430–431.

McGill-Franzen, A., & Lanford, C. (1994). Exposing the edge of the preschool curriculum: Teachers' talk about text and children's literary understandings. *Language Arts, 71,* 264–273.

McKissack, P. (1988). *Mirandy and Brother Wind.* New York: Knopf.

McMillon, G., & Edwards, P. (2000). Why does Joshua "hate" school . . . but love Sunday School? *Language Arts, 78,* 111–120.

Meier, D. R. (2000). *Scribble scrabble, learning to reading and write: Success with diverse teachers, children, and families.* New York: Teachers College Press.

Morrow, L. M. (1989). Using story retelling to develop comprehension. In K. Muth (Ed.), *Children's comprehension of text* (pp. 37–58). Newark, DE: International Reading Association.

Morrow, L. M., & Rand, M. (1991). Preparing the classroom environment to promote literacy dur-ing play. In J. F. Christie (Ed.), *Play and early literacy development* (pp. 141–165). Albany: State University of New York Press.

Morrow, L. M., & Smith, J. K. (1990). The effects of group size on interactive storybook reading. *Reading Research Quarterly, 25,* 213–231.

Murphy, S. J. (2000). *Beep beep, vroom vroom!* New York: HarperCollins.

Murray, B. A., Stahl, S. A., & Ivey, M. G. (1996). Developing phoneme awareness through alpha-bet books. *Reading and Writing: An Interdisciplinary Journal, 8,* 306–322.

National Center for Children in Poverty. (1998). Child poverty rates remain high despite booming U.S. economy. *National Center for Children in Poverty, New and Issues, 8,* 1.

National Center for Educational Statistics. (1995). *Approaching kindergarten: A look at preschoolers in the United States. National household education survey.* U.S. Department of Education, Office of Educational Research and Improvement.

National Center for Educational Statistics. (NAEP). (1996). *NAEP 1994 reading report card for the nation and states.* U.S. Department of Education, Office of Educational Research and Improvement.

National Committee on Science Education Standards and Assessment. (1994). *National science education standards: Discussion summary.* Washington, DC: National Research Council.

National Council for the Social Studies. (1994). *Expectations for excellence: Curriculum standards for social studies* (Bulletin 89). Washington, DC: Author.

National Reading Panel. (2000). *Report of the National Reading Panel.* Washington, DC:

Neuman, S. B. (1999). Books make a difference: A study of access to literacy. *Reading Research Quarterly, 34,* 286–311.

Neuman, S. B. (2001). The role of knowledge in early literacy. *Reading Research Quarterly, 36,* 468–475.

Neuman, S. B., & Roskos, K. (1993). Access to print for children of poverty: Differential effects of adult mediation and literacy-enriched play settings on environmental and functional print tasks. *American Educational Research Journal, 30,* 95–122.

Neuman, S. B., & Roskos, K. (1997). Literacy knowledge in practice: Contexts of participation for young writers and readers. *Reading Research Quarterly, 32,* 10–32.

Neuman, S. G., Copple, C., & Bredekamp, S. (2000). *Learning to read and write: Developmentally appropriate practices for young children.* Washington, DC: National Association for the Educa-tion of Young Children.

Neuman, S., & Celano, D. (2001). Access to print in low-income and middle-income communi-ties: An ecological study of four neighborhoods. *Reading Research Quarterly, 36,* 8–26.

Newcomer, P., & Hammill, D. (1988). *Test of Language Development-2, Primary.* Austin, TX: PRO-ED.

Newkirk, T. (1989). *More than stories: The range of children's writing.* Portsmouth, NH: Heinmeann.

Paley, V. G. (1990). *The boy who would be a helicopter.* Cambridge, MA: Harvard University Press.

Pappas, C. C. (1991). Young children's strategies in learning the "book language" of information books. *Discourse Processes, 14,* 203–225.

Pappas, C., & Barry, A. (1997). Scaffolding urban students' initiations: Transactions in reading information books in the read-aloud curriculum. In N. J. Karolides (Eds.), *Reader response in elementary classrooms: Quest and discovery* (pp. 215–236). Mahwah, NJ: Erlbaum.

Payne, C., & Schulman, M. (1998). *Getting the most out of morning message and other shared writing lessons.* New York: Scholastic.

Pellegrini, A. D., & Galda, L. (1982). The effects of thematic-fantasy play training on the development of children's story comprehension. *American Educational Research Journal, 19,* 443–452

Pienkowski, J. (1980). *Dinnertime.* Los Angeles: Price/Stern/Sloan.

Plourde, L. (1997). *Pigs in the mud in the middle of the rud.* New York: Blue Sky Press.

Polacco, P. (1990). *Thunder cake.* New York: Philomel.

Potter, B. (1902). *The tale of Peter Rabbit.* London: Frederick Warne.

Purcell-Gates, V. (1988). Lexical and syntactic knowledge of written narrative held by well-read-to kindergartners and second graders. *Research in the Teaching of English, 22,*128–160.

Purcell-Gates, V. (1996). Stories, coupons, and the *TV Guide*: Relationships between home literacy experiences and emergent literacy knowledge. *Reading Research Quarterly, 31,* 406–428.

Purcell-Gates, V., & Dahl, K. (1991). Low-SES children's success and failure at early literacy learning in skills-based classrooms. *Journal of Reading Behavior, 23,* 1–34.

Purcell-Gates, V., McIntyre, E., & Freppon, P. A. (1995). Learning written storybook language in school: A comparison of low-SES children in skills-based and whole language classrooms. *American Educational Research Journal, 32,* 659–685.

Rhodes, L., & Nathenson-Mejia, S. (1992). Anecdotal records: A powerful tool for ongoing literacy assessment. *Reading Teacher, 45,* 502–509.

Richgels, D. J. (1995). A kindergarten sign-in procedure: A routine in support of written language learning. In K. A. Hinchman, D. J. Leu, & C. K. Kinzer (Eds.), *Perspectives on literacy research and practice, forty-fourth yearbook of the National Reading Conference* (pp. 243–254). Chicago: National Reading Conference.

Richgels, D. J. (2002). Informational texts in kindergarten. *Reading Teacher, 55,* 586–595.

Richgels, D. J. (2003). *Going to kindergarten: A year with an outstanding teacher.* Lanham, MD: Scarecrow Press.

Richgels, D. J., & Wold, L. S. (1998). Literacy on the road: Backpacking partnerships between home and school. *Reading Teacher, 52,* 18–29.

Richgels, D. J., Poremba, K. J., & McGee, L. M. (1996). Kindergartners talk about print: Phonemic awareness in meaningful contexts. *Reading Teacher, 49,* 632–642.

Robbins, C., & Ehri, L. C. (1994). Reading storybooks to kindergartners helps them learn new vocabulary words. *Journal of Educational Psychology, 86,* 54–64.

Robbins, K. (1998). *Autumn leaves.* New York: Scholastic.

Roskos, K., & Neuman, S. B. (2001). Environment and its influences for early literacy teaching and learning. In S. B. Neuman & D. K. Dickinson (Eds.), *Handbook of early literacy research* (pp. 281–292). New York: Guilford Press.

Rowe, D. (1998). The literate potentials of book-related dramatic play. *Reading Research Quarterly, 33,* 10–35.

Ruwe, M. (1989). *Ten little bears* (D. Hockerman, Ill.). Glenview, IL: Scott Foresman.

Scarborough, H. (1991). Early syntactic development of dyslexic children. *Annals of Dyslexia, 41,* 207–220.

Schickedanz, J. (1998). What is developmentally appropriate practice in early literacy?: Considering the alphabet. In S. Neuman & K. Roskos (Eds.), *Children achieving: Best practices in early literacy* (pp. 20–35). Newark, DE: International Reading Association.

Schulman, M., & Payne, C. (2000). *Guided reading: Making it work.* New York: Scholastic.

Senechal, M. (1997). The differential effect of storybook reading on preschoolers' acquisition of expressive and receptive vocabulary. *Journal of Child Language, 24,* 123–138.

Senechal, M., LeFevre, J., Thomas, E. M., & Daley, K. E. (1998). Differential effects of home literacy experiences on the development of oral and written language. *Reading Research Quarterly, 33,* 96–116.

Seuss, Dr. (1957). *Cat in the hat.* New York: Random House.

Shores, E. F., & Grace. C. (1998). *The portfolio book: A step-by-step guide for teachers.* Beltsville, MD: Gryphon House.

Sims, R. (1982). *Shadow and substance: Afro-American experience in contemporary children's fiction.* Urbana, IL: National Council of Teachers of English.

Slavin, R., Karweit, B., Wasik, N., Madden, N., & Dolan, L. (1994) Success for all: A comprehensive approach to prevention and early intervention. In R. Slavin, N. Karweit, & B. Wasik (Eds.), *Preventing early school failure* (pp. 175–205). Boston: Allyn & Bacon.

Smith, S. S., & Dixon, R. G. (1995). Literacy concepts of low- and middle-class four-year-olds entering preschool. *Journal of Educational Research, 88,* 243–253.

Smolkin, L. B., & Donovan, C. A. (2002). "Oh excellent, excellent question!": Developmental differences and comprehension acquisition. In C. Block & M. Pressley (Eds.), *Comprehension instruction: Research-based best practices* (pp. 140–157). New York: Guilford Press.

Snow, C. E., Burns, M. S., & Griffin, P. (Eds.). (1998). *Preventing reading difficulties in young children.* Washington, DC: National Academy Press.

Stahl, S. A., & Murray, B. A. (1994). Defining phonological awareness and its relationship to early reading. *Journal of Educational Psychology, 86,* 221–234.

Stein, N. L., & Glenn, C. G (1979). An analysis of story comprehension in elementary school children. In R. O. Freedle (Ed.), *Advances in discourse processes: Vol. 2. New directions in discourse processing* (pp. 53–120). Norwood, NJ: Ablex.

Strickland, D. S. (1994). Educating African American learners at risk: Finding a better way. *Language Arts, 71,* 328–336.

Sulzby, E. (1985). Children's emergent reading of favorite storybooks: A developmental study. *Reading Research Quarterly, 20,* 458–481.

Taback, S. (1997). *There was an old lady who swallowed a fly.* New York: Viking.

Tabors, R., & Snow, C. (1994). English as a second language in preschool programs. In F. Genesee (Ed.), *Educating second language children: The whole child, the whole curriculum, the whole community.* New York: Cambridge University Press.

Taylor, D., & Dorsey-Gains, C. (1988). *Growing up literate: Learning from inner-city families.* Portsmouth, NH: Heinemann.

Tolhurst, M. (1991). *Somebody and the three Blairs.* New York: Scholastic.

Tompkins, G., & McGee, L. (1986). Visually impaired and sighted children's emerging concepts about written language. In. D. Yaden, Jr., & S Templeton (Eds.), *Metalinguistic awareness and beginning literacy: Conceptualizing what it means to read and write* (pp. 259–290). Portsmouth, NH: Heinemann.

Tompkins, G., & McGee, L. M. (1989). Teaching repetition as a story structure. In K. D. Muth (Ed.), *Children's comprehension of text: Research into practice* (pp. 59–78). Newark, DE: International Reading Association.

Ukrainetz, T. A., Cooney, M. H., Dyer, S. K., Kysar, A. J., & Harris, T. J. (2000). An investigation into teaching phonemic awareness through shared reading and writing. *Early Childhood Research Quarterly, 15,* 331–355.

van Allen, R., & van Allen, C. (1982). *Language experience activities* (2nd ed.). Boston, MA: Houghton Mifflin.

van Kleck, A., Gillam, R. B., & McFadden, T. U. (1998). A study of classroom-based phonological awareness training for preschoolers with speech and/or language disorders (1998). *American Journal of Speech–Language Pathology, 7,* 65–76.

Villaume, S. K., & Wilson, L. C. (1989). Preschool children's explorations of letters in their own names. *Applied Psycholinguists, 10,* 283–300.

Vygotsky, L. S. (1978). *Mind in society: The development of higher psychological processes.* Cambridge, MA: Harvard University Press.

Wadsworth, O. (1992). *Over in the meadow: An old counting rhyme.* New York: Scholastic.

Walker, D., Greenwood, C., Hart, B., & Carta, J. (1994). Prediction of school outcomes based on socioeconomic status and early language production. *Child Development, 65,* 600–621.

Waters, G., & Doehring, D. (1990). The nature and role of phonological information in reading acquisition: Insights from congenitally deaf children who communicate orally. In T. Carr and B. Levy (Eds.), *Reading and its development: Components skills approaches.* San Diego, CA: Academic Press.

Wells, G. (1986). *The meaning makers.* Portsmouth, NH: Heinemann.

Wells, R. (1981). *Timothy goes to school.* New York: Puffin.

Whitehurst, G. J., & Lonigan, C. J. (2001). Emergent literacy: Development from prereaders to readers. In S. B. Neuman & D. K. Dickinson (Eds.), *Handbook of early literacy research* (pp. 11–29). New York: Guilford Press.

Whitehurst, G. J., Arnold, D. S., Epstein, J. N., Angell, A. L., Smith, M., & Fischel, J. E. (1994). A picture book reading intervention in day care and home for children from low-income families. *Developmental Psychology, 30,* 679–689.

Whitehurst, G. J., Crone, D. A., & Zevnbergen, A. A., Schultz, M. D., Velting, O. N., & Fischel, J. E. (1999). Outcomes of an emergent literacy intervention from Head Start through second grade. *Journal of Educational Psychology, 91,* 261–272.

Whitehurst, G. J., Epstein, J. N., Angell, A. L., Payne, A. C., Crone, D. A., & Fischel, J. E. (1994). Outcomes of an emergent literacy intervention in Head Start. *Journal of Educational Psychology, 86,* 542–555.

Wood, A. (1992). *Silly Sally.* New York: Harcourt.

World Book's young scientist: Vol. 6. Animals. (1991). Chicago: World Book.

Yaden, D., Smolkin, L., & Conlon, A. (1989). Preschoolers' questions about pictures, print convention, and story text during reading aloud at home. *Reading Research Quarterly, 24,* 188–214.

Yaden, D., Tam, A., Madrigal, P., Brassell, D., Massa, J., Altamrano, L., & Armendariz, J. (2000). Early literacy for inner-city children: The effects of reading and writing interventions in English and Spanish during the preschool years. *Reading Teacher, 54,* 186–189.

Yolen, J. (1987). *Owl moon.* New York: Putnam.

Yopp, H. K. (1988). The validity and reliability of phonemic awareness tests. *Reading Research Quarterly, 23,* 159–177.

INDEX